# THE MAUDSLEY

## Maudsley Monographs

Maudsley Monographs number forty-six

# Culture and Self-Harm

## Attempted Suicide in South Asians in London

Dinesh Bhugra

Routledge
Taylor & Francis Group
LONDON AND NEW YORK

First published 2004 by Psychology Press

Published 2016 by Routledge
2 Park Square, Milton Park, Abingdon, Oxfordshire OX14 4RN
711 Third Avenue, New York, NY 10017, USA

First issued in paperback 2016

*Routledge is an imprint of the Taylor and Francis Group, an informa business*



Typeset in Times by RefineCatch Limited, Bungay, Suffolk



*British Library Cataloguing in Publication Data*
A catalogue record for this book is available from the British Library

*Library of Congress Cataloging-in-Publication Data*

Bhugra, Dinesh.
Culture and self-harm: attempted suicide in South Asians in London/ Dinesh Bhugra.
p. ; cm.–(Maudsley monographs; no. 45)
Includes bibliographical references and index.
ISBN 1-84169-521-1 (hardback: alk. paper)
1. Suicidal behavior–England–London. 2. Parasuicide–England–London. 3. South Asians–Suicidal behavior. 4. Immigrants–Suicidal behavior–England–London. 5. Suicide–Social aspects. 6. Suicide–Cross-cultural studies.
[DNLM: 1. Suicide, Attempted-ethnology–Asia. 2. Suicide, Attempted–ethnology–London. 3. Cross-Cultural Comparison–Asia. 4. Cross-Cultural Comparison–London.] I. Title. II. Series.

HV6548.G72L663 2004
362.28′089′9140421 2003022579

ISSN 0076-5465
ISBN 13: 978-1-138-88150-1 (pbk)
ISBN 13: 978-1-84169-521-1 (hbk)

*For*

Sh. Manoharlal and Smt. Promilla Wadhwa
Arvind, Reenu and Kiran

**With Love**

# Contents

# List of figures

# List of tables

# Acknowledgements

Thanks are due to Drs Manisha Desai, Madelyn Hicks and Jayshree Singh for their invaluable help in collection of data. Ms Veena Bahl at the Department of Health was instrumental in helping setup the projects, I am most grateful to her for her help. Neil Thompson helped to analyse the data – thanks. Dr Madelyn Hicks' contribution to Chapter 13 is tremendous and gratefully acknowledged.

Thanks are also due to Dr David Baldwin, Dr Elizabeth Fellow-Smith, Dr Carol Bayliss and other colleagues who helped formulate various ideas.

I am grateful to the families and patients who gave their time freely and helped us understand their trauma.

Earlier versions of some of the chapters were published elsewhere. My grateful thanks to publishers for permission to reproduce these, especially Prof. E. S. Paykel, editor of *Psychological Medicine*, and Cambridge University Press, and the editors of the *European Journal of Psychiatry*, the *International Review of Psychiatry*, and the *International Journal of Social Psychiatry*.

Thanks to all at Psychology Press, especially Kathryn Russel.

CHAPTER ONE

# Suicidal behaviour

## INTRODUCTION

Suicide and attempted suicide have often been described as the two ends of the same spectrum. However, not all attempted suicides will lead to suicide and not all suicides will have a history of attempted suicide. Suicidal behaviour has been well described in human history in a number of settings and across different cultures.

Suicide has been seen as one kind of death where psychological motivation may well be present, i.e. the death results from a conscious initiation of activity by the deceased that was *intended* to bring about his/her own demise (Farberow, 1975). The motivation becomes an important factor in that intention plays a valuable role, consciously or unconsciously. Farberow (1975) gives examples of a diabetic who chooses to disregard his/her diet or antidiabetic medication, or a cardiac patient who chooses to carry on with heavy physical exertion such as shovelling snow – deaths in either case may well be termed as natural. On the other hand, a car driver who drives at high speeds may well be putting his/her life at risk and were death to occur under these circumstances the attributed cause may well be accidental. The equivocal motivation in these cases, as well as in cases of suicide, is difficult to judge. Their definitions are discussed further in chapter 3.

There is considerable evidence in the literature that rates of suicidal behaviours vary across cultures. Some of this variation is genuine, whereas some is attributable to the actual process of reporting and identification of cases. There are several countries around the world, including some in the Indian subcontinent, where the act of suicide remains illegal. Thus acts of both suicide and attempted suicide will often be subsumed under other causes.

Suicide as a word is of recent origin in the English language. Derived from the modern Latin *suiciduim*, which in turn stems from the Latin pronoun for 'self' and verb 'to kill', suicide inherently indicates a thread of self-destruction, but the definitions of self vary according to cultures. This is discussed further later in this monograph (see chapter 2).

Suicide is seen as a multi-axial behaviour rather then a category of mental illness and its treatment becomes complex too. The types of therapy available include psychological, pharmacological, sociotherapies, and other different kinds of intervention, which must deal with factors like age, gender, place where behaviour takes place (e.g. prisons), and cultural and social factors. Self-harming behaviours too are many, and apart from ingestion of prescribed or over-the-counter medication well above the therapeutic dose, cutting, ingestion of herbicides and pesticides, and more violent means such as hanging, drowning, gunshot, and other actions such as jumping from heights can be seen as means to commit suicide. The spectrum between attempted suicide and complete suicide is sometimes very wide and sometimes very narrow.

Nonfatal suicide attempters (Maris et al., 2000a) are individuals who have survived the attempt and are available for treatment or intervention, though not necessarily willing to undertake this. Maris et al. (2000b) suggest that different types of suicidal behaviour are interrelated but the exact degree of such a relationship is not very clear. The attitudes towards the act and the repetitive nature of the act do have implications for the development and acceptance of intervention strategies. Although the discipline of suicidology cannot just study suicide attempts because the individuals are alive and available and sometimes willing to undergo batteries of tests (Maris et al., 2000a), it is worth bearing in mind that not all successful suicides would have previously attempted suicide prior to the successful act. They may not have sought help or been identified as having any needs on the basis of assessment.

## FACTORS IN SUICIDE ATTEMPTS

Suicidal behaviour may be preplanned or impulsive or related to psychiatric disorders. The gender differences in different kinds of suicidal behaviour are worth bearing in mind. Various social and cultural factors contribute to suicidal behaviour. These are not the same as the Durkheimian sociological perspective, which is discussed in chapter 4, but it is only relatively recently that other cultural factors like religion, caste, culture conflict, and alienation have been discussed and studied. It is not always possible to be absolutely certain about the causes of completed suicide or even attempted suicide and only educated guesses are possible at times. Factors like unemployment, alcoholism, and domestic violence need to be studied. These contribute to frustration and self-directed aggression, which may lead to suicidal behaviour. At the same time, factors such as family organisation, kinship systems, and access to organisations that may provide short-term, dedicated support, may interact with stresses to provide an element of protection. Suicidal behaviours may well be a response to a chain of events that may not be easily separable from each other or identifiable even for purposes of intervention.

Another key factor that is becoming an increasingly important focus for study is the act of migration and associated migratory status. This reflects the increased mobility of populations across a range of settings, be it internal – rural to urban – or external – from one country or culture to another. These migratory processes are the result of a number of factors, which either push or pull the individual towards migration. The reasons for migration can be economic, political, or academic. The patterns of migration may be voluntary or involuntary, singly or in groups. Each of these patterns has a different yet definite set of responses, which contribute to stress the individual experiences. At the same time, the welcome (or a lack thereof) by the host culture may introduce a further element, which pushes the individual to self-injurious behaviour. The roles of alienation, acculturation, and deculturation are worth bearing in mind. These are further discussed later in this volume (see chapter 5).

In addition to the patterns of migration and interactions with the host community, individuals also interact with members of the same ethnic and cultural group, which produces its own set of problems and difficulties. The concept of culture conflict emerges from such an interaction. An individual, by virtue of a number of factors (such as age at the time of migration and economic and educational status) may well hold less traditional attitudes and beliefs, which may then be at odds with those of his/her parents, extended family or community elders, thereby producing a sense of alienation within his/her own community.

In addition, this may also produce alienation from the host community, which might find it difficult to deal with these emotions and feelings. The role of protective factors and an understanding of these are essential in understanding the causes of suicidal behaviour and how to plan and evaluate interventions.

The factors that push the individual towards suicidal behaviour are also linked with factors of the culture or the personality of the culture. Hendin (1964a) suggests that the national character contributes to the actions of its subjects and that the social values of the national character allow the clinician to understand these acts and also help to develop preventive strategies.

What people think they should feel is indicative of certain social values present in the culture (Hendin, 1964a, p. 2). Hendin argues that if the same question – whether the subject was a good nurse – is asked of Norwegian and American nurses, the responses are remarkably different, indicating that social and cultural identities vary within the same profession. He urges the use of the term 'psychosocial character' rather than 'national character' because psychological, psychoanalytic, and cultural attitudes will contribute to the behaviours and moral values of individuals.

An individual's race and ethnicity also contribute to his/her beliefs and responses to suicidal behaviour. Sex, age groups, and social economic status all interact with race and ethnicity and allow clinicians and researchers to develop strategies for assessment and intervention. The definitions of race and ethnicity emphasise not only biological factors but also social and cultural factors. The interactions between individuals and their social and cultural backgrounds become extremely complex. In primary care settings a lack of prevention strategies that are culturally appropriate and culturally sensitive, and insufficient understanding of cultural factors, mean that not only are the rates of suicidal behaviour much greater in some settings and ethnic groups, but also that these are influential in help seeking and pathways into psychiatric care.

Historical accounts of how a community migrates, its aspirations for the future in the new country and how these are met can be seen as contributing to the national character of the country. In societies where feudal systems have lasted for a long time, e.g. the Indian subcontinent, politicians sometimes continue to behave as if they are still feudal lords, despite the introduction of democracy. As Benedict (1934) explained in her accounts, cultures too have personalities and, like that of the individual, lead individuals to behave in specific ways. In societies such as the Indian (which is a large heterogeneous group with several languages and religions) the response to acts of attempted suicide remains a patriarchal-controlled, feudal response where the elders know best and the younger members have to behave in a particular way to 'survive'.

Any conflict therefore becomes important within the individual psyche as well as within the larger kinship and society. Cultures based on the establishment of society by violent methods will encourage violent means for suicidal and homicidal acts. A major problem in understanding and studying suicidal behaviours is the individuality of the act, which is deeply embedded in the cultural context. Therein lies a paradox with which researchers and epidemiologists have to struggle in order to make sense of the behaviour.

The spread of suicidal behaviour across the life span and the life cycle is well known. It appears that in many cultures and societies the rates have been high among the youth or the elderly, both in ancient and modern times. It is likely that the frequency of suicidal behaviour not only fluctuates over the life cycle of an individual, depending upon his/her psychological, social, and cultural settings, but is also embedded within the national or psychosocial characteristics of the society or culture itself, as highlighted by Durkheim (see chapter 4).

Cultures or societies at the zenith of their power of development, or just beyond it, may well show permissive attitudes towards suicide, as well as an increase in the frequency of suicidal behaviour (Bayet, 1922). Conversely, Diekstra (1992) argues that cultures in early states of growth and development have more restrictive attitudes towards suicide, with a concomitant lower frequency of the phenomenon. The underlying argument is that the varying rates of suicidal behaviour across different cultures and societies may well be associated with the growth and development of the societies. However, this does not explain the high rates reported in some ethnic and racial groups compared with their host societies.

Social factors like isolation, alienation, poor support, estrangement, unemployment, and alcohol have been associated with rates of suicidal behaviour. Suicide rates are highest in the upper and lowest social classes. The role of imitation and societal and religious attitudes to suicidal behaviour are worth studying too. As a result of failure to respond to help in an appropriate and sensitive way, repetition of the suicidal act may also lead to further alienation and distancing from those around the individual, especially during the period immediately before his/her death. This malignant alienation remains understudied. Recurrent depression may contribute to the withdrawal of individuals from the society and culture.

In this volume, the main emphasis of study is on South Asian individuals who have migrated from South Asia, especially to the UK. Their rates and sociocultural factors are compared with those in South Asian countries and the Indian diaspora and placed in historical and religious contexts; preventive strategies that may be helpful are described.

CHAPTER TWO

# South Asia and concepts of self

## INTRODUCTION

South Asian countries, for the purposes of this monograph, constitute the Indian subcontinent. India forms the largest component, with its eastern neighbours Nepal and Bangladesh (which until 1975 was a part of Pakistan), and to the west Pakistan, with Sri Lanka to the South. The geographical area of the subcontinent is larger than the geographical area of Europe and extends from the Arabian Sea to the Himalayas. Its population exceeds 1.5 billion and the religions within the subcontinent are Hinduism, Islam, Buddhism, Sikhism, Christianity, and other minority religions like Judaism and various subsets. In India itself, more than 20 languages have been recognised in the country's constitution as key languages spoken within the country, thus establishing a heterogeneous group. Such broad heterogeneity needs to be borne in mind when attempting to understand any patterns of behaviour. The similarities and differences interact to make studies more complex in their interpretation.

This chapter aims to cover basic events of different religions and their attitudes towards suicidal behaviours. This is followed by historical aspects of suicidal behaviours across different religious groups and nations. Until 1947, India included not only Pakistan and Bangladesh but also Burma (now Myanmar) within its borders, so wherever possible historical descriptions will include these nation states as well.

## BASIC TENETS OF HINDUISM AND SELF

Very comprehensive accounts of these religions are beyond the scope of this chapter and interested readers are directed to Brockington (1996), Wilkins (1882), and Kalupahana (1987). For both Hinduism and Buddhism, most of these volumes barely scratch the surface in terms of philosophy, morals, rituals, and other tenets.

Hinduism is said to be a way of life and is neither a monolithic religion nor a unitary concept. This is exactly what makes it not only interesting, but also difficult to understand at times. Brockington (1996) argues that Hinduism has an incredible variety of expressions. Hinduism has no doctrine universal to the whole of Hinduism, but most people will accept Hinduism as a definite and reliable entity. With hundreds of thousands of gods and goddesses that people choose to worship (according to their spiritual need and personality trait), Hinduism cannot be deemed to have an exhaustive description of the religion. Brockington (1996) recommends using internal and external criteria for Hinduism. The external criteria can be a test of orthodoxy and the internal criteria used for definition. The stereotype of Hinduism is its rigidity as regards its caste system. For most Hindus, religion is all-pervading, but the individual in general is not obsessively concerned with it. However, the practice of religion is internalised and it is neither extraneous nor imposed from outside. The flexibility of attending rituals and prayer ceremonies is evident in daily Hindu life.

### The caste system

The traditional caste system consists of four *varnas* or castes – *brahmins, kshyatriya, vaisyas*, and *sudras*, which are by profession scholars, warriors, businessmen, and the servants or untouchables, respectively. Each of these is further subdivided into a number of subcastes and groupings. The two key functions within Hinduism are *dharma* (which means duty although often understood as a religion) and *karma* (which is actions, but on a metaphorical level covers a range of one's actions and beliefs to determine the outcome). A cumulative effect of all the *karmic* changes is said to influence reincarnation and what happens to the individual. Although, mistakenly, *karma* is seen as associated with fatalism, *karma* is not a passive concept. One's present state and status in life may be influenced by *karmic* deeds of the past, but these deeds are also essential in determining the actions of one's deed and people can make themselves whatever they choose.

### The Vedic systems of belief

Four *Vedas* are the traditional source of all wisdom about Hinduism. Of these, *Rgveda* is said to be the oldest and yet until relatively recently was not very well known to most philosophers and teachers. *Rgveda* is also said to have Zoroastrian influences and to be related to the Aryan invasion of India. The other three Vedas are *Yyajuaveda, Samaveda* and *Atharvaveda*. Initially, all these books were recited and handed down in oral tradition. It is only in relatively recent times that they have been written down. In *Rgveda* there is a clear mention of various illnesses and descriptions of pharmaceutical agents and processes. It appears that the ancient civilisation of Hindus was well organised, with wealthy people who had a nutritious diet and a lot of food taboos related to religious rituals, which were to do with hygiene and spread of water-borne diseases. The medicinal hymns and knowledge were presented in the form of poems to the god of medicine, *Aswini*. The goddess of knowledge, *Saraswati*, is also described as the first female physician associated with procreation. She is said to have propounded formulae for the cure of sterility in women and seminal insufficiency in men. Another goddess, *Shivali*, was described as a birth attendant (midwife) or obstetrician and women would pray to her to avoid miscarriages. The *Rgveda* is divided into ten books. *Agni*, the god of fire, represents purity as well as purifier by driving away diseases, reducing high temperatures and curing indigestion. Most of the *Upanisads* continue the creation hymns from the *Rgveda* and are the dialogue from where various dilemmas are debated.

The *Atharvaveda* describes a series of maladies due to supernatural agencies. Their treatment includes not only incantations, hymns and procedures for exorcism, but also plant and herbal extracts. *Ayurveda* (knowledge of long life) first appears in the *samhitas*. Generally it is considered as an *upveda* (subdivision) of the *Atharvaveda*. *Caraka samhita* deals with medical conditions and S*ushruta samhita* with surgical procedures and texts. The original *samhitas* were said to contain 1000 chapters and 1000 verses, but these were said to have been reduced to 1000 chapters with divisions that included *salya tantra* (surgery), *salakya* (minor surgery), *kumara bhartya* (paediatrics), *agada tanra* (toxicology), *sasayana* (tonics and vitalisation), yoga, and *vajakarana tantra* (aphrodisiacs).

The aims of the *sidhic* system of medicine are to deal not only with the biochemical nature of living cells, but also degeneration and regeneration. Diet, yoga, and meditation, as well as drugs, contribute to this. The latter included metals and elements. The five components of the *sidha* system are: *janamja* (from previous birth); *ausidhija* (medicine can make body healthy); *mantroja* (*mantra* and chanting hymns can make mind peaceful and healthy); *tapaja* (attaining peace and perfection through prayers by getting rid of unclean elements in oneself); and *samadhi* (merging with the supreme being through meditation).

Other systems within *Ayurveda* include treatises on dance, art, and music; thereby making it implicit that these forms are equally important for the physical and emotional well-being of the individual.

Of all the *samhitas, Caraka samhita* deals with the physical conditions and includes chapters on mental illness and demonology as well (see *Caraka Samhita*, 1949). *Caraka* advocated a holistic view of life and also included physical, social, ethical, and spiritual aspects of health and disease. Mind was seen as having two purposes – atomic and indivisible unity – and was responsible for the direction of the senses, control of the self, reasoning, and deliberation. Beyond mind is the field of intellect. An individual is composed of 24 elements: mind plus ten organs (five each cognitive and conative), five sense objects, and eight *prakriti* or evolutes of nature. *Caraka* did not see the laws of *karma* to be immutable and allowed a limited time of freedom to human efforts. The cognitive triad for well-being included desires for self-preservation, wealth, and happy future.

Thus, the three components of Hinduism are described: its roots in the Ayurvedic system; the individual self; and the religious tenets. The interactions between these three components are to be seen as the key to the individual's happiness and contentment. The individual is but a cog in the big wheel of time and life, and the self remains a minor part of the whole system.

## BASIC TENETS OF BUDDHISM AND SELF

The Buddha was probably born in the sixth century BC. The legendary account suggests that the young Buddha saw poverty, old age, and death and was so upset by them that he decided to give up his wife, young son, and kingdom and took to meditation. Having attained enlightenment he then travelled around spreading the word. The Hindu king, Asoka, is said to have adopted Buddhism and dispatched messengers around India, Sri Lanka, Burma, and Malaysia to spread the word.

During the early period (around 500 BCE down to the first century CE) there appeared the Doctrine of the Elders, which still pertains in Sri Lanka and South-east Asia. The second period covered the first century CE onwards, and during this time Buddhism spread into China, Japan, and Korea. Buddhism achieved high articulation. During the third period (from the seventh century CE) a form of Buddhism developed called *vajrayāna* or *mantrayana*, with much emphasis on magical and sacramental rites in which spiritual consequences were thought to flow from the recitation of *mantras*. This was gradually absorbed into Hindu practice, which may be one of the reasons for the gradual disappearance of Buddhism from the Indian states. It remains in Sri Lanka and also became the dominant form of Buddhism in Tibet and Nepal. This era lasted until the eighteenth century, after which the modern period deals with the impact of colonialism on various religions.

The dimensions of Buddhism include the narrative, doctrines, practical dimensions and material dimensions (see Smart, 1989). Various terms pertaining to Buddhism are illustrated in Table 2.1.

Table 2.1
Basic Buddhist terms

| *Word* | *Meaning* |
|---|---|
| *Dhyana* | Meditation in eight stages of ascending purity of unconsciousness. |
| *Nirvana* | Final liberation when no rebirth takes place. |
| *Prajna* | Insight into the nature of the cosmos. |
| *Samsara* | The living flux of existence in which individuals are involved in the process of rebirth. |
| *Sangha* | The order founded by the Buddha. |
| *Sila* | Virtue or precept encouraging a virtue. |
| *Sunyata* | Emptiness – the pervading characteristic of all events. |
| *Tantra* | Ritual text or method. |

The narrative dimension describes the Enlightenment of the Buddha. Born as Siddhartha Gautama, in 586 BCE, into the family of the ruler Suddhadan of Kosala, the birth itself was described as miraculous. His father protected him from the unhappiness existing outside the palace. After Siddhartha's marriage and the birth of his son, Rahul, he made a trip beyond the palace and was struck by the sight of a very old man, a sick person, a corpse, and a holy beggar. He questioned their meaning and on receiving unsatisfactory answers he decided to leave his luxurious life behind. He attained full insight into the nature of the world and the way to overcome the suffering and tribulation. After attaining Enlightenment he returned to Varanasi and in a nearby place called Sarnath he gave his first sermon. This is referred to as the Sermon of the Turning Wheel in which he set forth the notion of the wheel of *dharma*. After this sermon the first disciples of the *Sangha* (Buddhist community) were converted. Thereafter, for the next 45 years until the age of 80 he roamed the countryside preaching and teaching the organisation of the Sangha. In Pali texts he is not the only Buddha; other Buddhas are also referred to.

The doctrinal dimension, according to Smart (1989), includes Buddha's primary insight into the impermanence and interdependence of everything. Buddha gave radical new interpretations about life and ethics in his doctrines. He was attracted to the practice of austerity and to questions of rebirth and liberation, or *nirvana*. He suggested that meditation without understanding was blind, and understanding without meditation was fruitless. The key insight was that everything was impermanent and interdependent. Since everything in the universe is impermanent, no satisfaction could last forever and its disappearance was painful. This was the first of the Four Noble Truths that Buddha enunciated. The next was that the causes of suffering lay in the craving or thirst for existence. The third Truth was that this cause could be eliminated. The fourth Truth was that this could be achieved by treading the Noble Eightfold path, which has eight aspects and also consists of elements of trust, ethical conduct, and meditation. The first two aspects of the

Path concern trust. They are Right Belief and Right Attitude. The next three concern ethical conduct – Right Speech, Right Bodily Action, and Right Livelihood. The last three are to do with yoga and self-training and are Right Effort, Right Self-Awareness, and Right Meditation. The Path was seen by the Buddha as middle, or central, in that it exists between the extremes of self-indulgence and self-mortification, and between the extremes of thinking that the soul is eternal and that it is cut off at death (Table 2.2). The followers of the Path may experience complete insight and serenity. Giving up the world and its demands and possessions leads to a life of simplicity and austerity.

The most important practice invoked in the Buddha's teachings is that of yoga, through which an individual attempts to control his/her mind through meditation. The structure of the *Sangha* prevents too great an emphasis on individualism since the Buddha envisaged his followers to be living together according to the role or *vinaya*. At each phase of the moon they would make a mutual public confession of faults and at the end of the monsoons there would be more occasions for mutual forgiveness and confession. The Buddhists ate by begging for food – thus *dāna* was the primary lay duty towards the order.

The way emphasised that intentions count rather than a literal application of the rules. Five precepts *(pancašila)* should govern human actions – refraining from: taking life, stealing, wrong sex, wrong speech, and taking substances which obliterate self-awareness. The concepts of the self are sociocentric or collectivisitic. Individuals may have individual desires and wishes, but their actions affect and influence others. These actions have a multiplicity of dimensions – no action exists which has no consequence (Table 2.2). Variations of Buddhist teachings are followed in China and Japan (see Smart, 1989). The concepts of self in these traditions are discussed later in this chapter.

Table 2.2
The Middle Path (after Smart, 1989)

On ignorance depends Karma,
On Karma depends consciousness,
On consciousness depend name and form,
On name and form depend six organs of sense,
On which depends contact,
On contact depends sensation,
On sensation depends desire,
On desire depends attachment,
On attachment depends existence,
On existence depends birth,
On birth depend old age, death, sorrow, lamentation, misery, grief and despair,
Out of these emerges misery.

Attitudes to suicide and attempted suicide vary tremendously among other religions too. Dissanayake and DeSilva (1983) challenged the western assumptions that Buddhism encourages suicide. Buddhism of the orthodox southern school has influenced the beliefs and way of life among the Sinhalese and several studies have reported higher than expected rates of completed and attempted suicide. In contrast with the Judaeo-Christian religions, one theme dominates the worldview of both Buddhism and Hinduism: the doctrine of rebirth. According to this doctrine an individual is subject to repeated cycles of birth and death before he arrives at the ultimate salvation of *nirvana*.

Buddhism extols the value of human life, for birth as a human being is the culmination of the individual's efforts through many previous cycles of births. Suicide is therefore seen as an empty, fruitless act from the point of view of man's salvation or as a behaviour that will delay his ultimate enlightenment. Neither Hinduism nor Buddhism see condemnation of man to an eternity of suffering for whatever misdeeds he has done in this short span of life. In comparison with many other acts, suicide is considered more as an error or a mistake than a grave offence. Self-sacrifice for the cause of the greater good is seen as meritorious but still suicide.

The *Vinaya Pitaka* (Book of Disciplines) cites the incident of a monk who attempted suicide by throwing himself down onto a rock and survived. When he was brought before the Buddha, he was admonished for the act by the Buddha saying that while it was a wrongful deed it was not serious enough to oblige him to leave the monastic order (*Vinaya Pitaka* 9:I, 142). In both Hinduism and Buddhism, a belief in reincarnation may serve as a catalyst in some vulnerable individuals, hoping that the next birth may bring better life.

While Buddhism emphasises the fact that there is too much *dukkha* (pain, suffering) in life, this can help dissuade a Buddhist from giving in to despair. If *dukkha* is to be expected in life, then there is less reason to take particular problems so personally. The next birth may not provide salvation either because the individual may return as an animal to be preyed on or as a form of ghost. Harvey (2000) argues that the state of mind at the time of the act of suicide will be a crucial cause of yet another rebirth along with its problems. So as an attempted escape from the sufferings of life, according to Buddhist principles, suicide is ineffective. It will only be followed by another rebirth, probably lower than a human one, in which the sufferings will continue unabated if due to *karma*, and perhaps be intensified. Not only does suicide waste this opportunity for oneself, but it also deprives others of the benefits that one may bring to them.

Self-starvation is allowed if one has no time to collect food because of practising meditation intently, but not if one has already attained a specific meditative state and thinks one need do nothing more. It is not acceptable if one is ill but being helped is seen as too hard. It is acceptable in long-lasting, severe illness and when, due to illness, individuals know they are dying. Giving up life to save others, and burning oneself as an act of worship, are allowed. Chinese tradition allows persons to kill themselves as an act of protest so as to try compassionately to bring about an improved situation in society. Self-surrender culminating in voluntary death has been held as an honourable option in other Buddhist communities. A common cause of suicide in modern China (prior to the People's Republic) was the one committed for the purpose of taking revenge upon an enemy otherwise out of reach. This is seen as a most effective form of revenge because the law throws the responsibility of the deed on the one who occasioned it and the disembodied soul is better placed to persecute the enemy (Thakur, 1962).

In Japan, *harakiri* or *seppuku* (belly cutting) are two kinds of suicide – voluntary and obligatory. *Harakiri* was practised out of loyalty to a dead superior or to restore injured honour if revenge was impossible; the ceremony was usually performed in a temple. The obligatory variety was one of three forms of capital punishment. The other two forms of suicide are *shinju* or *aitashi* and *junshi*. The former is the death together of unhappy lovers who seek escape from the difficulties of their earthly lot. The latter is suicide committed upon the death of one's lord or master with the idea of following him into the next world. There were at least two incidents where whole clans almost disappeared in *junshi*. The Japanese classified suicide by motive.

In addition, *aisei-shi* (sacrificial suicide) is exemplified by *hito-bashira* (human pillar), where someone was buried under the foundation of a bridge to appease the river god and to facilitate the construction. Kamikaze pilots also belong to this category (Iga & Tatai, 1975). *Funshi* or *munerbara* is *harakiri* based on dire resentment, hatred, and enmity. It symbolises a society in which there is little available to inferiors who want to express their indignation towards their superiors. *Kashitsu-shi* or *sokotsu-bara* (suicide for exploiting mistakes) symbolises a society where a mistake has to be paid for by death. *Kanshi* or *kangenshi* (suicide for remonstration) is also typical of an authoritarian society where an inferior often had to kill himself in order to communicate a criticism to his superiors.

In addition to social factors, personal factors like narcissistic temperament, individual response to feudalistic philosophy of life, limited life experiences, and active mutism may play a role. Iga and Tatai (1975) analyse Yukio Mishima's suicide using these approaches. The multiplicity of factors and complex nature of the interaction at cultural, social, and personal levels means that sometimes it is impossible to tease out these factors. *Harakiri* is not common, but occasional reports emerge. Tatai (1983) studied the number of suicides between the twelfth century and nineteenth centuries and concluded that factors which underlie Japanese suicides are as follows:

1. A historical tradition of suicide as an honourable solution to harsh and difficult personal situations.
2. A romanticising of suicide as an escape from the stresses of life under a mantle of acceptability.
3. Inferences from the two religions of Shinto and Buddhism, which formulate an idea of life after death. Shinto views death as an opportunity to become a spirit or *kami*.
4. Lack of public institutions to help people suffering economic and psychological stress.
5. Absence of legal prohibitions against persecutions for suicide.
6. Economic distress.
7. A rigid, semifeudal society which demands conformity and success and prohibits failure and weakness.

## ISLAM

Islam, the religion of submission (as its name indicates) to the one God, took off from the north-west part of Arabia in the seventh century and rapidly spread north and west (Smart, 1989). The early period of Islam dates from about 750 to 1258 AD. Thereafter its impact is in relation to medieval or premodern period. Altogether, Islam became the dominant religion in the Arab Middle East. It spread across to the Indian subcontinent with the Mughal invasions.

The Prophet Muhammad was born in Mecca in 570 CE and his religious experiences guided him to become the messenger of Allah. The creation of the Holy Qur'an (which represents the divine thought and divine law) reflects the God's eternal speech. The experiential dimension of early Islam focuses on the overwhelming presence of God, who in his mercy communicates with human beings to lead them on the right path. Later on, however, a different mystical experience appears, which is gained through the practice of contemplation – due to the Sufi movement. The ethical dimensions of Islam lay in the weaving of the political task of founding a good and a just society under the guidance of God. Although rights may vary according to the individuals, all are equal before God. Kindness should be cultivated and, institutionally, Islam organised itself as a state to start with. Doctrinally, the single most important tenet of Islam is the unity of God, who is the creator of the universe.

Materially, Islam has its houses of prayer but bans the concrete representation of God. God gives a person strength through instantaneous empowerment before an act, but the choice is made later and is still that of the individual. Historically, Islam has provided a framework for the social life and culture of racially and linguistically diverse people. Such a framework constituted three characteristics: first, it had to be amplified considerably beyond the Qur'an; second, schools of law, mysticism and theology had to be seen in the context of unity and simplicity; third is the diversity or plurality, which was contained but not eliminated by the attempt at a juridical and ideological unity (Esmail, 1996). Within the diversity, argues Esmail, lay consciousness of God and the absence of any radical dichotomy between the world of matter and the world of spirit. Esmail illustrates some of these issues with an anecdote about a middle-aged Pakistani male who approached him with elements of pride, dependence, anxiety, and resentment about his son. Parental authority was not motivated in this case (and is generally not so in migrant groups) by a concern to maintain authority through the use of religion, but it undoubtedly impinges upon the concept of how one's self is formed and how the self is influenced by external factors, including language and religion. The paradox therefore suggests that the racial and ethnic identity and cultural identities need to be borne in mind. The parent–child conflict may be one aspect of the arduous struggle of an immigrant community for cultural comfort in an alien land, where the youth may mix and mingle more freely than their parents.

The Qur'an strictly prohibits suicide, stating that those who commit suicide will not be permitted to enter Heaven and will be punished in Hell. In Egypt, suicide is denied by the family and those around the individual. Al-Issa (2000) reports that although the suicide rates among Muslims in Algeria are low, the numbers are beginning to rise, especially among young women aged 15 to 22 and old soldiers from the liberation army, who often showed depression with delusions of retribution. The lowest rates have been reported in the month of Ramadan, revealing that the Muslim religion, which regards suicide as sinful, has some preventive influence on urban communities.

In Saudi Arabia too the rates of suicidal behaviour and deliberate self-harm were reportedly lower, but a majority of parasuicidal patients were young, single females who impulsively overdosed after an interpersonal conflict (Maghoub, Al-Freihi, Al-Myhayas, & Al-Nahdi, 1988; Malik, Bilal, Mekki, & Kinani, 1996). As the act of suicide is condemned, asking about the death wish is the only way to assess potentially suicidal patients without offending them. From Iran, Yasemi and Sanei (1994) reported that the rate of attempted suicide was 1.5 times more in women than men, while the rates of completed suicide were more common among men – self-immolation being the commonest cause. The social support and family perceptions can work both ways. In Algeria it is argued that middle-aged women, who already have many children and are frightened that as they are not likely to have more they will be divorced by their husbands, show a high rate of suicidal behaviour.

The psychopathology of individuals is likely to be coloured by their religious beliefs. Al-Issa (2000) illustrates this by giving an example of *Mu Ghayib* in Oman, which is an exaggerated form of attachment to the dead in response to untimely death. This involves a prolonged period of denial, which offers people hope and transition through bereavement. It has been suggested that those Muslims who do not practise religious duties are more likely to attempt suicide (Caruso & Moussaoui, 1992), but this is a simplistic formulation because religious beliefs do not always translate into religious behaviour.

Daradekh (1989), reporting on suicide in Jordan over a five-year period from 1980, observed that the peak rates of suicide were in the age group between 15 and 34 years. Nearly two thirds of the males who had committed suicide were single. Using data collected following reports of completed suicide, Daradekh (1989) found that males were marginally more likely to carry out the act and were also more likely to be employed in the army or police. Nearly two thirds of all cases were seen as mentally ill by the police. Two thirds of males used violent means such as shooting, hanging, stabbing, burning, and drowning. Overall rates from this Muslim country were reported to be lower than Christian countries, but the author does not state whether all cases were indeed Muslims. The underlying speculation put forward by the author is that strong faith in God, easy expression of anger and externalising anger (homicide rates were much higher compared with those reported from England and Wales), and extended family systems providing support both practically and emotionally, are important factors in explaining low rates. As the peak is among the young, Daradekh blames it on less religious behaviour and believes that mental illness plays an important role.

However, the rates of attempted suicide reported from Muslim countries are higher than expected. In comparative data between Muslims and Christians in several Middle Eastern countries, reported rates were lower for Christians than for Muslims. This suggests that factors other than religion may play a role (see Headley, 1983). Among these other factors, rural–urban differences, social support and familial factors, and economic factors may prove to be important. The gender differences in rates of completed and attempted suicide are not dissimilar to those reported in the west, but these may reflect under-reporting of suicidal attempts and suicide and different methods of data collection. The most common precipitating cause for suicidal acts is interpersonal problems. Family problems such as marital friction, child–parent disagreements, extended family disputes, in-law troubles, disappointments in love, failure in examinations, and poverty and economic factors also play a role.

Levav and Aisenberg (1989) reported that in Israel rates of completed suicide are higher amongst Jews than Arabs (4.2 times among men and 2.4 times among women). They attribute these differences to Islam seeing suicide as homicide and to Muslim Arabs being less likely to be single or divorced, being urbanised and having lower levels of education.

Thus religion becomes only one of the significant factors. In addition to religion, the legal status of these acts is also important. It is likely that the religious constraints will influence the legal system. Thus any comparisons of attitudes and sociodemographic factors have to tease out these differences.

The worldview of religions has a twofold basis – a spiritually and mythologically changed vision on the one hand and rationalism on the other. The same struggles continue within individuals and within the systems of the family or society. Although both views see the world as a unity, the spiritual principles address the existential conditions of life and rationalism argues for a tension, which is difficult to be sustained. Islam offers paradigms for a vision of community, self and self-realisation that differ significantly from the western concepts. These concepts allow individuals to maintain their functioning and existence, which clearly identifies them and gives them a sense of purpose.

## SIKHISM

Guru Nanak (1469–1504) is recognised as the first guru among Sikhs. The traditional accounts indicate that he experienced a religious experience while bathing in a stream and disappeared for three days. Upon his return, his first words were that there is no Hindu and there is no Muslim. Thereafter, he went on long preaching journeys and the key aspect in his teachings was the role of Guru. He was followed by nine other Gurus and the tenth – Guru Gobind Singh – told his followers to follow their holy book as their Guru – the *Guru Granth Sahib*. The ideology of Sikhism is within the framework of Hindu ideology. Guru Gobind Singh had organised Sikhs into a martial group. He suggested that Sikhs change their names to Singh (or Lion). Each Sikh has to wear five symbols – long hair, iron bangle, comb, long breeches, and a short sword. Sikhs are forbidden alcohol, tobacco, and meat slaughtered in the Muslim manner.

The *Guru Granth Sahib* gives a broad sense of Sikh devotional life and is also influenced by Hinduism, Sufism and Islam. At the social level it places a lot of emphasis on the irrelevance of caste and race and condemns distinction. It also underlines the vital role of purity of motives and emphasises the performance of truth, sincerity and attainment of *sahaj* (equipoise). The form of the *Guru Granth Sahib* is poetry. God is described in anthropomorphic terms and the Gurus use the imagery of family relationship to describe the union of God and man. The scripture is more than a viable focal point for Sikh devotions.

Sikh theology possesses coherence unique in the Sant tradition (Cole & Sambhi, 1989). Strictly monotheistic, this religion believes in the ultimate reality, which is a unity, and that God is one without a second and essentially without qualities. Consequently the truth is also personal, manifest, and possesses qualities through its attributes, which are never physical. In manifest form of qualities, *shabd* (word), *nām* (personality or character), and *guru* are communicative and creative. God is the creator and survival depends upon his will, which is all-powerful. Man is unique in this creation since he alone possesses the ability to discriminate and enter into a voluntary relationship of love with God. In his natural state man sees himself as creation's lord, disregarding the evidence of his own finiteness, which mortality and nature's independence of him provide. He is characterised by self-reliance and at best sees the world including himself erroneously as distinct from God. This duality leads to attachment to temporal values, which by definition are illusory. The rebirth depends upon cumulative actions, which lead to liberation only by becoming more God conscious and God filled (Cole & Sambhi, 1989).

Because God is within ones self, no rituals are necessary but right conduct is. A life of service in the world as a householder is acceptable because the world and the self are not separate but part of the same reality. God is personal and any understanding is therefore derived from experience. The Lord may be experienced but He cannot be known by the mind; He is beyond comprehension.

Sikhism has no difficulty in coming to terms with scientific theories of evolution. In fact they find them congenial to the belief that the universe is expanding and is derived from the mind of God. The opposition here is to materialism, which regards the universe as self-explanatory and self-existent (Cole & Sambhi, 1989). Man lives in constant dread of hunger, sickness and death, but God is fearless and without hatred. God is personal, does not grow old, and is unwearied either by effort or supplication. God is known to man by the Guru's grace.

Man is a result of God's intention. How and why this came about and how a separation between God and man occurred are subject to debate. God lives in everything and dwells in every heart, and yet he is a separate entity and not blended with anything. Ignorance is the root of man's problems and, knowing neither his true nature nor his destiny, he is bound to come and go repeatedly. Man is intelligent, knows right from wrong and has the moral law written in his heart. Yet he misses the opportunity to meet with his God because these failures lie in actions and the loss of cause of effect. Dependence upon God and obedience to his will are essential for liberation. The reality of the created universe is illusory, even though the universe is created by God.

All worldly possessions, food, clothing and everything else that human beings need, are illusory, except God who is responsible for the existence of this illusion. This illusion, or *maya*, is a subjective error resulting from a wrong point of view. The impact of the religion on Sikhs is further discussed by Cole and Sambhi (1989), Singh (1999), and McMullen (1989). The concepts of self are sociocentric in Hinduism and Sikhism. These views are to be seen in the context of what an individual does and what he/she is expected to carry out. Such an understanding is essential if patterns of deliberate self-harm are to be studied because what is important here is to understand who is being harmed.

## JAINISM

Among Jainas, suicide and its methods are considered vulgar and evil. While practising starvation, the Jaina must avoid desire for death. The Jainas see vocal sins being destroyed through silence, mental sins through respiratory restraint, bodily sins through starvation, and lust through mortification. The final condition to be expected by the sage is one of complete physical and mental collapse. Death by fasting was given a high place in the Jaina canon. Although encouraging abandonment of the body for the accumulation of merit in calamities, famines, extremes of old age, and incurable disease, suicide is not allowed to everyone. It is allowed only to ascetics who acquire the highest degree of perfection.

The ascetics have to give up begging and to lie down daily in a chosen place to await death by hunger and thirst. Suicide is only permitted to the ascetics, and non-religious suicide is regarded with special horror by the Jainas as they disapprove of all taking life. The concepts were quite different from the Buddhist ethics. The Jaina tradition most sharply draws the line between suicide, which it rejects because suicide implies passion and violence and arises out of ignorance, and the voluntary death of the sage (or sage amongst sages), which requires partial or total freedom from all desire (including the desire to abandon one's life), mastery over all the causes, a rigorous apprenticeship with a spiritual master, and finally keeping the rule of nonviolence to the point of self-mortification unto death.

Although some religions approve of suicide, it was by and large for those who had lived life fully and acquired high ascetics' powers. Aged individuals have been exhorted through one doctrine or another to take this duty and privilege to adopt a hermit's life unless they preferred to terminate of their own will an existence that had become burdensome to themselves and for others. The methods of suicide in religious custom have been many – starvation, drowning, burning, stabbing, and jumping from a precipice, generally into a river. Starvation to death has been used as a political tool in the Indian struggle for independence, and also by IRA prisoners.

## CONCEPTS OF SELF

The self-structure of western culture has been widely discussed as individuated, detached, separate, self-sufficient, and involving a dualistic metaphysic. No one would deny that a dualism between mind and body and self and other, and a radical individualism that puts a fundamental emphasis on autonomy, on appeals to an 'inner self' or instrumental reason, and on personality as a distinct entity, are not pervasive themes in western culture in the same way as concepts drawn from Vedanta permeate Indian culture (Morris, 1994).

The six orthodox systems of Hindu philosophy are traditionally divided into three groups of two – *Nyaya–Vaisesika*, *Samkhya–Yoga*, and *Vedanta–Mimamsa*. The world is seen as neither real nor unreal, and it is an appearance based on the reality of the ultimate spirit – Brahman. In a sense two selves are recognised in Hinduism – a material or phenomenal self and an 'inner self' which is identified with spirit, being formless, immutable, and absolute.

The realisation of the true self essentially implies detachment from the phenomenal world of being, not only from desires and material attachments, but also from the flux of psychic life itself. These secular goals in Hinduism are *karma, artha*, and *dharma*. *Karma* means desire or pleasure, *artha* is essential for the wealth and possessions, and *dharma* is living one's life according to the sacred or moral law. Dumont (1970) argues that there are two types of society – pre-capitalist and capitalist, and Hindu society will be seen as pre-capitalist.

In ordinary, everyday life the Hindu tends to see his or her identity largely in terms of kin relations and caste membership. The empirical ego comes last in the formulation of identity. Outside the ritual context, interpersonal identity tends to be social rather than metaphysical. In the Hindu context, self may well be identified in the spiritual realm. Persons in South Asia are not thought to be individual, that is indivisible, bounded units, as they are in much western social and psychological theory. In South Asian terms, persons are seen as divisible or dividual (Marriott, 1976). Thus the definition of deliberate self-harm needs to be looked at in this particular context. Similar conclusions can be drawn from Islamic teachings.

Cultures vary in the degree to which the individual aspect is emphasised, for a focal emphasis on egoism or individualism is by no means confined to the liberal doctrines of Europe. Although Buddhism and Hinduism play down this role and autonomy of the person, one cannot say that because some cultures are egocentric, everyone living in those cultures will be egocentric too.

Morris (1994) suggests that from a review of the cross-cultural data it appears that the dimensions of relevance in understanding the conceptualisation of humankind include the material dimension, which is related to the way in which the body is theorised in terms of its constituents, substances and life, which may also be expressed in spiritual terms. The concept of individuality is defined as personal autonomy. Lastly there is the spiritual dimension. In concepts of the self, all these domains and cultures must be referred to.

Not all cultures lay equal emphasis on all four domains, so clinicians need to be aware of the problems of simplification and generalisation.

Basu (1997) argues that concepts of self should be seen in cultural terms in the context of culture. The Buddhist view of self is a composite of five psychological and physical elements: *rupa* (physical form or really the matter of the composite); *vedana* (emotive or feeling part of experiences); *sanna* (perception); *vinana* (consciousness); *sankhara* (disposition). Physical form or *rupa* is the only physical component, whereas the rest are psychological. Of *Vedana* it is said that there are three varieties of experience: pleasant feelings engendering greed and attachment; unpleasant feelings arousing anger and repulsion; neutral feelings representing indifference and ignorance. The main goal for the individual is to be rid of all three classes of feeling, along with their contents, and to become detached from the world. Such detachment is active and needs to be distinguished from apathy. Perception is seen as a series of flights and perchings, whereas consciousness is attached to each sense and is the main agent in transmigration. Disposition is the transmission of habits, attitudes and the like, which are the main characters based from one birth to another.

Allen (1997) argues that the social construction of the self is influenced by a range of factors and consequently one could argue that one's self may in turn influence social factors, society and social functioning. Interestingly, self also needs to be seen in the context of the other which will determine the self.

## ELEMENTS OF SELF

Hsu (1985) developed a formulation of the way in which individuals live as social and cultural beings. The elements of human existence are based on ignoring wild swings from one extreme to another and avoiding the common failing of confounding the individual's psychology with that of the socio-cultural orientation of the group in seven concentric layers. These are illustrated in Figure 2.1.

The innermost two layers (six and seven) are the 'unconscious' and the 'preconscious', similar to psychoanalytic concepts. Layer six responds to semi-repressed and layer seven to repressed feelings and materials. Layer five is the 'inexpressible conscious' because its contents are generally kept within the individual. These are not communicated to others because the individual may be scared to do so: material may be too private and therefore others may not be able to understand it. The individual may feel something but is either ashamed to or unable to verbalise it.

Next is layer four, which is called 'expressible conscious' because it contains ideas, materials and feelings that the individual is able to communicate freely with others. Some of these ideas or feelings can be extremely personal,

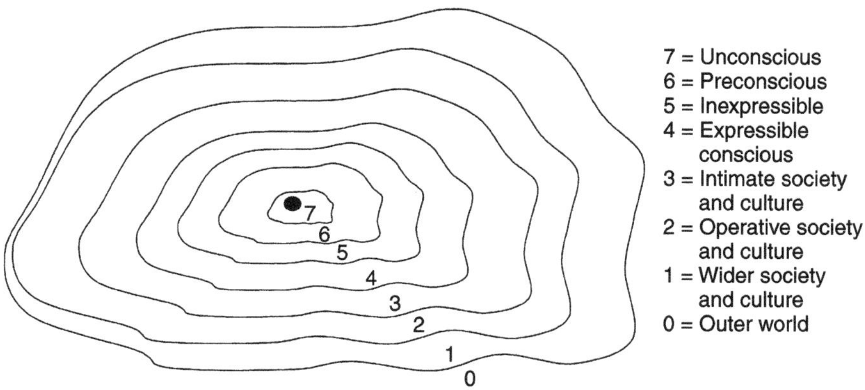


**Figure 2.1** Man, Culture, and Society (Hsu, 1985)

such as jealousy, whereas others can be more global, contributing to the individual's character traits, which may lead to stereotypes and prejudicial attitudes in others. Such a communication depends upon personal, educational, socioeconomic, or cultural factors.

Layer three is that of the external world to which each individual has strong feelings of attachment, which may appear to others as completely irrational. It contains feelings and attitudes that lead to shared intimacy, influenced by mutual receptivity, emotional support, and verbal communication. This layer is therefore consistent with cultural usage such as caste pollution among Hindu upper castes. Any changes in this layer can be quite traumatic to the individual and thus are likely to be resisted.

Layer two is characterised by role relationships. It is here that cultural rules and relationships with others are developed and maintained. Courtesy, rules of humour, rules of interaction, and patterns of greeting are all part of this layer. In the normal course of events here too the individual is likely to resist change.

Layer one consists of human beings, cultural rules, knowledge, and artefacts, which are present in the larger society, but many may not have connections with individuals. In the normal course of events, the individual may not have effective contact with others at this level.

Layer zero is the layer of society which influences the individual's worldview. This layer consists of societies with which the individual may not have any contact, no idea about, or erroneous ideas. Globalisation through the media and the internet is likely to influence such knowledge.

The clinician must be aware of these layers as understanding them puts the individual in the context of the interaction and religion can then be linked with the self (Figure 2.1).

## SELF AND SOCIAL CONTEXT

The self changes according to external stimuli and there is some inherent danger in assuming that such a self is static. Self-knowledge refers to the desire for the accurate and certain evidence of one's traits and abilities and the need for such an experience is highlighted in the need for consistency of the self. Such a process is required for reduction of any uncertainty the individual may feel and will allow the ability to predict and control the environment.

Self-enhancement refers to the desire for positive feedback about the self and is rooted in the more basic tendency to seek pleasure and to avoid pain. The pursuit of self-knowledge, self-enhancement, and self-improvement are all related to various aspects of Hindu religion and Ayurvedic concepts of being in harmony with other beings and organisms.

Allen (1997) suggests that the alternative concepts of the self (i.e. alternative to western concepts) are related to the world, which is an illusion, and the ego becomes pride, which is seen as destructive. There is a true eternal self that is free from historical and cultural constitution. The essential unity of mankind, the self and the world as embedded in nature remains a factor, even though all of these are illusory. Roland (1997) argues that the Indian self (which is equated to the Hindu self) has three variations – those of the individual self, familial self, and universal self – but the boundaries between these three remain porous.

Yogic teachings include self as consciousness, intelligence, ego-sense, mind, sense–motor organ complex, and an egoless reality. Thus, the relationship between external objects that can be found in nature, between individuals and their families, and the roles of various mind–body mechanisms become interesting to study. In addition, the roles of various components in the healing systems, such as personality traits, religious taboos, diet, seasons, and climate, can all influence the individual's health.

## HINDUISM AND SUICIDE

The views of Hinduism are ambivalent towards the act of suicide. At one level it is to do with liberation from the worldly, illusory existence and at another level it is linked with taking life, which is not in one's control anyway. Another very important factor in understanding the relationship between Hinduism and suicide is the polymorphism of Hinduism. With so many different sects and groups, and with a variety of beliefs, the broad brushstrokes explored in this chapter may not entirely reveal the views of the entire canon of Hinduism.

Persons of great spiritual elevation have sometimes been known to die in a way which can only be described as suicide, but in these circumstances the act is seen as supreme sacrifice. Although the Hindu personality has been described as narcissistic, deliberate self-harm reflects a major shift although, as Spratt (1966) highlights, this act may well be related to a narcissistic society. Such a society is described by Spratt as one where some members are concerned with spiritual matters while others focus on ego-ideal matters rather than individual egos. Thus death by suicide for the greater cause and for the greater good may well prove to be at a higher spiritual level as well. The relationship between the ruler and the ruled is therefore weak where the ruled are more passive. There is some truth in this observation in that ruled Hindus often refer to their rulers as *mai–baap* (mother–father). Thus the ruler is seen as be controlling as well as nurturing. The relationship to suicide is discussed further below.

## Ancient India

As one of the oldest civilisations in the world, the Indus Valley civilisation and the Hindu religion, especially in ancient India, carry a different but clear set of values. These are often well described in the literature, but sometimes Indologists tend to project their understanding of the issues onto those who they aim to study. Acts of suicide have been described widely in Hindu scriptures, often without any comments or criticisms, thereby suggesting that these acts were seen in the strictest possible neutral sense. The following sections have been heavily influenced by Thakur's (1962) observations and writings. The history of suicide in the Indian context is full of interesting observations and conclusions.

Religious suicide has been mentioned in the basic doctrine of Jainism (Embree, 1994, p. 71). Although opposed by Buddhists, religious suicide is known to both Hindu and Jaina ascetics. Mahāvira is said to have voluntarily starved himself to death by the protracted fast known as *itvara* or *sallekhanā*. As noted above, a Jain monk who wishes to end his life in this way, and thereby rid his soul of a great deal of *karma* and perhaps even obtain full salvation, must prepare for the final penance by a course of graduated fasting lasting for as long as 12 years. However, if he is sick and unable to maintain the course of rigid self-discipline to which he is vowed, he may starve himself to death without the preliminary preparation. There is a clearly defined protocol for the monk to gradually starve himself to death as described in the Book of Good Conduct. Such an approach sees suicide as a triumphant end to a life of spiritual struggle and there is no course for tears:

> Mindful of his body, immovable as a beam, the monk should strive to waste his body away. He should enter a village or town . . . and beg for straw. Then he should take it and go to an out-of-the-way place.
>
> He should carefully inspect and sweep the ground, so that there are no eggs,

> living beings, sprouts, dew, water, ants, mildew, drops of water, mud or cobwebs left on it. Thereupon he carries out the final fast . . . Speaking the truth, the saint who has crossed the stream of transmigration, doing away with all the hesitation, knowing all things but himself unknown, leaves his frail body. Overcoming manifold hardships and troubles, with trust in his religion, he performs this terrible penance. Thus in due time he puts an end to his existence. This is done by those who have no delusions. This is good, this is joyful and proper, this leads to salvation; this should be followed! (Acārāriga Sutra 1.7, 6).

Dubois (1906) points out that religious suicides under the wheels of the chariot which carries Lord Jagannath (the origin of the word 'juggernaut') during the annual pilgrimage in Puri are deplorable, as are instances of individuals who set themselves on fire to purify themselves. He calls individuals fanatics who place the sick whose recovery is despaired of 'on the banks of the Ganges, or of some other so-called holy river so that they may be drowned by the floods or devoured by crocodiles' (Dubois, 1906, p. 606).

In ancient India, suicide was often seen as an act which was not a medical or a psychiatric condition. This act was reflective of human nature and the stresses of life, with a series of predisposing causes which included congenital or hereditary causes, physical conditions, and impulsive passions such as love, jealousy, ambition, or shame.

Thakur (1962) uses a multiplicity of sources for his study, varying from scriptures and archaeological sources to travelogues. The history of suicide in ancient India is therefore very much dependent upon its accounts in the scriptures. Of these, the two key scriptures are the *Ramayana* and the *Mahabharata*. Although these two were in the oral tradition, the written-down versions are of recent vintage and any study also needs to take this into account. The *Ramayana* has various versions, of which the most popular is that of Tulsidas. The story revolves around Lord Rama – one of the incarnations of God Vishnu. He was born to the oldest wife of the King of Ayodhya, Raja Dasrath, who had three sons from two other wives. His third and the youngest wife wanted her son, Bharat, to succeed to the throne and she persuaded her husband to exile Rama to the forest for 14 years. Rama's wife, Sita, and his younger brother, Lakshmana, decide to follow him. While in the forest, Sita is kidnapped by the demon king Ravana and taken to Sri Lanka. Rama and Lakshmana raise an army and with the help of the Monkey King manage to liberate her. On their return, Rama overhears aspersions cast upon Sita's character so she walks through fire to demonstrate her purity. In the end she commits suicide, as do other citizens of Ayodhya, by walking into the river. The versions vary from Valmiki Ramayana to Ramcharitmanas.

Similarly, several incidents of suicide are described in the *Mahabharata* which revolves around the story of the battle of two sets of cousins – Pandavas and Kauravas – over the kingdom of Indraprastha. The Pandavas are five brothers who are married to the same woman – Draupadi – whom the oldest Pandava, Yudhishter, loses in a gambling bet. The war between the two families is the major battle where the Pandavas have both justice and Lord Krsna, another incarnation of Lord Vishnu, on their side. Just before the onset of battle, one of the Pandavas, Arjun, becomes extremely anxious and panicky. At this point the sermon by Lord Krsna is distilled in the Geeta, which focuses on Karma yoga defined as performing actions and not worrying about the results of the actions.

In the *Mahabharata* there are several instances of an individual committing suicide either for religious reasons or for the simple reason that the individual has reached the end of lifetime.

Both these stories hold a special place in the life of Hindus. They are told to the children and repeated with prayers and scriptures. *Ramcharitmanas* is often enacted in towns and villages by amateur actors for weeks in the autumn every year prior to *Diwali*, which celebrates the return of Lord Rama to Ayodhya and is also the start of the Hindu New Year. Neither scripture condemns suicide, which is not seen as inherently evil. Thakur (1962) discusses two types of suicide – religious and general. General suicide includes social, economic, and political instances.

Self-immolation is described in the *Rgveda*, as is suicide at the confluence of the Ganga and Yamuna rivers: 'with sacrifice, the gods worshipped the sacrifice . . . These great beings attained to the heavens where the gods, the ancient sādyas reside!' In hymns in the *Rgveda*, God is represented as the agent, the object or the subject of sacrifices himself and to offer up heaven and earth while in others it is stated that the 'Lord of Creatures gave himself. He became their sacrifice . . . He having given himself to them made a reflection of himself which is sacrifice.' In the *Upanishads* it is laid down that the *sanyāsin* who has acquired full insights may enter upon the great journey or choose death by voluntary starvation, drowning, fire, or a hero's fate. However, such acts are attacked in the *Iśāvāsya Upanishads*, thus confirming the ambivalence: 'Those who take their lives reach after death the sunless regions covered by impenetrable darkness.'

In the *Ramacharitmanas* referred to earlier, Lord Rama had promised that if a human ever violated his order or his wish, he would abandon him. Unfortunately, his younger brother Lakshmana was the first to act to the contrary, although unintentionally. Rama then deserted him for good. This separation from Rama was a big blow to Lakshmana who drowned himself in the River Saryu. As Rama's wife, Sita, and mother, Kausalya, had died earlier, Rama was alone and lost interest in life. Together with his remaining two brothers, he then walked into the same river and drowned himself. Upon hearing this, his subjects walked into the river in their thousands and drowned themselves. Thus mass suicide made Ayodhya a deserted city. Interestingly, the family history of suicide and depression is very strong in the descriptions and depictions of the Suryavanshi clan, to which Rama belongs in the Ramayana.

In other scriptures, such as the *Brahmapurāna*, suicide is frowned upon: 'Those who commit suicide by poison, hanging, drowning or falling from a cliff or a tree should be classified with those who commit *mahāpātakas* (cardinal sins). Such persons should not be cremated nor should usual funeral rites be performed for them.' Interestingly, no such condemnation is made for the religious suicide as this is done without any passion. There are exceptions, however:

1. *Sati* or self-immolation of women either with (*sahamaranam*) or after (*anumaranam*) the cremation of their husbands (see chapter 7).
2. Suicide by drowning is not only permitted but enjoined at the confluence of the rivers Ganga and Yamuna. Death by self-cremation at one of the holy places is commended.
3. The *Purānas* also allow persons with incurable diseases or those who are too old to do their appointed religious duties to terminate their lives voluntarily by drowning, starvation, jumping from cliffs or self-immolation.
4. It is specially recommended for ascetics.
5. Terminating one's life towards the end by *mahāprasthāna* (great exit or departure) is also a recognised form of exit from the world.

Apart from the suicide due to incurable disease, all other forms represent forms of religious suicide. The ambivalent messages dealing with acts of suicide, those who deal with it and those who enable such acts to happen, suggest that such individuals should be offered no alms or solace. In Yama-smrti it is said: 'When a person tries to do away with himself by such methods as hanging, if he dies, his body should be smeared with impure things and if he lives he should be fined along with his friends and family and they should all undergo prescribed penance.'

Thakur (1962) suggests that whereas religious suicides are discouraged and even denounced, general suicides are not. The conflicting views are not always clear, especially when it is difficult to differentiate between the two types of suicide.

## Medieval India

With the repeated invasions, the attitudes towards suicide started to change. The Holy Qur'an clearly states: 'It is not for any soul to die, save by God's permission written down for an appointed time . . . spend in the way of Allah and cast not yourself to perdition with your own hands. . . . Whoever shall kill himself shall suffer in the fire of hell . . . shall be excluded from heaven forever.' Thus there appears to have been unanimity of opinion throughout the Muslim world that suicide is a violation of a divine command contained in the Qur'an and the Sunnah of the Prophet. Due to the nature of the Muslim's belief in God and the future life, suicide is seen as an act of revolt against God. In medieval India, suicide did occur among the Muslims. At the same time *sati* and *jauhar* were prevalent among their subjects, as further discussed in chapter 7.

Religious suicides described include *mahaprāsthāna* (the great exit or departure). The ascetic or pilgrim is advised to walk until he drops, or to leave his life by fire or in the snow. He is also advised to give up food, then water, and eventually to live only on air, which he is also expected to give up eventually. Suicide by fire, water, or jumping off a cliff is extolled. Various places of pilgrimage are said to be where acts of suicide may take place. Similarly, trees in these places are revered because these are the places from where pilgrims can jump into the river and commit suicide. In Allahabad such a tree is said to be close to the temple where pilgrims came to die. It was believed that one who committed suicide in this temple attained heaven and enjoyed eternal pleasure. Thus *Prayagraj* at the confluence of the Ganga, Yamuna, and Saraswati rivers was, and is, still considered as the holiest place. It was the greatest centre of suicides and attracted persons from all over the country to indulge in self-destruction to achieve what they desired.

*Saiva Purānas* advocated suicide by fire or falling down from the top of a mountain cliff to ardent devotees of Siva so they obtain a heavenly existence. They recommend that such an advocate should build up a great fire and, after worshipping a picture of Bhairava, offer himself as a sacrifice in that fire. The special and significant feature of this form of approach to heaven is its availability to sinners as well as virtuous men, to women as to men, and to men of all castes. The sorrow of a sinner for his moral lapses must be as intense as his faith in this form of redemption. The spread of such beliefs was helped by the anarchy engendered by the fall of great Hindu empires and foreign invasions. These views, although ancient and medieval, are still observed.

Thakur (1962) suggests that suicide as an act of expiation for penances was noted in north Bihar during the medieval period. From the Aine-Akbari it becomes clear that suicides by starving, by covering oneself with cow dung and setting oneself on fire, by burying oneself in the snow, by drowning, or by cutting one's throat were observed and reported. This was noted at the time of the Mughal emperor Akbar in the fifteenth century. Similarly, Crooke (1896) reports that those who were ill chose to bury or drown themselves with due ceremonies in anticipation of receiving a happy transmigration into a healthy body. Suicide in medieval India meant not so much absorption in an impersonal absolute as union with a personal deity. The widespread custom of dying under the carriage of Lord Jagannātha led to legislative changes under British rule.

## SUICIDE AMONG BUDDHISTS

Although the Buddhists allow a man to take his own life under certain circumstances, they also maintain that dire miseries are generally in store for the self-murderer and look upon him as one who must have sinned in previous births. Not withstanding this opposition, the Buddhist literature is full of description of various kinds of suicide. Harishchandra (1998) has described various psychiatric aspects in the *Jataka* tales, which embodied what the Buddha reached whenever a particular crisis prompted him to give advice or guidance. A method of attempted suicide mentioned in the *Jataka* tales involves pulling out and eating one's own tongue. Harischandra (1998) calls this act *glossophagia* and suggests that the cause of death may be cardio-respiratory failure secondary to shock and haemorrhage. He cautions that even a stripped, isolated individual cannot be prevented from carrying out this act. These acts were related to grief in the *Jataka* tales.

## CONCLUSIONS

Although the literature is variable and the interpretation of various acts have to be understood in the specific cultural-economic and political context, it is fair to conclude that acts of suicide were not uncommon and were influenced, and often approved, by culture and religion. It is also fair to assume that attitudes towards acts of suicide and attempted suicide have not been always negative. These acts allowed various individuals in different religious groups to find a way out of a life that had got too stressful.

CHAPTER THREE

# Definitions of suicidal behaviour

## INTRODUCTION

Suicide is the act of death that is seen and/or meant to result from a conscious initiation of activity by the individual that was intended to bring about his/her own demise. The question is whether this motivation leads to an act by the said individual to the said individual, and not by others. Farberow (1975) suggests that in some cases the intent is not entirely clear and this intention may play a variable role, both consciously and unconsciously.

## CONCEPT OF BODY

When a body is seen as a representative of the society or culture and the attacks on the body are in fact attacks on the society, then deliberate self-harm (although harming oneself) may actually be harming the larger group. Turner (1997) suggests that, in the western context, the body is seen as the effect of deeper structural arrangements of power and knowledge; as a symbolic system of metaphors through which power is conceptualised; body can be understood as the consequence of long-term historical changes in human society and as a lived-in experience of daily life. Hence, any harm to the body can be seen as an attack on any of these four aspects. However, when body is simply seen as flesh the religious aspects become more important, especially in the Christian context.

Women's sexuality may be seen as problematic within a patriarchal society because it is necessary to guarantee the legitimate reproduction of men in order to secure the economic basis of society. Thus, to understand women's sexuality, Turner (1997) argues that we need to understand the distribution of property within societies, regulated typically through the patriarchal structure of the household, and how these changes affect changes in relationships. Thus any self-harm by women may be seen as a response to patriarchy, whereas for men, self-harm may reflect a failure of economic achievement. This may explain the high rates of attempted and completed suicide in unemployed men and housewives.

In feudal systems, the social accumulation of property and land within the family relies on arrangements of marriage where female sexuality, especially virginity, becomes one element of exchange. The female body under these circumstances is exchanged and for a female who wants to respond, one way is by deliberate self-harm, especially at the age and level where such exchanges are being contemplated or occurring, i.e. pubertal or late adolescents. With women's position being subordinate to that of men in some cultures, the continuity of patriarchal authority allows little liberation. When self is conceived as reflexive in response to modernism (Beck, 1992; Giddens, 1992), then self becomes conceptualised as a project, which can be made, constructed and endlessly refashioned through the life cycle. The self thus becomes the body – hence any self-harm will fit into this perspective. This allows males or females to take control, especially if they see themselves as modern compared with their traditional roots. The impact of racism, which reflects another kind of power, therefore becomes a similar factor producing the same levels of stress. Overdose, self-poisoning or self-harm can be a reflex response.

Asad (1997) hypothesises that interest in body (by the professionals certainly) is linked to a noticeable ideological development in contemporary life – the urge to aestheticise modern life. The body as an image, as seen in the media, may lead individuals to depersonalise their body and may confirm that any damage to the body may necessarily be permanent. There are accidental deaths, of course, as a result of a suicidal act, where the intent to die may not have been strong but circumstances conspired against the individual by delayed discovery or unexpected reaction to the substances taken.

Farberow (1975) suggests that the word suicide was first used in 1651. The act of suicide can be purely individualistic or it can be social or institutional. Farberow (1975) offers a cultural history of suicide and draws attention to the fact that causation of the act was seen as a result of social factors, as well as of insanity. Cultural history provides a perspective for viewing suicide as an act influenced by a multitude of factors such as religion, law, philosophy, and thought.

## ATTEMPTED SUICIDE, PARASUICIDE, OR DELIBERATE SELF-HARM

While suicide may be preceded by attempted suicide, parasuicide, or deliberate self-harm (often these terms are used interchangeably), not all cases of attempted suicide, parasuicide, or deliberate self-harm lead to suicide. The frequency of deliberate self-harm is considerable and creates enormous demands and distress on those who carry out the act, those who look after for those who carry out the act, and those who care for these individuals whether they are formal or nonformal carers (Pritchard, 1995).

Although deliberate self-harm is often seen as a 'cry for help', it is not always thus, and this explanation can often be viewed in a derogatory manner. Various forms of deliberate self-harm can be seen as causes of high morbidity amongst both men and women and young and old alike. The severity of these acts varies. Kreitman (1978) suggested using the word parasuicide – both parasuicide and attempted suicide have connotations related to the act of suicide and therefore sometimes the term deliberate self-harm is preferred. However, as discussed earlier, concepts of self do differ across cultures. In sociocentric cultures, the individual's concept of self is very much related to kinship and the family. Hence the act of self-harm may well be aimed at one or more individuals within the kinship. The deliberateness of the act in harming these individuals or oneself (if one comes from an egocentric society) contributes to the action, which may or may not eventually lead to the act of suicide. The repetition of the act is related to a number of factors such as impulsivity, poor impulse control, high levels of psychiatric problems, substance misuse problems, etc. Deliberateness of the act can also be questioned at times.

Diekstra and Gulbinat (1993) define it as: 'suicidal gestures and manipulative attempts to serious but unsuccessful attempts to kill oneself – any act with nonfatal outcome that attempts to cause or actually causes self-harm or without intervention from others would have done so or consists of ingesting a substance in excess of its generally recognised or prescribed therapeutic dose'. Habitual self-mutilation and drug or alcohol abuses are not part of this definition. This is a comprehensive definition that focuses on the act rather than the intent, which is its advantage and also its disadvantage. The act can be identified by carers – formal or informal.

Pritchard (1995) observes that male suicides are generally more common than female and older people are less likely to harm themselves. However, differentiating between deliberate self-harm that is an actual failed attempt to kill oneself and deliberate self-harm in which people make a suicidal gesture can be extremely difficult.

## SUICIDAL INTENT

As noted above, the distinction between an act of deliberate self-harm that has failed, suicide, and a suicidal gesture where the person did not intend to kill him- or herself can be quite difficult. The differentiation has to be due to suicidal intent. Beck, Resnik, and Lettieri (1974) developed this in a suicidal intent scale by relying on a feeling of hopelessness (which may mediate between depressive state and suicidal state) and sense of control. However, in clinical settings not only is an assessment of suicidal intent problematic, but it can also be a false negative. The relationship between suicidal intent, thought and action is problematic and may well be related to a number of factors (see Figure 3.1). Those who attempt suicide are more likely to be female, of lower socioeconomic status, of substance abuse, and exhibit personality disorder problems, impulsivity, and situational stresses.

Pritchard (1995) has offered a distinction between deliberate self-harm and suicide as illustrated in Table 3.1.

## SUICIDAL IDEATION

Suicidal ideation as a necessary prerequisite of other forms of suicidal behaviour has been reported in all communities (Goldney, Harris, Badri, Michael, & Fisher, 1998): from 5.4% in a general population in the USA (Van-

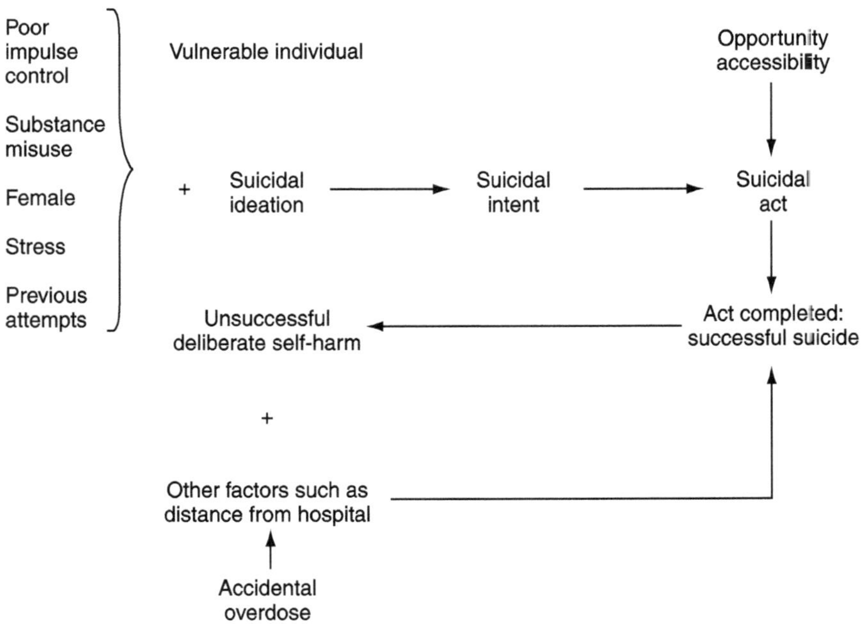


**Figure 3.1** Interrelationship of suicide ideation, intent, and act

Table 3.1
Differences between suicide and deliberate self-harm

| *Characteristic* | *Suicide* | *Deliberate self-harm* |
|---|---|---|
| 1. *Act* | Emotionality | Impulsive |
| | Violent means | Poisoning |
| | Wishes to die | Not clear |
| | More in spring | No seasonal peaks |
| 2. *Demographic factors* | Males | Females |
| | Divorced | Divorced |
| | Living alone | Usually in relationships |
| | Certain professions | Any profession |
| | All ages | Younger |
| 3. *Social factors* | All social classes | More social class 4 & 5 |
| | Unemployed | Unemployed |
| 4. *Psychological factors* | Psychiatric illness | Affective symptoms |
| | Stress | Stress |
| | Alcohol/drug use | Alcohol/drug use |
| 5. *History* | Previous attempts | Previous deliberate self-harm |

divort & Locke, 1979) to 63% in the same country (Bonner & Rich, 1987) – whereas rates from other countries such as Australia (Goldney et al. 1998), Egypt (Okasha, Lataib, & Sadek, 1981), Sweden (Hallstrom, 1977), and the UK (Salmons & Harrington, 1984) are reported to be somewhere in the middle.

Repeated suicidal attempts frequently occur in the presence of suicidal ideation and this may increase the risk (Batchelor, 1954; Ettlinger, 1984). Following on from 3130 students who had participated in a postal survey, Goldney, Winefield, Tiggeman, and Winefield (1991) repeated a 4–8-year follow-up. Interestingly, 40% of the sample denied ever having had a suicide ideation in their lifetime. The researchers found that 3% had acknowledged attempting suicide and suggest that the relationship between suicidal ideation and self-esteem has to be understood in this particular context. In a sample of Sudanese women, Goldney et al. (1998) found that displaced persons showed higher levels of suicidal ideation than the students (55% vs. 27%). Although the numbers are small, the study illustrates the universality of suicidal ideation. The reasons may reflect trauma of migration and increased expression of freedom, but religious taboos may lead to an underestimate of the levels of suicidal ideation. It is useful for clinicians to ascertain suicidal ideation as part of any clinical assessment, especially in vulnerable groups such as females and migrants.

## MASS SUICIDE

In addition to acts such as *jauhar* (see p. 42), mass suicide is seen in other settings which may be largely related to sociopolitical events rather than to personal psychopathology, such as is seen in psychiatric patients. Meerloo (1962) reports that when people fail as a group and believe that they have no future, they surrender en masse to death. Defeats in war may lead to self-destruction to save one's honour, to face death rather than slavery or defeated status, with associated fear of punishment by the victor. Loss of freedom may lead to catastrophic reactions of either murderous rebellion or chosen death. Meerloo (1962) suggests that among primitive peoples [sic], a suicidal post-battle tendency often becomes strong when failure of aggression and attack fortifies feelings of guilt. He goes on to argue that such people often believe that their failure in war is caused by a magic, punishing power. Fear of the unknown divine punishments forces them to surrender passively to his wrath and to death.

In a psychoanalytic ascription of the act of war, Meerloo (1962) proposes that a nation full of guilt feelings and unsolved aggression escapes from inner collapse only by the explosion of outer war. Mass suicidal war can be a paradoxical attempt at rejuvenating the self-esteem of the nation. The love for the deity (of death) leads to the wish to die, or to be reunited with the primordial mother or goddess. Fear of war, and in recent times terrorism (be it real or perceived), leads individuals to behave in either a weakened way or a perceived aggressor type of stance. The childhood fantasy of magic/horror is seen as coming true and the individual may feel frightened of future punishment.

Worldwide fear replaced the magic fear of the primitive world and mass scares have become much more transferable; one only has to look at the threats of virus attacks on the web. Thus, fear experienced by individuals may become paralysing and the passive surrender to fate may be comparable with the position of learned helplessness. In any feeling of catastrophe, both progressive and retrogressive tendencies are included. The retrogressive tendencies fit in with the Freudian death instinct. The archaic suicide implies not only the conscious killing of the self, but also our attempt to transcend our own capacities.

In mass thinking there lives something destructive and deeply masochistic, yet, quite paradoxically, joining and merging with the masses is inwardly experienced as immortality. Meerloo (1962) argues that in the masses an archaic instinct prevails more easily, a primitive solution is resorted to above civilised judgement. He sees mass suicide as one of the symptoms of collective psychotic behaviour. It is mass aggression directed against the very existence of the masses.

In addition to understanding the definitions of suicidal ideation, suicidal acts and suicidal behaviour, it is helpful to understand the often-used terms of 'culture', 'race', and 'ethnicity', and what they represent. Culture is defined as a common heritage or set of beliefs, norms, and values (Department of Health and Human Services (DHHS), 1999). It refers to the shared and largely learned attributes of a group of people. Anthropologists see culture as a system of shared meanings, i.e. a set of people who are placed either by census categories or through self-identification into the same racial or ethnic groups. They are often assumed to share the same culture. There is no doubt that this is a gross simplification. Culture is equally applicable to groups of whites as it is to black and ethnic minority groups. The term 'culture' is equally applicable to common social groupings such as adults trained in the same profession or youth who belong to a gang (DHHS, 2001). 'Cultural identity' is a term used to identify a level at which someone identifies and to which he or she belongs for standards or behaviour. Thus, cultural identities can be multiple and culture is a dynamic process. Culture continually changes and is influenced both by people's beliefs and the demands of their environment (Lopez & Guarnaccia, 2000).

Ethnicity refers to a common heritage shared by a particular group (Zenner, 1996), and this heritage includes similar history, language, rituals, and preferences for food and music. Any historical experience has to be seen in that particular context.

Although race may overlap with ethnicity, its definition is much more biological. Although defined as a biological category according to common inborn biological traits (e.g. skin colour, shape of eyes, lips, nose), there are no standardised biological criteria for dividing races into distinct categories. The strongest, most compelling evidence to refute race as a biological category comes from genetic analysis of different racial groups. Within one racial group there are great genetic variations (DHHS, 2001). Race has meaning as a social category. Different cultures classify people into racial groups according to a set of characteristics that are socially significant. The concept of race is especially potent when certain social groups are separated, treated as inferior or superior, and given differential access to power and other valued resources (DHHS, 2001).

## CONCLUSIONS

Thus, for ascertaining rates of suicide and attempted suicide, not only do clinicians and researchers have to be aware of the acts and how they are defined, but they also need carefully to identify denominators in the population, as well defining race, culture, and ethnicity. It is possible that, in cultures and societies where such acts are illegal or criminal, there will be tremendous underreporting or misreporting.

CHAPTER FOUR

# The sociology of self-harm

## Contributions of Durkheim

### INTRODUCTION

Durkheim (1879/1951, p. 44) suggests that the term 'suicide' is applied to all cases of death resulting directly or indirectly from a positive or negative act by the victim himself which he [sic] knows will produce this result. Suicide can be attributed to organic–psychiatric dispositions and the nature of the physical environment (Durkheim, 1879/1951, p. 57). He proposes that in the individual constitution, or at least in that of a significant class of individuals, it is possible that on the one hand there might exist an inclination, varying in intensity from country to country, which directly leads to individuals committing suicidal acts, and on the other hand that the actions of climate and temperature may indirectly have some effects.

The argument that suicide is a type of mental disease is put forward by Durkheim as monomania. A monomaniac is therefore described as a sick person whose mentality is perfectly healthy in all aspects but one – a flaw which is clearly localised. As these monomaniacs do not imply any essential disturbance of intellectual functions, monomania is therefore seen by Durkheim as an extreme emotion in the order of impulses, one false idea in the order of representations, but of such intensity as to envelop the mind. Thus normal ambition becomes abnormal. Fleeting suicidal ideation can lead to suicidal attempts once or repeatedly, but yet may or may not lead to the suicidal act itself. Suicides generally seem influenced by some abnormal passion, whether its energy is abruptly expended or gradually developed. It may thus even appear reasonable that some such force is always necessary to offset the fundamental instinct of self-preservation which Durkheim (1879/1951, p. 60) goes on to attribute to monomania and a manifestation of insanity.

## CLASSIFICATION OF SUICIDE

Although already well known, it is useful to understand the classification of suicide as propounded by Durkheim (1879/1951, p. 63). He divides it into the following categories:

1. *Maniacal*: this is due to hallucinations or delirious perceptions where the patient kills himself/herself to escape from an imaginary danger or disgrace, or to obey an order from voices or forces other than oneself. The mind in these cases is influenced by changeable experiences. The motives too appear, disappear and change with amazing speed. The most trivial incident may cause these sudden transformations.
2. *Melancholy*: this type is associated with a general state of extreme depression and exaggerated sadness, causing the patient to no longer realise sanely the bonds with other people and things around him or her. Life is viewed as through a dark cloud and seems to become boring and painful. It is possible that hallucinations and delusions are associated with this general despair and sense of despondency and, contrary to maniacal experiences, in this case these beliefs are fixed. The fears by which the patient is haunted, the self-reproaches, felt grief he feels are always the same.
3. *Obsessive suicide*: in this case the motive is a fixed idea of death and the individual is obsessed by the desire to kill himself/herself. It is an instinctive need beyond the control of reflection and reasoning and the individual may well resist it initially, but this resistance itself produces sadness and depression associated with constantly increasing anxiety. This anxiety ceases as soon as the individual has decided to give up the struggle and to kill themselves.
4. *Impulsive or automatic suicide*: this too is unmotivated, but instead of being produced by a fixed idea obsessing the mind for a shorter or a longer period and only gradually affecting the will, it results from an abrupt and immediately irresistible impulses to kill oneself.

Durkheim (1879/1951, p. 66) argues that, in short, all suicides of the insane (maniacal) are either devoid of any motive or determined by purely imaginary motives. The depressed or melancholy suicide is linked with alienation that the individual is feeling. Such a sense of individual or personal alienation can also be attributed to a general cultural alienation, where the individual's sense of belonging to his/her own culture in the face of a new culture is severely shaken. The differences between the melancholy suicide and those described above are that in the former the resultant act is not without an objective cause. The suicides of the insane differ from others just as illusions and hallucinations differ from normal perceptions.

The suicides not associated with insanity are deliberate, and spring from representations involved in this deliberation which are not purely hallucinatory. The insane suicide was seen by Durkheim (1879/1951, p. 68) as a possible reflection of a nervous condition he calls neurasthenia. Neurasthenia sufferers experience pain and, as neurasthenia is a much more prevalent condition than insanity, the combination of pain and conflict predisposes to suicide. In addition, he takes a systems approach whereby the extremely sensitive nature of the nervous system is combined with ideas and feelings that a destabilisation may occur, which influences the mental organisation: 'Life in a fixed and constant medium is only possible if the functions of the person in question are of equal constancy and fixity, for living means responding appropriately to outer stimuli and this harmonious correspondence can be established only by time and custom' (Durkheim, 1879/1951, p. 69).

The psychological type of individual who commits or attempts suicide is that of someone who is not organised. Thus, the individual is not able to respond appropriately, and/or is unprepared to respond to stress. New forms of conduct need to be developed. The more fixed the social system, the more difficult is life there for so mobile an individual. This fixed rootedness in the Asian diaspora may reflect rigidity in the older generation, which the younger generation may well find difficult to deal with or understand. The cultural rigidity may act as a barrier against an individual who is freer within that culture. Durkheim (1879/1951, p. 70) argues that rates of suicide are proportionate to those of neurasthenia, which may also reflect rural–urban differences in the former.

Subsequently, he goes on to counter his own argument by suggesting that insanity is much more prevalent among Jews, but suicide is not and that, if anything, it is in inverse proportion to psychopathic [sic] states. A tendency to suicide is based on the constitution of the individual, which may well be influenced by factors such as race. Race is identified by processes of resemblance and affiliation. Race is the aggregate of individuals with a clearly common stock. The race was identified as the total of similar individuals of the same species who transmit characteristics of a primitive sort by sexual propagation. Thus, as Durkheim himself (1879/1951, p. 83) argues, the existence and area of race can be established only by historical and ethnographic research. The rates of suicide in some races may well be explained by high genetic contribution. The heritability of suicide needs to be ascertained across different races and ethnic groups.

The contagion of suicide is often noted either in the same family, in suicide pacts or otherwise, and across different groups through the influence of the media. Durkheim (1879/1951, p. 97) also illustrates the common factors in contagion by the story of a hospital where 15 patients had hanged themselves in swift succession in 1772 from the same hook in a dark passage of the hospital. Once the hook was removed, there was an end to the epidemic. Thus, imitation remains as a possible cause contributing to the act. Durkheim (1879/1951, p. 124) embeds the act of imitation in the quality of the states of consciousness felt simultaneously by a given number of different persons, leading them to act upon one another or combine among themselves to produce a new state – such a combination resulting from a reciprocal imitation of each of them.

Imitation is also an impulse that drives individuals to seek harmony with the society to which we belong. Thus we follow the moral and legal codes of our society, even if we are ignorant about their logical explanation. Both manners and customs are obeyed and followed. The third definition of imitation is act, which we copy in order to copy rather than for any other reason. It is the last two definitions that are worth bearing in mind in the context of suicide and attempted suicide. Imitation is said to exist when the immediate antecedent of an act is the representation of a like act previously performed by someone else with no explicit or implicit mental operation which bears upon the instinctive nature of the act reproduced intervening between representation and execution. Obviously no imitation can exist without a model to imitate. The imitation of suicide reflects certain characteristics of the society in which the 'primary' or 'autochthonous' suicide has occurred and the characteristics of the individuals living in that society are vulnerable in one way or another to carry out the act of imitation. Thus suicide that is being copied has to be seen for it to have some social effects. Lastly, the act of physical, geographical, or cultural suicide has to be in the immediate vicinity – the greater the distance, the less likely the impact on contagion.

The key difference between Durkheim's concept and modern perception is that the print and the electronic media make immediacy both more likely in a short period of time and graphic, thereby influencing copycat acts. In cross-cultural work, the closest example (barring local clusters from time to time) is that of *jauhar* when wives of Rajput soldiers (who were away at war or had died) would commit mass suicide to avoid capture and dishonour. This act might be led by the queen or another member of the Rajput household and others may follow (see chapter 7 for a detailed discussion).

Other tendencies to commit suicide are associated with social and cultural factors. This is where Durkheim defines egotistic, altruistic, and anomic suicides.

## EGOTISTIC SUICIDE

Comparing rates of Protestant and Catholic suicides, Durkheim (1879/1951, p. 158) suggests that the proclivity of Protestantism for suicide must relate to the spirit of free enquiry that animates this religion. Second, the collective credo of Protestantism is weaker because the more extensive the credo, the more unified and strong the society. Therefore, the fact that a less integrated church is more likely to have higher rates of suicide emerges. Interestingly, in religions such as Hinduism where the orthodox settings of the credo remain strong, although in some castes the collective credo is not as strong, the rates of attempted suicide remain high, even though in most epidemiological studies no distinction is made between castes. Among Muslims, where the credo is stronger in some settings, the rates of suicide are said to be low. In addition to religion, educational status also impinges upon the rates of completed and attempted suicide (see later in this volume). Durkheim (1879/1951, p. 208) posits that rates of suicide vary inversely with the degree of integration of religious, domestic and political societies, when the individuals' own goals become preponderant over those of the community and the lack of integration is unable to hold down the individual. The more weakened the groups to which the individual belongs, the less he/she depends upon them and more likely to depend upon him-/herself (see also Berrios & Mohanna, 1990).

This in turn leads to nonrecognition of any other rules of conduct (except those founded on his/her private interests). In state of egoism the individual ego asserts itself to excess in the face of the social ego and thus suicide is egoistic, springing from excessive individualism. The collective force of the society and the impact of its disintegration allow individuals to behave in such a way that they see themselves as masters of their destiny and do not feel they have to endure life's suffering patiently. The disintegrative or less cohesive society allows the individual to feel alienated and isolated without any moral support.

Excessive individualism not only results in following the action of suicidogenic causes but it itself forms such a cause. The vulnerable individual feels less moored and less attached to others around and the response to stress may well be a direct egotistical (possibly immature) one. The interaction between the society and culture on one hand and the individual on the other, and acceptance of one by the other, together with the religious, moral, political (and economic) beliefs of society, will influence the religious, moral and political beliefs of the individual. As Durkheim (1876/1951, p. 212) observes: 'To play our social role we have striven to extend our intelligence and it is still society that has supplied us with tools for this development by transmitting to us its trust fund of knowledge.' As these values have a collective origin, they also have a collective function and a collective passion.

In the religious context, the more the believer doubts, i.e. the less he/she feels a real participant in the religious faith to which he/she belongs, the more the community and society become alien to the individual. The escape therefore becomes of paramount importance, and seeking such an escape may be the causation of the suicide.

Durkheim (1879/1951, p. 213) argues that social man necessarily presupposes a society which he expresses and serves. If this dissolves then an artificial combination of illusory images remains. This alienation allows the individual to look for something else, which in egocentric settings may well be the individual him-/herself. In other settings of sociocentric societies, egocentrism allows the individual to enter into a conflict, which has to be resolved in one way or another. The detachment and alienation may be more common in better educated individuals whose egocentric perceptions produce a discrepancy between their expectations and achievement. Marriage (if unhappy) may further add to a sense of alienation and detachment and may not necessarily be protective. The conflict between the society (whether collectivist, individualist, egocentric or sociocentric) and the individual leads to the individual's ego becoming a generating cause. Thus the bond between the individual and life becomes feeble. The gender differences can thus be seen in the context of gender role expectations and the underlying conflict may continue to arouse feelings of alienation.

Suicide has varying significance in related but distinctly different cultures. The ways to express individual and social maladjustment are clearly limited: suicide, neurosis, crime, alcoholism, and a few others. Hendin (1964b) argues that these ways vary qualitatively (in their meaning and significance) as well as quantitatively, not only from country to country but also among the subcultures (in the same country). In a study carried out in Scandinavia, Hendin (1964a) proposed that suicidal patients are an excellent barometer of the pressures felt by everyone in that culture, whether they succumbed to them or not. He observed that suicidal Swedish patients presented an exaggerated picture of the pressures of life in Sweden where there is 'performance' suicide related to the rigid concern with achievement that characterises the culture. Puritanical rural areas in Norway may show what can be described as a 'moral' form of suicide reflecting the individual's concerns with sin and punishment.

## ALTRUISTIC SUICIDE

This is defined by Durkheim (1879/1951, p. 219) as relating to peculiar characteristics as seen in primitive [sic] cultures. These peculiar characteristics are related to wives' suicide on their husbands' deaths, suicide by men on the threshold of old age or stricken with sickness, and suicide of followers or servants on the death of their chiefs. Perceived as a duty, especially in the cause of the larger group, kinship or society, this type of suicide is sacrifice for the purposes of the greater good (see chapter 3). Thus, for the society to compel one of its members to commit suicide suggests that individual personality is secondary to societal expectations. For individuals to occupy so small a place in collective life, they must be almost completely absorbed in the group and very highly integrated.

Thus in ancient India the practice of *sati* (the wife sitting on the funeral pyre of her husband) reflects an altruistic motive. Although such motives may also be indicative of avoiding the grotesque fate of Hindu widowhood – where the widows had to shave their heads, were seen as ill omened and often had to migrate to places of pilgrimage to live off charity – the impact of sociocentric society dictating to the individual is abundantly clear (see also chapter 7). Altruistic suicide characterised by a sense of duty has been defined as obligatory altruistic suicide. Not every altruistic suicide is obligatory. These suicides are associated with the moral values of the society. Another variety of altruistic suicide is optional and is required less expressly by the society. In some cases, attempted suicide may be seen as an attempted sacrifice where the individual is attempting to sacrifice him-/herself to the altar of others' needs. Among Hindus, a number of varieties of suicide, especially among religious practices, come under the umbrella of altruistic suicide. Brahminic influences command suicide only with some reservations. A man must have reached a certain age and have left at least one son. The Brahmin thus freed from his body, grief and fear is honourably received in the abode of Brahma. The custom of seeking death in the waters of holy rivers, especially the Ganga, is well known and followed by kings and their subjects alike.

Jumping from high rocks or being run over by the chariot of Jagannath have been important ways of seeking religious salvation. Altruistic suicide differs from egoistic suicide, which is related to the crude morality that disregards everything and relates solely to the individual. Altruistic suicide is associated with the refined ethic, which sets human personality on so high a pedestal that it can no longer be subordinated to anything. Durkheim (1879/1951, pp. 228ff) hints that altruistic suicide may be more common in soldiers than civilians. He links such an increase with alcohol use among soldiers and easy access to arms.

## ANOMIC SUICIDE

The third type of suicide defined by Durkheim was anomic suicide. He argues that no living being can be happy or even exist unless his needs are sufficiently proportioned to his means (Durkheim 1879/1951, p. 246). As noted earlier, any change in equilibrium is likely to contribute further to a sense of alienation. Human activity cannot be entirely released from all restraint. When society is disturbed by some painful crisis or by beneficent but abrupt transitions, it is momentarily incapable of exercising the influence of its restraint on its members. The rise in suicides due to changed economic circumstances may be attributed to this. Weariness itself may contribute to a sense of disillusionment.

A lack of regulation and consequent sufferings may lead to anomic suicide. Unlike egoistic suicide, the society's influence is lacking in the basically individual passions. Individual forms of the different types of suicide include melancholic languor, where the individual withdraws and detaches from business, public affairs, useful work, and domestic duties. This may well be a form of egoistic suicide, whereas altruistic suicide involves expenditure of energy, as its source is a violent emotion. This is an active suicide. The third variety is that of an individual who commits suicide in a passionate manner, but this is not altruistic passion. Violent recriminations against life in general or individuals, characterise this anomic form of suicide. Of course, one or more forms may combine together to influence other individuals.

Suicide is influenced by both extrinsic and intrinsic factors. Intrinsic factors include psychological profile, personality characteristics, patterns of attachment, etc. Extrinsic factors include social factors, societal pressures, economic factors, and religion. Sociocentric and egocentric societies will allow individuals to respond to stress in some specific ways. Society may be formed by individuals, but it reflects a combination of structures and institutions. Stockard and O'Brien (2002) gathered data from the United States and 13 other developed nations to study the cohort and contextual effects on the rates of suicide. They measured the collectivist, solidaristic, and egalitarian nature of the public policy of the countries. The collectivist view captures the extent to which nations have political systems that provide universal programmes for social assistance and strong programmes of social protection. Traditional family roles were measured – using rates of marriage, divorce, fertility, and female participation in the labour force. They reported that rates of suicide were low among Irish teenagers but very high among Finn males and New Zealand females. They found that cohorts that were relatively large had higher suicide rates even when age, period, and national differences were controlled; this finding was stronger for males than for females. Stockard and O'Brien hypothesised that this variation is related to social integration and regulation. Their observation that the influence of cohort-related measures of integration and regulation is weaker in societies with a strong commitment to social political equality, especially involving institutions that support women, suggests that such social programmes may reflect such a degree of integration and social regulations which may be more difficult to accept in some cases. This in turn may well contribute further stress especially if racism and perceived discrimination are not allowing or encouraging individuals to integrate.

The avenues of communication and transportation of ideas become crucial in the way they are understood by individuals, but this needs to be seen in the context of social and cultural settings. Cultural factors imbibed by the individual include religious, moral, faith, kinship, and structures, and allow individuals to develop their own mores, which have to fit in with the broader cultural and social structures if they are not to lead to conflict. Egoistic suicide may well be the commonest type of suicide. However, suicide and homicide have been argued to be two sides of the same coin (Hendin, 1964b).

Durkheim (1879/1951:363–364) argues that in societies and environments where the dignity of the person is the supreme end of conduct, where man is a God to mankind, the individual is readily inclined to consider the man in himself [sic] as a God and to regard himself as the object of his own cult. The attitudes towards God inherent in the individual allow the individual to get away from conflict by rationalising the act of self-harm.

Pritchard (1995) argues that Durkheim's great project was concerned with the social causes that contribute to suicide, yet he did include an inetgrationalist approach. However, as Berrios and Mohanna (1990) point out, Durkheim was selective in choosing as protagonists those who would see suicide and mental illness as having a physiological ideology, rather than schematically generating antagonists which create an inadvertent schism. It is worth mentioning that Durkheim did not refer to his contemporaries' work very much, and did not take into account specific cultural and social differences across different nations whilst he producing his seminal work.

In Durkheim's overall interpretation of ritual suicide in lower societies where 'insufficient individuation' leads to *sati*, he sees the ego as not its own property but as being blended with something not itself. When Durkheim suggests that the forms of voluntary death he has grouped under the category of 'obligatory altruistic suicide' are to be explained by the fact that between a widow and her husband, a client and his patron and a servant and his prince the relationship of dependence is so close and the very idea of separation so painful and unthinkable that the fates of the two proponents are bound together. Yet he still reintroduces the concept of fanatical suicide with regard to devotional suicide, although often the concepts of sacrifice and suicide are clearly defined in the minds of individuals. Stockard and O'Brien (2002) propose that the four types of suicide in modern societies, as defined by Durkheim, were related to low levels of social integration and social regulations. These two concepts are seen as integral to Durkheimian theories. Stockard and O'Brien (2002) suggest that both egotistic and anomic suicides also reflect some causal factors within the society, i.e. diminished regulation and reduced integration.

The role of geography too has to be seen in this context. Baller and Richardson (2002) observed that the results of the French analysis of suicide contradict the Durkheimian view that imitation plays a role in shaping the geographic patterning of suicide. They found that suicide rates for northern and southern French departments cluster geographically even when the clustering of multiple dimensions of social integration is controlled. They replicated similar findings in non-western countries. However, for the American and western countries they found that suicide clusters exist only in geographic space because important structural predictors of suicide, including measures of social integration, do. Baller and Richardson measured the presence of social ties as well as three other measures of social integration, which included contact with religious persons, life-long friends, and spouses. Carrying out spatial analysis they found that for the years 1872–1876, French suicide rates were 0.749, which compared with US county rates in 1989–1991 of 0.152. Residential and marital stability in the French data indicate imitations, according to Baller and Richardson (2002). They further argue that marital stability offers significant protection. They conclude that Durkheim's rejection of invitation theory was premature.

Giddens (1978), in his monograph on Durkheim's life and works, argues that the perception that nonsocial factors such as race, climate, etc. do not have any influence on rates of suicide is simply not true. Durkheim's use of data was also defined by Giddens (1978, p. 115) as that developed by moral statisticians. The usefulness (or lack thereof) of the suicide data and its official sources and accuracy are in doubt. The definition of suicide used by Durkheim did not take intention into account. The suicide data are more than an index of the incidence of self-destructive acts. As Durkheim did not take into account acts of attempted suicide, Giddens (1978, p. 117) argues that the study of attempted suicide is fundamental to the understanding of completed suicidal acts.

## CONCLUSIONS

Durkheim made a clear distinction between sane and insane suicides, and associated these differences with other social and cultural factors not always clearly defined but nevertheless identified. The role and contribution of Durkheim to the study of suicide have been extremely influential. His description and definitions are used in lay language and often described. However, his writings too are one of the products of his environment and the context in which they were written. The use of intention in defining acts of suicide is a useful concept, but the act itself is extremely complex and clinicians must take this into account.

CHAPTER FIVE

# Social and personal factors and suicidal behaviour in adolescents

## INTRODUCTION

The meanings as well as the experiences of suicidal behaviour vary between adolescents and adults. As a result, social and personal factors in the causation also vary to some degree. In addition, attitudes to suicidal behaviour differ massively across age groups. As with adults, and as previously identified by Durkheim, religious integration and integration with a stable social structure may act as protectors against suicide. Increasing social stress, social expectations and possible changes in family structure may well contribute to stress in adolescents, thereby pushing them towards an increased likelihood of suicidal behaviour.

The data on adolescents' rates of attempted suicide are even more difficult to obtain. The additional complicating factors include provision of services, 'accidental' nature of the act and the age group itself. There have been several attempts, in different parts of the world, to collect adequate information, but these attempts have not always been very successful.

## SELF-HARM BY ADOLESCENTS

Shaffer and Fisher (1981) caution that both researchers and clinicians must remain aware that there is a moderate under-representation of acts of suicide in the 15- to 19-year-old age group and a very considerable under-representation of suicide in the 10- to 14-year-olds. They conclude that the significance of childhood suicide is not in its importance as a public health problem – for the condition is a rare one – but rather in what it may tell us about factors that protect individuals from suicide. They go on to suggest that this protection seems to be a universal phenomenon. The proportion of suicides that occur in childhood is remarkably similar in all countries from which reliable data are available. The three general aetiological models they propose include psychiatric illness, internal or unconscious conflicts (which will vary according to age, gender, and stress), and that suicide is an understandable, intended, and logical behaviour, bearing in mind the context of the stressors. Shaffer and Fisher (1981) go on to argue that the reasons why black children are less likely to attempt/complete suicide are twofold. The first suggests that there is an idea of reciprocal relation between inwardly and outwardly directed aggression. They suggest that as black children have higher levels of delinquency, i.e. outwardly directed aggression, this may explain reciprocally held low rates of suicide. The second reason, they argue, is that even though blacks have high levels of stress, cultural factors or convention make suicide less (or more) acceptable or 'necessary'.

Adolescent suicide and suicidal attempts have become a major worry for mental health practitioners, teachers, parents, and others involved with this age group. Consequently, the evaluation of suicide risk and the identification of youths likely to be at risk have become priorities. Suicide is the second leading cause of death among adolescents (National Centre for Health Statistcis, 1992). Estimates of the incidence of suicide attempts in teenagers range widely. Incidence reports from clinics are difficult to interpret because many of the individuals who engage in suicidal behaviours do not seek medical treatment and they may be misdiagnosed when they do (McIntire & Angle, 1970). Standardised clinical assessments of outpatient samples of youths have revealed that about 60% have suicidal ideation and up to 20% have made suicide attempts (Myers, McCauley, Caldron, & Tredes, 1991).

Other factors complicate attaining accurate figures further. Stigma is attached to suicide. In order to save the family from the associated stigma and distress, family members prefer to give a different description (Chambers & Harvey, 1989). In spite of these two factors, research on annual figures has demonstrated that on a national level the data are reasonably reliable (Speechley & Stavarky, 1991). Second, careful analysis shows that adolescent suicide figures are also reasonably stable (Males, 1991). Hence the use of the annual suicide rate of a country can be taken as an accurate indicator of changes in those environmental factors that are associated with suicidal behaviour (Pritchard, 1995).

## GENERAL RISK FACTORS

In a review and critique of the literature on attempted suicide in adolescence, Spirito, Brown, Overholsen, and Fritz (1989) argue that attempted suicide amongst adolescents is a frequent event. The medical lethality of an event can be assessed using a number of criteria. The likelihood of rescue, method used, suicidal intent, and indications of intent may all give a clue towards the prognosis of the act. Psychological factors associated with adolescent suicide behaviours include hopelessness, depression or depressive illness, and anger (Bancroft et al., 1979; Roberts et al., 1995). Depression among adolescents may well be difficult to ascertain and hopelessness or anger may also be marked, making it likely that these conditions remain underdiagnosed. Anger may take many forms and lead to intense verbal outbursts or acting out (Spirito et al., 1989). Cognitive factors include lack of flexibility and rigidity in problem solving. Impulsivity too is a frequent risk factor (Arffa, 1983), and is also a personality characteristic of adolescent suicide attempters (Cumley, 1979; Haider, 1968). Lack of impulse control makes the lethality of the act more likely. It has been suggested that impulsive suicide attempters hail from families where action takes precedence over verbal mediation (McCulloch & Phillip, 1972). Impulsive attempters are less depressed and less hopeless than non-impulsive attempters (Williams, Davidson, & Montgomery, 1980). Cognitive distortions associated with maladaptive information-processing patterns may predispose a person to focus on the negative aspects of a situation. Spirito et al. (1989) propose that problem-solving deficits, impulsiveness, and cognitive distortions appear more frequently in suicide attempters. Furthermore, they argue that behavioural substrates in suicide attempters indicate that these individuals may lack effective coping strategies. They suggest that suicide attempters were less likely to use wishful thinking and more likely to use social isolation as a coping strategy. However, whether social isolation and lack of peer support or increased peer pressures lead to the act, or the social isolation is a result of coping, is difficult to tease out.

Interpersonal factors that put the individual at risk of suicide include impaired social skills and poor peer relationships. Social adjustment problems may be complicated by environmental factors such as family functioning, aggressive behaviour, conflict with and between parents, family history of distress, and psychiatric illness along with alcohol abuse, chronic physical illness in the family, and sexual abuse. Some of these factors, such as peer relationships and expectations of such relationships, gender roles, and gender role expectations, are likely to be more or less culture specific. Conflict between parents, and the impact of this on children, and violence, neglect, and alcohol abuse in the family, although not specific to certain cultures, are also influenced by the culture's interpretation of these acts. Spirito et al.

(1989) conclude that the families of adolescent suicide attempters are characterised by substantial levels of dysfunction, which include physical abuse, excessive discipline, marital conflict, and communication difficulties. If stressful life events occur at vulnerable periods these may create further problems. Another factor that needs to be taken into account is 'contagion' or imitation of the act. There is little doubt that media portrayal of suicides does influence the rates of attempted suicide.

Models of behaviour within the family may include high rates of attempted suicide from which the young vulnerable adolescent may learn. It is also entirely possible that the large number of young people who depend for a sense of worth on being valued by others are particularly vulnerable to psychological stress. Their internal world often appears devoid of conscious fantasy and they depend for psychological stimulation on external forces, including drugs. The blurring and attenuation of the adolescent developmental period means that adolescents inappropriately maintain an early adolescent attitude through chronological early adulthood, a profound conviction about the ease of the act and the probability of survival. They may then play a risky game by repeatedly attempting suicide (Peterson, Awad, & Kendler, 1973).

Acosta-Rua (1991) indicates that age-typical pressures may trigger suicidal acts in vulnerable individuals. Kerfoot (1988) reported on 100 children under the age of 16 admitted to a hospital following an episode of deliberate self-poisoning. When compared with non-attempters, the author found that self-poisoners showed higher levels of delinquency, school problems, previous attempts, truancy, and previous experiences of care. Their families too showed more evidence of marital failure, previous psychiatric disorder, self-poisoning, and delinquency. Taylor and Stansfeld (1984) reported very similar findings, although their numbers were smaller.

It is generally agreed that the risk of completing suicide in adolescents is substantially elevated in those who have active suicidal ideation or have attempted suicide in the past. Adolescent victims of suicidal acts are much more likely than community controls to have a history of suicide attempts or suicidal ideation (Bjarnason & Thorlinsson, 1994; De Wilde, Kienhörst, Diekstra, & Wolters, 1992; Marttunen, Anott, & Henriksson, 1994a; Pfeffer, Hurt, Kakuma, Peskin, Sielker, & Hagabhairava, 1994). The risk for recurrent suicidal behaviour is particularly high among those adolescents who had been hospitalised for suicidal attempts (Brent et al., 1993; Granboulan, Rabain, & Basquin, 1995). Suicide ideation, plans and threats, and deliberate self-harm are associated with actual suicide attempts. However, some researchers found very low percentages of suicide attempters who went on to make further suicide attempts (Cotgrove, Zirinsky, Black, & Weston, 1995). Although the rates of recurrence vary by sample composition, length of follow-up, and outcome, it is apparent from most of the studies that suicidal children and adolescents are likely to have made suicidal attempts at follow-up (Pfeffer, Kleinman, Hurt, Lesser, Peskin, & Siefker, 1991).

Several studies have shown that those who have recurrent suicidal behaviour and ideation were more likely to show a history of or presence of psychiatric disorders, personality disorders, affective disorders, conduct disorders, adjustment problems, drug and alcohol use, depressive cognition, identity problems, low self-esteem, externalising and internalising problem behaviours, adverse childhood circumstances, be born to a teenage mother, display poor adaptive functioning in home and school, have experienced undesirable life events, and other have psychosocial problems (Brent et al., 1993; De Man & Leduc, 1995; Fergusson & Lynskey, 1995; Garrison, Addy, Jackson, McKeown, & Waller, 1991; Lewinshan, Rohde & Seeley, 1994; Slap, Corters, Khadid, Marguiles, & Forke, 1992).

During the past decade, there has been a growing concern that adolescents exposed to a peer suicide may be at increased risk of engaging in suicidal behaviour (Brent et al., 1993; Brent, 1995; Wagner, 1997). More immediate exposure to suicide, such as that occurring within a school community, may also trigger suicide clusters (see Martin, 1996). A personal relationship with a suicidal victim, without direct exposure to the suicidal act, may result in another suicide (Brent et al., 1992). Among a cohort of adolescent suicide completers, Sahfi, Carrigan, & Derrik (1985) found a higher than expected frequency of exposure to suicidal behaviour in family members or friends. Adolescents exposed to suicide showed an increased incidence of major depression, suicidal ideation, and post-traumatic stress disorder (PTSD). Ladely and Puskar (1994) propose that risk factors for adolescents attempting suicide include not only age and gender, but race, low ethnic density populations, histories of disturbed behaviour, and psychiatric symptoms. Adolescents with suicidal ideation have been found to have greater levels of anger, poorer ability at anger control (Lamb & Parker, 1991), and feel more responsible for their own actions (Conrad, 1991) than nonsuicidal adolescents. Divorced or separated parents, poor social links, and perceptions of self are other key factors.

Interpersonal conflicts with a parent or significant other, suspensions at school, legal problems, recent changes in schools, sexual assault, aggressive behaviour at home, and alcohol consumption are other factors which place a vulnerable individual at risk of suicide.

## PSYCHIATRIC DISORDER AND SUICIDE

The relationship between psychiatric disorder and adolescent suicide is now well established. Psychiatric disorders have been shown significantly to increase the risk for suicidal ideation by age 15 and suicide attempts by age 18 (Reinhertz et al., 1995). Wetzler et al. (1996) identified three suicidal groups: suicide attempters who require medical treatment; suicide attempters who did not require medical treatment; suicide ideators who had never made a suicide attempt. All three suicidal groups were differentiated from nonsuicidal groups on the basis of suicidality and psychopathology. Marttunen, Aro, and Lonnqvist (1994b) reviewed cases of adolescents who had completed suicide. Less than half of the adolescent suicide victims had been under psychiatric care. Brown, King, and Barraclough (1995) examined 722 consecutive suicide cases and found nine pacts of suicides. Of the total 18, 11 subjects appeared to have been mentally ill at the time of death and another three had a history of mental illness. Mental disorder is common in those who enter suicide pacts.

The prevalence of suicidal behaviour displayed by pre-adolescent psychiatric outpatients has been estimated to range between 25% and 33% of the outpatient population, with 15% having recently engaged in some form of suicidal behaviour and almost 3% having made a suicide attempt that was viewed as realistically endangering life. (Milling et al., 1991). In a later study, Milling, Campbell, Laughlin, & Bush (1994) found 18% to 80% of suicidal behaviour in pre-adolescent psychiatric inpatients. King, Naylor, & Segal (1995) reported that 18% of adolescents acknowledged suicidal behaviour during the follow-up period after psychiatric hospitalisation.

In a review article, Harrington and Dyer (1993) posit that the increase of attempted suicide among young males is not necessarily explained by psychiatric disorders. The importance of mood disorder in predicting subsequent suicidality has been underlined in several studies (Kovacs, Goldston, & Gatsons, 1993; Myers et al., 1991). Studies of adolescents who committed suicide have confirmed that, as in adults, there are substantial links with affective disorders.

When comparing psychological characteristics of adolescent suicide attempters with those of adolescents with depression, several researchers (Kienhörst, De Wilde, Diekstra, & Wolters, 1992; De Wilde, Kienhörst, Diekstra, & Wolters, 1992, 1993) have found that suicide attempters had more turmoil in their families and had suffered more adverse events during adolescence.

## REPETITION OF ATTEMPTS

Risk factors for repetition of suicide attempts have been identified as personality disorder, a history of psychiatric treatment, alcohol and drug dependence, being divorced or separated, having a history of deliberate self-harm, having a diagnosis of dysthymia, and interpersonal conflict. In a follow-up study, 20% to 40% of the sample repeated suicide attempts during the follow-up period, and 6% to 8% committed suicide (Kelleher et al., 1994).

A high proportion of the patients who re-attempted during the follow-up period abused alcohol, and one third were treated for a psychiatric illness. In comparison to nonrepeaters, they were estimated as unstable people with limited resources for coping with social and mental stress. They acknowledged difficulties in the area of personal relations and partnership (Kelleher et al., 1994). Between 18% and 33% of young suicide completers have made at least one prior attempt to kill themselves, primarily by overdosing, wrist cutting, or a combination of both methods (Brent et al., 1988; Hoberman & Garfinkel 1988; Rich, Sherman, & Fowler, 1990).

Rodger and Scott (1995) reported that in their follow-up study of 44 patients who had been admitted after frequent deliberate self-harm, of the 42 who they had been able to trace, 38 had attempted suicide an average of 13 times. The average cost solely attributable to the inpatient accommodation and psychiatric assessment during follow-up for this group was £34,036.60 (1986–7 prices). In another study, 130 adolescents (aged 13–18 years) seen in general hospital emergency departments or psychiatric hospitals after a suicide attempt were followed up at one month and three months. After one month 6% reported another suicide attempt and after three months 10% had re-attempted suicide. Of the subjects who were followed-up at one month, 20% had been hospitalised to a psychiatric unit. Suicide attempts after one month were significantly more frequent for the psychiatric hospital group than for general hospital group. Granboulan, Rabain, and Basquin (1995) followed-up 265 adolescents who were hospitalised in a psychiatric unit following suicide attempts. After an average of 11.5 years, 30% of these subjects showed signs of improvement, 22% appeared to be unchanged, and 33% were worse. Only 32% of the patients were followed up for sufficient amounts of time. The causes of all deaths were closely related to adolescent disorders. Johnsson Fridell, Ojehagen, and Traskman-Bendz (1996) observed that re-attempters had more psychiatric symptoms and their overall functioning was poor compared to those who did not re-attempt. The predictors found to increase the likelihood of a re-attempt were young age, personality disorder, parents having received treatment for psychiatric disorder, and a poor social network.

## DEPRESSION AND SUICIDE

An association has been consistently reported between adolescents' suicidal behaviour and depressive symptoms or disorders in particular (Goldston et al., 1996; Kovacs & Goldston, 1991; Recklitis, Noam, & Borst, 1992). Adolescents who attempted suicide in the follow-up period were seven times more likely to have a mood disorder during the follow-up period than those who did not attempt suicide (Pfeffer et al., 1991). More specifically, suicidal youngsters with depressive disorders had high rates of suicidal ideation and had made more attempts (Myers et al., 1991). Cappelli et al. (1995) reported a high correlation between depression and suicidal ideation. The probability of suicidal attempt was highly prevalent in patients with psychological complaints. Brent et al. (1993) discovered that the most significant psychiatric risk factors associated with adolescent suicide were major depression, bipolar mixed state, substance abuse, and conduct disorder. Recklitis et al. (1992) indicated that suicide attempts and suicide occurrence were more common in adolescents with affective and dysthymic disorder. Taiminen, Strandberg, and Kujari (1996) observed that almost all attempters were depressive and about half of them also had alexithymia. Depression and alexithymia correlated significantly with each other, but there was no correlation between alexithymia and lethality of suicidal attempts or suicidal intent. They concluded that alexithymia in suicide attempters appeared to be associated with depression, but not with suicidality per se. Further, Lewinsohn et al. (1994) observed that adolescents with depression accompanied by suicidal ideation had much longer and recurrent episodes of depression.

Loneliness further increases the risk of depression and suicidal ideation. Lonely adolescents are more likely to report higher rates of both depression and suicidal ideation (Kienhörst, De Wilde, Diekstra, & Wolters, 1992). Suicidal probability was most prevalent in patients with psychological complaints (Cappelli et al., 1995). Even in children, an association between suicidality and depression has been documented in child psychiatric samples and community surveys (Fennig & Carlson, 1995; Kovacs et al., 1993). Depression in childhood was found to be a strong predictor of attempted suicide in adulthood (Harrington & Dyer, 1994; Reinhertz et al., 1995). However, some of the studies have been unable to establish a relationship between the medical seriousness of suicide attempt and presence of depression (e.g. Brent et al., 1993). Hodgman and McAnarney (1992) pointed out that most depressed persons are not suicidal and many suicidal persons are not depressed.

Comorbidity with depression further increases the risk of suicidal ideation and attempts. Depressive thinking and conduct behaviour were found to be predictors of suicide attempts (Myers et al., 1991). Many researchers have found that depression is associated with alcohol and substance abuse, conduct disorder, delinquency, aggression, identity problems, psychological stressors, somatic and psychological complaints, family history of depression, family problems, and problematic circumstances, e.g. family disruption or physical and sexual abuse (Marttunen, Aro, Henriksson, & Lonnquist, 1991).

Rey and Bird (1991) found that affective disorder diagnoses doubled the probability of suicide for both boys and girls. Further, Larsson et al. (1991) indicated that there was a tendency for boys to show more stable depressive symptoms and suicidal ideation than girls. Reinherz et al. (1995) discovered that an early onset of psychiatric disorder significantly increased the risk for suicidal ideation at age 15 and suicide attempts by age 18 in adolescents of both genders.

Seshadri, Srinath, & Girimaji (1989) reported on six children who had presented with deliberate self-harm out of a total of 202 children who had presented to a child and adolescent psychiatry unit in the South Indian city of Bangalore. Five out of six were male and in three cases the act was impulsive, whereas in the other two it was planned and the remaining one had lacerated himself in a depersonalised state. Five out of six had a psychiatric diagnosis ranging from psychosis to mixed disorder of conduct and emotion. All children were over the age of 12. Small numbers of cases thus make generalisability of the findings impossible. In addition, as the cases were collected from a tertiary psychiatry unit specialising in child and adolescent psychiatry, the likelihood of underlying psychiatric conditions remains high.

## SUBSTANCE MISUSE

Alcohol and substance abuse have been identified as risk factors for suicidal behaviour in adolescents (King et al., 1993; Murphy, 1992; Rossow, 1995; Rossow & Wichstrom, 1994.) Alcohol and psychoactive substance abuse also appear to be associated with a greater frequency and repetitiveness of suicide attempts, more medically lethal attempts, a greater seriousness of intention, and greater suicidal ideation (Brent, 1995; Bukstein et al., 1993; Crumley, 1979; Wasserman, Varnik, & Eklund, 1998a, 1998b). Schwartz & Reifler (1988) found that multiple suicide attempts were associated with habitual craving in young girls. Madianos, Gefou-Madianou, and Stefanis (1994) observed 12 months prevalence of suicidal ideation and suicidal attempts in adolescents in accordance with severity and frequency of substance consumption. They found that the characteristics of substance and alcohol abuse associated with suicide and suicidal behaviour were recent and heavy use and overall severity of use. An association between alcohol intoxication and use of firearms in completed suicide has also been reported (Berman & Schwartz, 1990; Crumley, 1979). Other factors such as sex abuse and conduct disorder associated with alcohol and substance abuse further increase the risk and predictability of suicidal ideation, attempts, and completed suicide (Hawton & Fagg, 1988, Drinkwater, Gardner, & Bammer, 1992; Kokkevi & Stefanis, 1995; Sibthorpe & Windle, 1995; Windle & Windle, 1997).

Suicidal ideation and suicidal attempts have been associated with alcohol and substance abuse, both alone and in combination with affective disorders. Studies have reported high prevalence rates of affective disorders amongst drug and alcohol users in adolescents (Hovens, Cantwell, & Kiriakos, 1994). Psychoactive substance abusers, particularly adolescents with any type of depressive disorder, appear to be at higher risk of suicidal behaviour and suicidal ideation (Berman & Schwartz, 1990; Brent, 1995; Bukstein et al., 1993; Young, Mikulich, Goodwin, & Hardy, 1995).

Kjelsberg, Winther, and Dahl (1995) indicated that drug-dependent individuals who committed suicide had more psychotic symptoms, suicidal ideation, learning difficulties, and somatic disorders than those who were drug dependent and took overdoses. Psychosocial stressors in alcohol and substance abuse further increase the risk of, and often precipitate, suicidal behaviour.

As already mentioned, ongoing and chronic family discord, family dysfunction, alcoholic parents, lower socioeconomic status, loneliness, early parental separation, disruption in adolescence, poor interpersonal relationships, lack of family support, excess accumulation of stress, and inability to solve problems are also some of the risk factors associated with suicidal behaviour in alcohol and drug abusers (King et al., 1993; Kosky, Silburn, & Zubrick, 1990; Lamminpaa, 1995; Rossow & Wichstrom, 1994).

## PERSONAL FACTORS

Recent contributions to the psychology of adolescence suggest that the achievement of greater interdependency, rather than increased separation, is an important goal for many nonsuicidal adolescent girls. Interdependency is a healthy developmental goal during adolescence and the pathway towards increased interdependency has been disrupted in the lives of many adolescent girls who engage in nonfatal suicidal behaviour. Interdependency, reciprocity, and mutual empathy are seen as characteristics of a healthy relationship. Relational theorists propose that women and men experience increased psychological difficulties when opportunities to enter into and sustain healthy relationships are unavailable (Bergman, 1991; Stiver, 1990a, 1990b).

The psychology of female adolescence may show that increased interdependency is an important task for adolescent girls. Their psychological development may take place through a process of affiliation and mutuality within relationships.

## THE ROLE OF GENDER

As mentioned earlier in this chapter, gender, gender role, and gender role expectations are important features in adolescent development. It has been theorised that suicidal behaviour by adolescent girls signals conflict or failure in their ability successfully to separate and individuate during adolescence (Wold, 1971). Although it is generally accepted that female adolescent suicidal acts are a desperate form of communication regarding unmet interpersonal needs (Rosenthal, 1981), it can also be assumed that these areas of interpersonal need result from an inability to establish more mature relationships. It would appear that such an inability manifests itself in a need to be with others. Such females are dependent and rely upon others to help, approve, and support (Cantor, 1972).

Female nonfatal suicidal acts have been seen as a means of gaining power and control 'over' others. Implicit in this view is the notion that suicidal girls are not simply seeking to create and maintain relationships, but they are also inappropriately dependent on them. Studies indicate that in a majority of female adolescent nonfatal suicidal acts, the immediate precipitating factors are relational conflict and loss (Lukianowicz, 1972). These relational precipitants usually occur against a background of ongoing interpersonal dissatisfaction (Lester, 1984). Adolescent girls who engage in nonfatal suicidal behaviour report a lack of parental support and a feeling of estrangement from these significant relationships (Simon & Murphy, 1985). They also report feeling distant from those important to them (Marks & Haller, 1977), unfulfilled in their interpersonal needs (Ganzler, 1967), and lacking the security of a close confidant (Topol & Reznikoff, 1982).

The view that suicidal adolescent females are exceedingly dependent on relationship arises largely from assumptions that have been made based on observations of male adolescent development (Kaplan & Klein, 1989). Dependency has been defined as a 'tendency to desire self-esteem primarily from interpersonal relationships' (Barnett & Gotlib, 1988). Dependency needs are essential to the development of relationships. Stiver (1994), for example, has argued that dependency is a label frequently applied to women as they attempt to create and maintain relationships. 'The prevailing belief seems to be that dependency needs belong in childhood and if these needs are not satisfied in childhood they continue to exert influences in the form of clinging, demanding, helpless personalities.'

Bettridge and Favreau (1995) measured dependency using Barnett and Gotlib's (1988) Trait Dependency Scale and a written story completion test among 21 female adolescents (12- to 20-years-old) who had presented at an emergency ward as a result of a suicidal act (self-poisonings). The comparison group consisted of 22 female adolescents (also 12- to 20-years-old) who had no history of suicidal behaviour. They found that suicidal and nonsuicidal adolescent girls reported similar dependency needs. However, suicidal behaviour in adolescent females has commonly been defined as a 'cry for help', arising from, among others, unmet interpersonal needs. Rather than being a dependent cry for help, however, a young woman's nonfatal suicidal act can be understood as a cry for connection. From this perspective, an adolescent girl's suicidal act signals 'a desperate plea for mutual engagement in which she can make herself known to others and others will respond so as to make their feelings known to her' (Kaplan & Klein, 1989). The suicidal adolescent's unmet need is for greater interdependency in relationships. The relationships need to be a two-way interaction. For women, the primary experience of the self is relational; that is, the self is organised and developed in the context of important relationships (Surrey, 1991). Traditionally, theories of development have proposed that adolescence entails a process of separation–individuation. This view, as outlined by such writers as Blos (1962), Erikson (1968), and Glenn and Urbach (1981), theorises that healthy adolescent development involves becoming less dependent on others: 'The formation of an independent, autonomously functioning, emotionally self-reliant character is the successful adaptive achievement of a sense of identity' (Glenn & Urbach, 1981).

From this perspective, adolescent development involves a linear progression away from dependence towards interdependence. However, this view reflects a westernised ideal of egocentric development, that may well be more difficult to sustain in other cultural settings.

## ETHNICITY AND ATTEMPTED SUICIDE

Sudak, Ford, and Rushforth (1984) question that the disparity of rates between blacks and white is perplexing. Hendin (1982) argues that blacks age quickly, but Sudak et al. (1984) propose that the future may appear more bleak to black males and better status integration (less being out of phase with one's equally disadvantaged peers because of poorer job opportunities, and in general less chance of upward socioeconomic mobility) may influence lower rates. Another option offered by Hendin (1982) is that homicide and suicide are two sides of the same coin, indicating that high levels of homicide among young black men by other black men is an indication of death wish by the latter.

Differential levels of suicide among immigrants in England and Wales were identified in the first national analysis of immigrant mortality in the 1970s (Marmot, Adelstein, & Bulusu, 1984). Local studies of attempted suicide among immigrants in the UK have contributed further to our understanding of the causes leading to self-harm (Burke, 1976a, 1976b, Lockhart & Baron, 1987, Merrill & Owens, 1986, 1987, Wright et al., 1981).

In a detailed analysis of national data covering 1970–78, Soni-Raleigh, Bulusu, and Balarajan (1990) reported that suicide levels were significantly lower among male immigrants from the Indian subcontinent and significantly higher among young Indian women, as compared with levels prevalent in England and Wales.

In another study, Soni-Raleigh and Balarajan (1992) studied suicide cases in England and Wales during 1979–83 and discovered that suicide levels were low among males (standardised mortality ratio (SMR 73) from the Indian subcontinent and significantly high in young Indian women (age specific ratio 273 and 160 at ages 15–24 and 25–34, respectively). Suicide levels were low in Afro-Caribbeans (SMRs 81 and 62 in men and women, respectively) and high in East Africans (SMRs 128 and 148 in men and women, respectively). The excess in East Africans (most of whom are of Indian origin) was largely confined to the younger ages. Immigrant groups had significantly higher rates of suicide by burning, with a ninefold excess among women of Indian origin. The pressures leading to higher suicide levels among young women of Indian origin highlight the need to make appropriate forms of support and counselling available to this community. (It should be noted that both these studies were on adults.)

There have been few studies on Asian adolescent differences in self-poisoning and suicidal behaviour, but some findings have been consistent. As mentioned elsewhere in this volume, suicide rates are higher amongst Asian women (Maniam, 1988), who are also over-represented in self-poisoning amongst females of all ages (Merrill & Owens, 1986), particularly in the 15–19-year-old age group. Other differences, i.e. a higher female to male ratio, a lower frequency of previous overdose, and culture conflict with parents, seem to play a role in suicidal behaviour (Biswas, 1990; Handy, Chithirandian, Ballard, & Silveira, 1991; Merrill & Owens, 1986).

Kingsbury (1994) examined the social and psychological features of Asian and Caucasian adolescents who had taken overdoses. His two main findings were first that the social and parental relationships showed a picture of isolation in Asian adolescents. They saw their best friends less often – on average less than weekly – and tended to confide in them less. In their general friendships too they seemed to have fewer friends near their home and did not meet friends after school or visit their friends' houses. Their parental relationships did not make up for this as they tended to confide in their parents less and experienced them as more controlling. This needs to be investigated further for several reasons. If these individuals live in high ethnic density areas and their friends are not from the same ethnic background, they may well be presenting cultural conflict to their parents. It could also mean that the geographical distance may also reflect emotional distances. These findings perhaps account for the differences seen in problem types. Asian adolescents had fewer problems with boyfriends or girlfriends and had problems with siblings.

Second, in the psychological domain, Kingsbury (1994) discovered (surprisingly) that although no Asian adolescent scored above the cut-off score for high suicidal intent, they were more likely than the Caucasian group to be depressed, feel hopeless and to have contemplated taking an overdose for longer. In contrast, for adults Merrill and Owens (1986) found the Asian group had a higher rate of previous overdose.

Handy et al., (1991) presented a study of self-poisoning in 25 Asian and 25 Caucasian adolescents. Culture conflicts were the most important factors in the parasuicidal behaviour of Asian children, whereas a variety of factors accounted for the parasuicidal behaviour of Caucasians, with a predominance of a disrupted family background. There was little difference in the type of poisoning and the degree of pre-planning between the two groups. Soni-Raleigh et al.'s (1990, 1992) findings are generally consistent with the patterns reported for India (almost 80% of the deaths examined in this study were of immigrants born in India, and the balance of immigrants from other countries of the Indian subcontinent). Studies in India also show that suicide rates are highest at 15–30 years and low among the elderly (Adityanjee, 1986; Bhatia, Khan, Mediratta, & Sharma, 1987), a consequence perhaps of the support and companionship traditionally accorded in Indian society to the senior members of a family. These studies also report high suicide rates among young married women. Arranged marriages with the tradition of dowries are generally regarded as contributory factors in suicide among young women in India. Higher suicide and parasuicide rates among Indian women than men, particularly at younger ages, are also reported among Indian immigrants to the UK and elsewhere (Burke, 1976a; Cheetham, Edwards, Naidoo, Griffiths, & Singh, 1983; Merrill & Owens, 1986; Price & Karim, 1975). Many of these studies cite cultural conflict as a contributory factor.

## CULTURAL FACTORS

As discussed elsewhere in this monograph, most immigrant Indian communities have maintained their cultural identity and traditions even after generations of residence overseas. This tradition incorporates a premium on academic and economic success, a stigma attached to failure, the overriding authority of elders (especially parents or in-laws), and unquestioning compliance from younger family members. Thus, interpersonal disputes, particularly in relation to marriage and life styles, the pressures of economic competition with the loss of self-esteem associated with failure, and the anxiety attached to nonconformist behaviour have been cited as causes of self-harm among the young (male and female), both in India and abroad.

These pressures are intensified in young Indian women, given their rigidly defined roles in Indian society. Submission and deference to males and elders, arranged marriages, the financial pressures imposed by dowries, and ensuing marital and family conflicts have been cited as major contributory factors in suicide and attempted suicide in young Indian women in several of the studies reviewed here, relating as much to India as to immigrant communities abroad. The causes of self-inflicted injury among people of Indian origin abroad, although not dissimilar to those seen in the country of origin, also suggest that they are not particularly attributable to migration, although they are probably exacerbated by the pressures following the move to a different social environment.

Epidemiological studies on psychological morbidity among adult Asians in Britain present mixed findings (London, 1986), with some showing higher rates of hospital admissions (Carpenter & Brockington, 1980; Dean, Walsh, Downing, & Shelley, 1981). This has not, however, been demonstrated consistently. On the basis of both his inpatient (Cochrane, 1977) and community studies (Cochrane & Stopes-Roe, 1981), Cochrane concluded that Indians and Pakistanis suffer less psychiatric morbidity than the general British population. He notes, however, that unmarried Indian women and those in the nonmanual group have significantly high symptom levels, although no higher than the average for English women. It is believed that the levels and causes of psychological stress among young Indian women, in particular, need further detailed study.

Merrill and Owens (1986) compared the characteristics of Asian patients admitted to Birmingham hospitals following deliberate self-poisoning with those of British-born, white self-poisoners. Asian patients were more likely to be young, female and married. They were less likely to have previously self-poisoned, received previous psychiatric treatment, been diagnosed psychiatrically ill, or suffered from a personality disorder. Culture conflict was common among the Asian patients and was present in the majority of unmarried Asian females. The rate of self-poisoning for Asian females was higher than white females, but for Asian males was lower than for white males.

## RACISM

As already discussed in this monograph, race is defined as a biological category according to common inborn biological traits (e.g. skin colour, hair, shape of lips, size of nose), but there are no standardised acceptable biological criteria for dividing race into distinct categories. Genetic evidence suggests that even within one racial group there is so much variation that it is almost impossible to have a homogeneous racial group. However, race has been turned into a social category. Racism can be seen as a negative attribution made by people of one social group towards another social group by virtue of putative physical characteristics. The key factor of racism is related to the position of one set of individuals within society and to the perceived or real power by the other group. The most significant component underlying racism is power – political, social or economic – that gives one group advantages which it is keen to hang on to.

Goldberg and Hodes (1992) suggest that the life cycles of families have to be seen in the context of specific needs and special experiences. The cultural influences on individuation, identity, peer relationships, expectations, extended family, and kinship make individual children react in different ways with their parents and siblings. The internal organisation of the family is affected by the needs of the individual and the subsystems along with demands made by the society and culture.

Goldberg and Hodes (1992) suggest that the changes which occur in a family because of racism and other external threats and attacks are related to pre-existing structure and values of the family. Gender and generational differences are important organising principles required for understanding the effects of racism on the family. They argue that culture conflict itself can be precipitated or exacerbated by racism. Younger generations may find it easier to identify with the majority culture and, paradoxically, this may exaggerate their alienation from their parents, siblings, and community. Other adolescents may identify with aspects of their minority culture, so distinguishing themselves from and opposing their parents' assimilation. Thus cultural identity and a need for individual identity in the context of the larger community may influence vulnerable individuals in a way that may lead to taking overdoses to escape from the stress. Racist attacks on the family may also influence the adolescent who is trying to assimilate to respond in an aggressive manner, which may well be internalised. In adolescents who are feeling alienated anyway, these attacks confirm their alienation even further, and lead to aggressive impulses which may be internalised. Racism may therefore strengthen the boundaries between different ethnic groups.

The younger generation, in contrast with the parental generation, viewed suicidal behaviour in terms that were less judgemental of the individual, less stigmatised, and less calamitous after death (Boldt, 1982). The younger generation did not see suicide in religious–moral terms and they placed greater emphasis on the individual's right to suicide. The perception that the individual has of the act itself is extremely important in understanding the genesis of the act. Kalish, Reynolds, and Farberow (1974, p. 301) point out:

> The person contemplating suicide, the recovered survivor of the suicide attempt, the family member of a publicised suicide and the volunteers and professionals at a suicide prevention center all share one vitally important characteristic. They are functioning in a society that has established the meaning of the act of suicide and the act of attempted suicide, with varying degrees of success they have been socialised to live in this society.

The experiences, perceptions, and attitudes in the context of social norms and mores not only determine how help is sought, but also what economic and personnel resources are dedicated to services. In addition, development of preventive strategies will be determined by the societal views.

## OTHER FACTORS

Various other factors that have not been discussed so far which influence suicidal behaviour in adolescents include the following:

- age
- education
- childhood sexual abuse
- sexual identity
- family and culture.

## Age

Bagley and Ramsey (1997) reported that in their sample from Calgary, Alberta, young people had significantly poorer mental health than the older ones and reported more suicidal ideas and behaviour in their lifetime. In a community survey of 679 adults, Bagley and Ramsey (1997, p. 51) found that, in comparison with other age groups, 18- to 24-year-olds had already experienced more personal stresses of various kinds. In growing up, the young report a higher prevalence of permanent separation from a parent because of divorce. The younger subjects had poorer mental health, lower self-esteem, and reported a higher number of psychiatric consultations. The young were more mobile and had less stable attachments.

These authors point out that their younger subjects were by contrast unsure of themselves, geographically more mobile, and often felt unattached to their neighbourhoods. Reported stress involving conflict with a parent was an important correlate of a poorer mental health and suicidal behaviour and they were more prone to economic stresses.

There is no doubt that the age profile of suicidal behaviour is changing in all western countries. Completing suicide rates have traditionally been higher in older people, tending to increase rapidly in males over 45 (Kreitman, Carstairs, & Duffy, 1991). In the late 1970s this consistent pattern started to change when the rate in younger males began to increase (McLure, 1984; Sainsbury, 1983). Parallel with these changes, the rates of attempted suicide increased, especially among young females in North America and Europe.

Bagley and Ramsey (1997, p. 52) go on to point out that each age cohort, as it gets older, appears to retain its higher suicide rate (Reed, Camus, & Last, 1985). Increasing rates of suicide in young people may reflect demographic and socioeconomic changes of the population in general, including the proportion of adolescents (Hollinger & Offer, 1982). Interestingly, the differences of rates between the young and very old have been attributed to (at least in North America) increased resources available to the old and relative neglect of the needs of younger people.

## Education

Additional pressures on young people are education and the environment at school. Peer pressure, bullying, and pressure to achieve all add to the stress which may lead to suicidal behaviour. Often, factors that contribute to the stress at school and family include childhood sexual abuse, physical abuse, and illicit substance usage. Schools should be important agencies of child welfare. However, there is little evidence that all schools serve this function well (Bagley 1997, p. 97). Many schools fail in the most fundamental task of retaining to school completion that group of children whose motivation and ability to study has been impaired by coming from a broken family. Among children, ethnicity may also play an additional complicating role for bullying, stigmatisation, and institutional and personal racism. Deviancy and truancy further contribute to a sense of rebellion and social isolation. This vulnerable group, like its peer group, also has the additional pressure of developing self-identity and self-esteem along with a sense of individuation. A sense of confusion and despair felt by young people prior to their attempts reflects a number of factors.

Bagley (1997, p. 97) describes the taxonomy of completed youth suicide in Canada and reported that in this age group the commonest methods of suicide were gunshot (38%), overdosing (24%), and hanging (21%). Various social and clinical characteristics were: prior acts of deliberate self-harm (21%); being in care (13%); separation from 'significant other' in the previous one month; failed grades (29%); history of mental illness or suicide in the family (21%); five years or more in foster or adoptive home (15%); separation from biological parents for longer than six months (43%); clinical treatment or indicators of depression in previous 12 months (24%); quit school (39%); and previous communication of suicidal intent (31%).

On comparing suicides with community controls, the former were more likely to have had clinical diagnosis or indicators of depression, past history of deliberate self-harm, being in care, history of suicide or mental illness in the family, chronic personality problems, problems of alcohol or drug abuse, school drop-out, and separation from biological parents for more than six months. These findings highlight a picture where family and school life are both disrupted. A cause of alienation and isolation may settle in and in response to bullying the individual may attempt, contemplate, or complete suicide. Bagley (1997, pp. 104–105) analysed completed suicides and divided them into six groups, which are illustrated in Table 5.1

## Childhood sexual abuse

Childhood sexual abuse or physical abuse may well lead to depression and suicidal behaviour. Physical abuse or childhood sexual abuse have been identified as key factors in the genesis of adolescent psychopathology only over the last 30 years or so. Both these types of abuse, in particular sexual abuse, can provoke suicidal crises, which may lead to active self-injury. As a significant portion of childhood sexual abuse takes place in the nuclear or extended family, it is not surprising that a sense of betrayal and alienation

Table 5.1
Types of suicide (after Bagley, 1997)

| *Type* | *Gender* | *Features* |
|---|---|---|
| A | Male 14–18 | Violent means<br>Past history<br>Separation from parents<br>In care<br>School drop-outs |
| B | Female any age | Any method<br>Overdose or poisoning<br>1 or more acts of deliberate self-harm |
| C | Male 18–20 | Violent means<br>Breakdown of relationship<br>Recent job loss<br>Use of alcohol/drugs<br>Family history of suicide |
| D | Male 12–14 | Violent<br>H/O delinquency<br>H/O school drop-out<br>Mental illness in parents |
| E | Male or female 15–20 | Recent clinical depression or schizophrenia<br>No scholastic problems |
| F | Native American | Substance abuse<br>Unemployment |

contributes to victimhood, low self-esteem, and poor self-identity where suicide may be seen as a way out. A sense of self-deprecation and guilt may well contribute to symptoms of depression. The long-lasting trauma may produce chronic dysthymia. Childhood sexual abuse has been linked with problems of body image, eating disorders, and increased rates of sexual dysfunction as adults.

Combined and prolonged physical and sexual abuse are bound to influence the individual's self-esteem. Such sexual abuse combined with serious physical abuse leads to serious and permanent mental health sequel in up to a quarter of the victims (Bagley, 1995; Bagley & Ramsay, 1986; Finkelhor, 1984). Although eliciting the history of child sexual abuse is important, it is also vital that clinicians are aware of the disclosure, which in itself is also likely to contribute to the stress and make the individual more vulnerable to self-harm. Such a disclosure is bound to influence the family, which is then likely to respond in a number of ways. They may withdraw their support at the time of the allegations, they may increase their support in a more controlling way, or they may respond in an ambivalent manner, contributing to the chaos the child may be feeling and experiencing.

The disclosure will influence the interaction between the child and the family members. Another complicating scenario may be if the parents of the child have split and the disclosure is made to the single mother or to the 'new' family with stepparents. Half-siblings may further complicate the child's inner world. Under these circumstances, any disclosure will precipitate further crises for the child and key members of the family, especially the mother. With gender role identification, such a response may well lead to an increased vulnerability in the child to self-harm.

As a victim the child is likely to experience further symptoms of low self-esteem, poor self-confidence, a sense of despair, and possible depression. These are prone to be further complicated if the family and others around do not respond in a caring and supportive manner. The perceived as well as real lack of support may have led to delay in disclosing the abuse, but the pressure to remain silent, as well as the chronic deceit, may further contribute to a sense of increasing isolation and alienation, as well as ongoing anomic difficulty.

Child sexual abuse associated with physical trauma is characterised by repeated and ongoing abuse, especially from an authority figure who is in a trustworthy position. If the child is threatened and expected to remain silent this further contributes to an increased risk of self-harm. The role of the family in understanding its own pathology and supporting or rejecting the child is extremely important.

Sexual abuse in children can have an immediate or long-term sequel and lead to serious depression, of clinical severity, in adolescent and adult survivors. There are clear grounds for assuming that the abuse and factors associated with it have caused the onset of depression, although the abuse may have interacted with other vulnerability factors (Bagley & Young, 1997).

Bagley and McDonald (1984), after following up 57 female children (who had been removed from the parental home because of sexual or physical abuse, or parental separation, desertion, or abandonment) 12 years later, reported that experience of sexual abuse had both an independent and powerfully negative effect on adult functioning (including episodes of depression and chronically impaired self-esteem). A combination of physical abuse, sexual abuse, and separation from the mother had the most negative effects of all. Such individuals have been shown in other studies to have high rates of depression and suicidal ideation (Meiselman, 1978; Monroe-Posey, 1985).

Male children who have been abused are likely to invert their anger inwards, thereby feeling depressed, withdrawn, hopeless and out of control. These feelings are then likely to lead to self-hatred, self-harm, and self-mutilation. De Young (1982) reported on 45 females aged 7 to 38 and found that 58% were involved in self-injurious behaviour such as overdoses, cutting, burning, and attempts to break bones. A majority in this sample had used more than one method. The motivation in this group varied from feelings of wanting to disfigure themselves or to make themselves ill as a cry for help to punishing themselves for either being a victim or enjoying it. Similar feelings have been reported in other studies (Sedney & Brooks, 1984). The authors found that 16% of 301 adult students had reported some kind of sexual abuse in their childhood years. Those who had been abused were more likely (than those who had not been abused) to feel depressed and were also more likely to experience suicidal ideation (39%, compared with 16% controls). One fifth had attempted suicide compared with 8% of controls. The rate of abuse in attempts has varied widely from 43% to 72% (Van Egmond, 1987). Briere and Runtz (1986) hypothesised three models that may be used to explain motivations towards suicidal behaviours: first, through stigmatisation, self-blame, and low self-esteem; second, through a sense of real or perceived powerlessness which may lead to inadequate coping styles and strategies; third, the interpersonal consequence in that individuals may not form trusting or intimate relationships.

Mullen, Martin, Anderson, Romans, and Herbuson (1993) from epidemiological data in New Zealand and Van Egmond, Garnefiski, Jonken, and Kenkhof (1993) from the Netherlands found that rates of suicidal behaviour among those who had reported child sexual abuse were extremely high. The data for sexual abuse across different cultures are not robust enough to draw further comparisons. However, there is no evidence to suggest that a similar sense of isolation, alienation, and victimhood in those who have been abused as children will not apply to other cultures or settings. Self-esteem (the person's evaluation of the self) and self-concept (the aspects of the self which an individual thinks are important) are important tenets of an individual's socialisation and social functioning.

Bagley and Ramsey (1997) studied 1025 females and 1087 males in grades 7–12 at high school and found that among both groups those who had experienced a high number of sexual assaults in the previous six months were significantly more likely to have conduct disorder, somatic disorder, and emotional disorder. Boys were more likely to attempt suicide (33%) if they had been sexually abused compared with 0.9% of those who had not been abused. Among females, 13.2% of abused victims had attempted suicide compared with 1.3% of those with no history of sexual assault.

## Sexual identity

Until relatively recently, homosexual acts were illegal even among consenting adults, especially men. When the UK laws were liberalised in the 1950s there still remained a discrepancy between heterosexual males and homosexual males as to the age of consent for sex, and also between homosexual men and homosexual women. It is only within the last ten years or so that various countries, especially in western Europe, have begun to equalise the age of consent for heterosexual and homosexual men.

Bettridge and Favreau (1995) found that the suicidal adolescents reported a history of physical and/or sexual abuse more often than nonsuicidal adolescents. Only 3 out of 21 suicidal adolescents did not report having been abused, whereas only 4 of the 23 nonsuicidal adolescents reported a history of abuse. These findings are consistent with recent studies (Briere & Zaidi, 1989; Cutler & Nolen-Hoeksema, 1991; Straus, 1988) documenting high rates of depression and suicidal ideation and behaviours in adolescent girls and women who were physically and sexually abused during childhood.

In various US and UK studies in the 1960s and 1970s, rates of suicidal behaviour were shown to be much greater among the gay youth than in with their heterosexual counterparts (Bell & Weinberg, 1978; Plunmer, 1989; see Bagley & Tremblay, 1996, for a review of the studies). Reasons for this were again related to alienation, social isolation, stigma, and overt homophobia. The rate of suicidability in this vulnerable group will depend very much on the definition of sexual behaviour and on how 'open' or 'out' these individuals are, and to whom, about their sexual orientation and suicidal ideation. Thus, across cultures and societies which clearly pathologise homosexuality, it would be almost impossible to obtain adequate epidemiological data. Further complications may well emerge when transgendered individuals are included.

## Family and culture

For adolescents, cultural factors play a crucial part in forming identity, developing protective systems, and dealing with peers. Zimmerman and Zayas (1995), from their studies on Latino women, suggest that acculturation and child socialisation, along with the relationships between mothers and daughters, are important. The notion of the fragmentation and conflict between mothers and daughters becomes important.

Mothers may have been socialised within patriarchal cultural systems and may have therefore accepted the gender roles expected of them. However, they may not have found adequate resolutions for themselves of conflicts between acquiescence and self-affirmation and may develop a degree of ambivalence towards what is expected of them and what they expect of their daughters. Such ambivalence may lead to resentment and reduced support for their daughters, which may create a strained relationship, especially if the daughter aims to move away from the traditional culture. As the daughters grow up, the mothers may come face to face with their own missed opportunities. Zimmerman and Zayas (1995) suggest that this creates a number of reactions – a sense of commitment to the culture they know so intimately, envy at their daughters' opportunities, resentment of both their culture and their daughters, and yet hope that their daughters will genuinely succeed where they were unable to. Similar observations can be made about Asian mothers and their daughters. The complex relationship between culture, family (as embodied by the mother) and the individual (the vulnerable adolescent or young adult) needs to be teased out. It is possible that the daughters also represent the 'new generation' for the mother, which may well be seen as more frightening. It is possible that some mothers, irrespective of their ethnicity and cultural background, are poorly equipped to support their daughters in the transition from adolescence to adulthood. It is possible that this lack of ability to help their daughters is complicated by the presence of cultural differences; even if they themselves were brought up in a similar culture, their own transition may have been dramatically different. The relationship between mothers and daughters may reflect a number of factors.

It is quite likely that the development of the self in the context of sociocentric cultures is dictated by a sense of identity, which involves others around the individual in spite of the egocentric factors. Such an interaction may lead to renegotiating various relationships and establishing adequate channels of communication between various family members. The daughters may look up to their mothers for developing their gender role identity and socialisation. When a mother's viewpoint is contrary to that of the daughter, the conflict as perceived by the daughter may lead to a sense of abandonment and a lack of guidance, thereby contributing to a sense of despair and isolation. Also, looking at the mother's experience and her relationship to males in the society may either confirm the daughter's views or may alienate her further. Various restrictions placed on daughters by mothers are more likely to generate a sense of control, which in an alien culture may be something that the individuals wish to avoid. The cultural sense of control may be seen by the vulnerable individuals as something awful, something that is inferior, especially if they are trying to assimilate with their peers. The daughter may try and shift some of this interaction in a way that allows her freedom, but if the mother is seen as weak or unempathic the individual may feel unsupported and abandoned. The suicidal behaviour then becomes a clear idiom of distress through which the daughter attempts to express her lack of connectedness and lack of belonging. It may elicit family help, especially from the females, to cope with the demands of both the host and the traditional cultures. Zimmerman and Zayas (1995) suggest that in a way the suicidal act is a cry for companionship. However, the act itself may further separate mother and daughter, especially if the mother feels that she has to support the traditional culture as a carrier of that tradition. In addition, it is possible that the patriarchy may have stronger influences on the mother, thereby alienating the more modern and less traditional daughter.

At best, adolescence is a time of turmoil, dealing with processes of individuation and development of self-identity and self-esteem. These are influenced by a number of factors – individualistic, familial, and societal. A range of factors come to an interplay to make a vulnerable individual prone to acts of suicidal behaviour. Cultural expectations and gender role, socialisation, and expectations play very significant roles in understanding the risks of suicidal behaviour. The understanding of these factors will lead to a number of intervention strategies being put into place, both at an individual level as well as through familial intervention. Any public health models developed to provide prevention and intervention strategies need to be fully aware of cultural and social norms, mores and expectations.

## CONCLUSIONS

If the findings of the research are true, i.e. that: Asian adolescent overdose is over-represented (Glover, Marks, & Nowers, 1989) and has a unique set of causes, e.g. cultural conflict (Biswas, 1990), then does this imply that the nature of Asian adolescent overdose is qualitatively different from that of Caucasians? In other words, do psychological variables of risk, such as premeditation, hopelessness, and depression, have the same associations with high suicidal intent, or does an assessment of an Asian adolescent overdose need to consider not only cultural issues but have a different model of psychopathology? Cultural conflict is believed to be the primary cause of deliberate self-harm in Asian adolescents. The main assumption is that Asian parents of British-born children hold more traditional views than their children with regard to a whole range of issues, including marriage, social relationships, aspirations, and employment, to name just a few. The differences of opinion between parents and offspring are the sources of the conflict, which along with other stressors increases the likelihood of suicidal behaviour in Asian adolescents. In order to assess the impact of culture conflict, a factor that must be ascertained is whether the rates of attempted suicide are genuinely different. If indeed they are, then does culture conflict contribute to this? These points are further discussed later in this volume.

CHAPTER SIX

# Women and suicidal behaviour

## INTRODUCTION

It has been argued that in most countries the rates of suicidal behaviour are much higher among women, although men tend to complete the act and also use violent means to achieve the end. The acts of attempting to self-harm in women are related to a number of factors – social, psychological, and biological. Social factors include rates related to social class, economic class, education, employment, social support, gender roles and role expectation, as well as factors to do with cultural norms and expectations.

One of the key problems in studying suicidal behaviour in women has been that the majority of studies have been carried out by men, which has led to a specific emphasis being placed on a number of factors. For example, pre-menstrual syndrome (PMS) has been blamed for a number of aberrant behaviours, but no equivalent studies have been carried out on men. Canetto (1992) has argued that often women's lower suicidal mortality has been blamed on them being perceived as dull, passive, conforming, and suggestible. However, this does not explain high rates of attempted suicide in women in some cultures. Is it likely then that these rates explain passive acts of violence to the self? Durkheim (1879/1951) argued that women are more imaginative (perhaps not imaginative enough to identify violent or potentially lethal methods).

Others have argued that women accept traditional and religious prescriptions more easily. Hence they are more likely to comply with the suggestions that suicide or suicidal behaviour will lead to a passive acceptance and reduction (Davies, 1904; Neuringer & Lethieu, 1982). Canetto and Lester (1995) point out that men (thus) may demonstrate imagination and initiative by killing themselves in the face of adversity, which goes against Durkheim. Canetto (1992) observes that women's suicidal behaviours are labelled pejoratively, even if associated with adaptation and survival. Men's behaviours are labelled positively, even when they lead to self-destruction in suicidal behaviour.

## SOCIAL FACTORS AND GENDER

As mentioned earlier, social factors related to suicidal behaviour, especially in the context of gender, include gender roles, role expectation, and gender socialisation, in addition to common factors of educational, employment, and economic and religious status across the gender divide. Cultural factors will include assimilation, cultural identity, and cultural mores and norms related to violence and alcohol and drug consumption.

Kushner (1995), while highlighting the differences in epidemiological rates of suicide between men and women, argues that suicide among women was seen as an individual emotional act, and thus inconsequential, while male suicide was seen as a barometer of national economic and social well-being. Second, he opines, as a result of the first observation it appears that male suicide was a consequence of the stress inherent in men's roles and responsibilities (i.e. the price of civilisation); females committed suicide when they deviated from traditional roles.

## GENDER ROLES AND GENDER SOCIALISATION

The social expectations that are often drilled into young females from their childhood are related to how their culture and society define their gender roles. It is possible that parents, family, peers, and the media play significant roles in this. When women are expected to behave in a feminine way and these expectations are constantly flaunted, any female who chooses to ignore this way of functioning is likely to become isolated and alienated from the broader culture. Gender role socialisation does not occur in isolation and associated family pressures and dysfunctions may well increase the conflict, which will further alienate the individual.

Females in many cultures are expected to fulfil their sexual obligations and to be subservient and passive. Especially among immigrant groups, women are often expected to contribute financially to the household income by going out to work and being active. Yet on their return home they are expected to keep the house, do the chores, and look after the family. Such an expectation does not necessarily have to be related to migration. In cultures and societies that are patriarchal, the male expectation of the female gender role will set them on a collision course. If the women are well educated and working in high-powered positions, their expectations of their own roles and those of others may well be different from those of a homebuilder. Both groups will face conflict if they are brought into any situation where their achievements and expectations diverge. Failure on the part of the family, partner, or husband to understand and support these gender roles will contribute further to a sense of isolation and alienation, leading to low self-esteem and despair. Although there are biological and hormonal differences between men and women from birth, the process of gender role socialisation starts from pregnancy.

In some cultures, different types of food are encouraged to ensure a healthy boy. Soon after birth, in many cultures, boys are dressed in female clothing to keep away the evil eye and to encourage bad spirits not to harm the 'female' (or the vulnerable) child, thus sparing the male child by a process of deception. Parent–child and social interactions through conversation, stories, television, media, and clothing lead to a clear process of gender development. Females may be discouraged from rough play or engaging in gross motor activity, thereby confirming a submissive passive role for females (Maccoby & Jacklin 1974; Macdonald & Parke, 1986). Whereas fathers may encourage visual and motor explorations in sons, daughters are offered only physical proximity and vocal interaction (Bronstein, 1988). Traditional girls' clothing such as dresses and frills are less likely to encourage them into physical activity and exploration (Shaken, Sharen, & Sternglanz, 1985). Clifton and Lee (1995) suggest that many females are prevented from early practice with challenging situations. They asked college students to anticipate a challenging public situation (such as defending a student issue in front of an all-campus governing body) and to select from a list of adjectives those that would describe their feelings prior to the event. Women were noted to report more negative feelings such as discouraged, frustrated, fearful, troubled, anxious, and embarrassed, whereas men reported feeling proud, pleased, enthusiastic, and eager. These authors argue that because early gender socialisation does not allow girls to engage in early practice with small challenges, they may be disadvantaged when faced with bigger challenges.

Interestingly, Clifton and Lee (1995) also observed that the anticipated negative feelings were more likely to be reported by individuals with low self-esteem, low self-confidence, and high self-destructiveness. On examining these findings by gender, the authors found that these were stronger in women compared with men. It appeared that most men, irrespective of their self-assessments, have learnt to psyche themselves up for challenges, whether small or large.

Parent–child interactions also direct boys and girls towards either an affective or an analytical orientation (Clifton & Lee, 1995). Studies have shown that patterns of verbal and nonverbal communication differ between parents and their sons and daughters. Daughters are often talked to about feelings and emotions (Shapiro, 1990), whereas sons are more likely to be told stories that include anger and violence (Macdonald & Parke, 1986). Parents also tend to question their sons more and use more numbers and action verbs in talking with them (Bronstein, 1988; Weitzman, Birns, & Friend, 1985). In media portrayals it is rare for girls to be encouraged to continue with physical activity, while boys are encouraged to be playful, aggressive, outgoing, and active. In children's stories, boys are still more likely to lead the adventure and be awarded for their achievements (Weitzman, Eifler, Hokada, & Ross, 1972), although this may be beginning to change. In schools, teachers interact less with girls and are more likely to complete their tasks for them than give them instructions. Boys are more likely to be given remediation, challenging tasks with detailed instructions, and praise.

Parents and teachers attribute girls' academic achievements to the ease of the tasks or to luck, and explain their failures as being due to lack of intelligence. In contrast they attribute the boys' successes to their abilities, and their failures to bad luck (Clifton & Lee, 1995). In addition, through school and college years the challenge to girls is often to find a suitable boyfriend or husband, so that the emphasis may be on physical attractiveness and denial of one's own interests and abilities. Zuckerman (1989) argues that this dichotomy may well contribute to a sense of vulnerability. This discrepancy in their inherent ability to achieve some things and being denied access to other achievements will in turn contribute in vulnerable individuals to a sense of social alienation and despair. Young women are led to de-emphasise their academic qualities, which produces career aspirations well below their abilities. Zuckerman (1989) further observed that college women and men with low self-confidence, low self-worth, less coping ability, and low levels of self-sufficiency were more likely to experience depression, anxiety, withdrawal, and anger when under stress. Women who reported less confidence in their coping ability, self-sufficiency, leadership, and public-speaking ability than men went on to curtail their activity levels and reported more symptoms of depression and low self-confidence under stress.

Furthermore, an additional suggestion in the field of gender put forward by various authors is that women are expected to hang on to their relationships and that their suicidal behaviour is related to the status of their relationships and what happens within them such as conflict, violence, and alcohol abuse (Beck, Lester, & Kovacs, 1973; Paykel, Prusoff, & Myers, 1975; Stephens 1985). Canetto (1992) and Canetto and Feldman (1993) suggest that the suicide context is a predictable adult outcome of a feminine socialisation that places undue emphasis on intimate relationships with men as a measure of personal success. Canetto (1992) states that in western cultures nonfatal suicidal behaviour is seen as more feminine than fatal suicidal acts (which could be seen as masculine).

The role of employment and education in the context of gender socialisation is extremely important. When the economic circumstances demand 'cheap' labour, often women are recruited to low-grade jobs in spite of their educational status. Discrimination in employment and education, and the existence of glass ceilings, are important factors in confirming for the vulnerable the very issues related to gender role socialisation. Some aspects of this socialisation, although perceived to be protective, may in fact become provocative factors into self-destruction and suicidal behaviours.

All behaviours, except perhaps those that are reproductive, are found in both males and females. Maris et al. (2000b) suggest that the expressions of thresholds for eliciting these behaviours are simply matters of 'more' versus 'less' in each gender. They illustrate this by using aggression as an example, because aggression tends to have a lower threshold in most males than in most females. Repertoires of aggression as a coping strategy will be sanctioned by social and cultural expectations and experiences.

Whereas some of the male/female differences are biological, others are sociocultural. Gender roles and gender role expectations are very clearly determined by the society and culture one lives in. In some ways, gender roles and gender role expectations form an integral part of the culture and society, and therefore of an individual's cultural identity. Childhood upbringing, peer pressures, and the media all play a role in the way gender roles develop and in societal expectations of how men and women will behave.

The differences between males and females are many and yet there are a lot of similarities too. In terms of suicidal behaviour in the West, the rates of attempted suicide have been shown to be higher in women but the rates of completed suicide are higher in men, whereas in other parts of the world the rates of male attempts *and* completed suicides are higher than for women. Some of the reasons for this are to do with gender roles and role expectations, whereas others are to do with age, socioeconomic status, educational status, discrepancy in achievement and expectation, alienation, and lack of social support. These factors are applicable to both the sexes, so what is it about women that makes them more vulnerable sometimes to self-harm? Maris et al. (2000b) postulate that as the modern society demands more androgyny and becomes less patriarchal (i.e. as gender equality becomes more the norm) the uniqueness of gender identity starts to dissipate; whereas in controlling societies patriarchy plays an extensive role in determining who does what. However, the complicating feature is that traditional societies, whether they are rural or urban, have not necessarily remained isolated – audiovisual and written media are now widely available, so that individuals are usually aware of all the changes that are going on in the outside world. Thus role strain might contribute to suicidal behaviour.

Stack (1978) hypothesized that when women enter the labour force they experience increased strain due to increased demands of both external (i.e. the job) and the internal (i.e. the household) responsibilities. This was confirmed by Davis (1981), who found high rates of suicide in women in the 1950s and 1960s when they entered the labour market.

Maris et al. (2000b) argue that, with changes in gender roles, the rates of suicide among males should go down because stereotypical roles of self-control and rationality are beginning to change. However, this has not been found to be the case. One possible explanation might be that the genders experience distress in different ways.

Gender might influence suicidal behaviour by a number of means:

- gender and method
- gender and suicide
- gender and mental disorder
- gender roles and role expectation
- social acceptability
- gender and biology and aggression
- gender and sexuality
- gender dysphoria
- sexual abuse
- marital status.

Some factors, such as childhood sexual abuse and physical abuse, have been discussed elsewhere in this volume. As mentioned earlier, epidemiological data suggest clear gender differences across different cultures. Gender and sexual abuse have also been linked with self-injurious behaviour, eating disorders, and sexual dysfunction. The most common sequelae of self-mutilating behaviour are a reduction in a tension or other intense affect and a reduction of the sense of alienation. Such self-harming patients are often diagnosed as having personality disorder and are likely to be women.

## Method and low self-esteem

Method of suicide and attempted suicide is often associated with gender, with more macho, assertive methods being linked with men (Pritchard, 1995). Violence in relationships can be a trigger for suicide. It has been suggested that men who perpetuate a violent act or psychological violence then go on to damage or kill themselves. Conversely, it is suggested that their female recipients also do so but that in their case the causation is related to low self-esteem (Fischer et al., 1993). Low self-esteem can also contribute to poor self-confidence and self-rejection in situations where harm to the self would appear to be the only way that individuals can control their destiny. This, combined with poor impulse control and depressogenic cognitive schemata, might well contribute to a sense of not belonging and, if the female is not able to deal with prescribed and expected gender roles, the pressure could become unbearable.

Pritchard (1995) cautions that it is easy to consider gender in purely physiological terms. With changes in behaviour across genders it is likely that there might be additional problems. Pritchard (1971) illustrates this by proposing that both adolescent and young women who engage in underage drinking, and the sensitive 'new men', are challenging and changing stereotypes.

### Gender and marital status

As mentioned elsewhere in this volume, when cultures give women specific roles, and social and cultural institutions allow women programmes for better functioning, these changes, in combination with the collectivist nature of the society, will influence rates of suicidal behaviour. Marriage appears to contribute a statistical protection against suicide for both genders and divorce, with its associated anxiety and trauma, is strongly associated with suicide (Stack, 1992). The trauma of divorce, even if it is accompanied by a sense of relief, will add to anxiety and might lead to a reduction of social support and isolation. A degree of alienation could well appear if, following the divorce, mutual friends of the couple disperse along with the changed relationship. Dysphoric mood related to divorce and separation, with resulting alienation, social isolation, and bereavement might well influence the genders differentially.

## CONCLUSIONS

With increased urbanisation and globalisation it is likely that changes will occur and that statistics will continue to change. Pritchard (1995) comments that in several Western countries, rates of suicide have fallen among women as a result of better community outreach and GP prescribing habits. The frustration of being forced into positions of inferior social and financial status, while having good educational achievements, might be a contributing factor because the discrepancy between achievement and expectation might generate a sense of dysphoria. Pritchard (1995) points out that, associated with social class, the sense of failing to achieve goals could contribute to a sense of disillusionment. He argues that 'new' woman might be in danger of overreaching herself, especially as it appears that 'new man' has not yet truly equalled her contribution in the home. The social dimension of suicide cannot be overstressed, argues Pritchard (1995), and he recommends that this needs to be examined and understood, in combination with other factors.

CHAPTER SEVEN

# Sati and *jauhar*

## SATI

A *Sati* is a good woman (*sadhvi*), a woman devoted to her husband (*pativrata*). Only in a subsidiary sense is the term '*sati*' used to designate a woman who 'is burned on the pyre along with the body of her husband'. Even then, conspicuously, no direct mention of widowhood is made (Hawley, 1994). Originally, *sati* was a feminine participle derived from the verb 'to be'. It is also a means of avoidance of widowhood. There is the practice of *sati* (*Sati pratha*) and it is also a noun. Subsequently, the act itself comes into 'being'. Thus Sati is person and practice, as well as the goddess.

Courtright (1994) suggests that Sati has an iconic representation and is not a single unitary phenomenon. He questions whether women enter the fire out of pure devotion and a compelling confidence in the reality of rebirth and the effectiveness of self-sacrifice, simply because their submissive and subject status may not allow them a sense if freedom to make an independent decision when they are going through suicide. On one side of reality, Courtright suggests, lies the religious view that emphasises reincarnation and self-sacrificial actions. On the other is the 'modern' view when individuals act in the context of social environments which are more or less hospitable to a person's self-fulfilment. Courtright (1994) argues that the former is the ideal heroic and the latter is a paradigm of powerlessness.

He suggests that the three representations of Sati are: of traditional Hinduism (where Sati is a sacred person); of western travellers and perspective, i.e. a measure of Hindu superstition and irrationality; the Sati of contemporary India shaped in large measure by the discourse of feminism. The colonial discourse saw Hinduism [sic] as 'passive docility of the natural character and the mental subjection of its members, seem to admit of no other impulse sufficient to kindle resentment' (Kennedy, 1843).

Sati designates a woman who immolates herself and not the rite or custom of widow burning: 'It was the British who at the close of the eighteenth century officialised the confusion between the immolated woman and the sacrifice of the widows adding to this fine mess such delightful orthographic minorations *as Sattee, Suttee, Suttee*, and other variants to which may be appended the elegant French transcription of Sutty' (Hodges, 1793). Weinberger-Thomas (2000) illustrates the terms used in Sanskrit language which resort to periphrastic expression 'going with' (*Sahagamana*) or 'dying with' (*Sahamarana*) if the woman burns herself with her husband, and 'going after' (*anugamana*) or 'dying after' (*anumarana*) if she burns herself on a different pyre. One also finds terms such as 'ascension' (of the pyre – *anavarohana*) and burning of the Sati (*Satidaha*).

Sati was variously expected to carry a dagger in one hand and a lemon or mirror in other. The dagger and lemon are both images of sacrifice, or rather of that component which provides sacrifice with its meaning and substance – the victim. Sati's sacrificial calling recognises the crucial role of love in the matter. Whatever the reason, the act was (and is) seen as admirable.

Parvati was seen as 'she who desired [only] to gain a husband's blessing long displayed the utmost devotion: [first] because she wanted to show favour to the world; [second] because it was advocated by sacred tradition; [third] because it was her father's command [as a result] she became one with the body of the Lord [Shiva] whose crest jewels in the crescent moon. "May Sati, gem of chaste women, today grant me knowledge in the way of the sacred law!"' Citing from Tryambaka's treatise, Leslie (1989) observes that Sati is the daughter of Daksa. After Daksa insulted Shiva by refusing to invite him to his great sacrifice, Sati immolated herself in the fire. Later, when the world was threatened by the demon Taraka, it was prophesied that only the child of Shiva and Parvati could destroy him. So 'in order to show favour to the world' Parvati set out to win Shiva, first by her beauty and, when that failed, by her religious devotion. Eventually Skanda was born and both gods and universe were saved.

Manu, in his texts on the roles and responsibilities of women, maintains that women are not fit for independence. They are guarded by their fathers, then by their husbands and, in their old age, by their sons. By guarding his wife, the husband guards his own descendants, practices, family, and himself, as well as his own duty. The husband enters the wife, becomes an embryo and is born here on earth. That is why a wife is called *Jaya*, because he is born [*Jayate*] again in her (Doniger & Smith, 1991). The institution of *sati* or self-immolation of widows has been seen as an important form of suicide perceived in terms of one's *dharma*.

*Dharma* is a difficult word to translate and refers to duty, law (a seamless combination of law in the sense of law of gravity, natural law, and law in the sense of paying taxes, cultural law, justice), sight, religious merit, and finally religion. It has been suggested that this practice of self-immolation was prevalent among ancient Greeks, Germans, Slavs, Egyptians, and other races of the world (Thakur, 1962). Westermarck (1906, cited by Thakur, 1962) states: 'From Greece we have the instances of Evadne throwing herself in the funeral of her husband and of the suicide of three Messetan widows mentioned by Pausanians. [The] sacrifice of widows occurred as it seems a regular custom among the Scandinavians, Herlinki and Slavians.' Similarly in Slavonic lands it is argued that a thousand years ago widows used to destroy themselves in order to accompany their dead husbands to the world of spirits. If the dead man were rich or noble, then his slaves were expected to sacrifice themselves as well. Twelve slaves were laid on the funeral pyre of Petroclaus.

Figueira (1994) suggests that European travellers of the fifteenth and sixteenth centuries had described *sati* in India, which suggested coercion as well as devotion. She highlights the portrayal of that act by Brunhilde in Wagner's opera *Götterdümmerung*. The battle between reason and religion was also compounded by seeing the act in particular, and the Orient in general, as exotic, which suggests that the portrayals may have had more to do with the colonial master's view of the poor deluded native. Figueira (1994) points out that a male India peopled by fanatics and despots incarnating, superstitious fatalism and arbitrary power, confronted a female India split between sexual licence and matrimonial rigour, even though Sati, as represented in the literature, drew these extremes together. Figueira (1994) draws the attention of the reader to the suicide in the nineteenth century of the German poetess Günderrode, whose romantic love was not responded to: using a Sanskrit poem (reflecting the act of *sati* devotion) as a suicide note, she killed herself. Lewis (1994) agrees with Figueira's interpretation, but suggests that the British rendering of *sati* appeared in texts rather than in imaginative genres, which would reflect the rulers' needs for 'factual reports' rather than fantasy or imaginative ones.

Westermarck (1906) also suggests that system similar to *sati* was deep-rooted in China. In spite of imperial prohibitions, the suicide of widows on the death of their husbands continued until the twentieth century. Petrie (1962) observed that in ancient Egypt it was the custom to kill-off the court and high officials at the king's death. In Japan and China the original immolations were subsequently replaced by allowing the nearest relatives and slaves of the deceased simply to settle on the tomb rather than sacrificing themselves. The women of Bali wounded themselves with a *kris* as a means of showing their determination to die. Weinberger-Thomas (2000) illustrates this process very effectively with eighteenth-century travelogues and historic material.

The Vedic scholars differ in their opinion about the practice of widow burning. Narasimhan (1998) points out that there is no reference to *sati* in the Brahmanic literature up to 700 AD. In the Vedic texts, although funeral procedures are described in detail, widow immolation does not gain a mention. Widow remarriage is mentioned on several occasions and injunctions on drinking alcohol and eating meat, honey, and salt after the death of the husband are described. *Manusmrti* and Kautilya's *Artha shastra* do not mention *sati* either, although there is selective mention in *Mahabharata*. Narasimhan (1998) asserts that till around 500 BC, the custom of *sati* was not prevalent even among the Kshatriyas, who practised widow burning long before the other classes took to it in imitation. With the rise of Buddhism in the fifth century BC, the denigration of women and emphasis on ascetism, the mention of *sati* also started to increase. Narasimhan (1998) observes that, chronologically, there appeared to be a shift for the widows from remarriage to celibacy to self-immolation. Around 700 AD there is the exhortation that 'for all women there is no other duty except falling into the funeral pyre when the husband dies'. Yet this applied to castes other than Brahmin (Kane, 1973). The early years of the sixth and seventh centuries AD were marked by practical and social uncertainties, together with an increase in threats of rape and abduction, as well as child marriage and *sati*. Intercaste marriages were forbidden because there may have been a sense of keeping purification of the genes and during a period of cultural decline certain elements of Hinduism surfaced.

Narasimhan (1998) cites that the most explicit authority for widow burning is said to be found in the *Taittriya samhita* (quoted in the *Marayaniya Upanisad*): 'O Agni, I will observe the vow of following my husband. Do thou enable me to accomplish it . . . to gain the heavenly mansion I enter in to thee – inspire me with courage and take me to my lord.' The exemption granted to Brahmin women may reflect an underlying wish to save their own caste from disappearing, as Brahmins themselves interpreted the texts. However, it is also possible that *sati* started as a *kshatriya* practice and gradually spread to other castes (Narasimhan, 1998). Between the sixth and seventh centuries AD the practice may have become more settled. Between the ninth and tenth centuries both pro- and anti-*sati* views appear to have prevailed. The detailed act and what is expected of the woman are described in various Puranas which date from around the sixth century AD.

The diversity of edicts and changes in edicts over several centuries suggest that the interpretation of the texts, and possibly even some rewriting, may have taken place in response to prevalent sociopolitical factors. On the one hand, the interpretation and reinterpretation of these findings validate social practices, which may be thought to be imposed for one reason or another. On the other hand, textual ambiguities are selected to be reimposed in support of prevailing customs and practices.

According to Thakur (1962), the simplicity of the ideas indicates that there is no mention of fire and none of wood or burning to suggest anything like incineration. The body is deposited in the earth and the earth is invoked to lie lightly on it. It is suggested that here that burial was the norm earlier and not cremation. However, another hymn in that part of the *Veda* suggests that fire is invoked, not to hurt the body consigned to it, and cremation is clearly indicated.

After the preliminary preparations, the task is to dig a trench, place fuel thereon, wash, shave and prepare the nails of the dead body and place it on the pyre along with the widow of the deceased. These were probably performed without any mantras, for the *Aranyaka* does not allude to them. When placed on the pyre, the body should have a bit of gold in its hands if a Brahmin, a bow if a Kshatriya, and a jewel if a Vaisya. The wife should lie down on the left side of the corpse, according to *Baudhayana* and *Sayana.*

*Asvalayana* recommends that she should be placed next to the head on the north side. The chief mourner, or he who is setting fire to the pyre, should then address the dead: 'O mortal, this woman [you wife] wishing to be joined to you in a future world [i.e. to obtain the *patiloka* (the region of husbands)] is lying by the corpse. She has always observed the duties of a faithful wife. Grant her your permission to abide in this world and relinquish your wealth to your descendants.' A younger brother of the dead man or a disciple should then proceed to the pyre, hold the left hand of the woman and ask her to come away: 'Rise up, woman, thou rest by the side of the lifeless. Come [back] to the land of the living, away from thy husband and become the wife of him who holds thy hand and is willing to marry thee.' In a subsequent mantra she is asked to bring away the gold from the hand of the corpse with the following words: 'For the promotion of thy wealth and glory as a Brahmana woman, and beauty and power, take the gold from the hand of the dead [and abide] in this [region]; we [shall dwell] here well served and prospering and overcoming all presumptions assailants.' The removal of the widow is thus contemplated.

Thakur (1962) argues that the custom of sacrificing the wife existed among the Aryans in the Indo-European period and later fell into disuse among the Vedic Aryans. There is evidence from the *Atharvaveda* that some formalities reminiscent of the archaic custom of *sati* were practised during the Vedic age. Narasimhan (1998) suggests that there was a clear shift from no *sati* practice to increased and rigid practice between the tenth and nineteenth centuries AD. Instead of immolating herself, the widow was asked to come down and a prayer was offered that she lead a prosperous life, enjoying the bliss of children and wealth. Thus the custom appeared to be discouraged.

Even in its basic sense, *pativrata* has a bearing on an ideological nuance, for literally it means that the woman has vowed [*vrata*] to her husband [*pati*]. The substance of this vow is protection. If a wife is devoted to her husband and therefore protects him (by her deeds and actions) he will prosper. If not, he will suffer and perhaps die (Harlan, 1994). There are two basic ways in which *pativrata* protects her husband – by serving him and attending to his personal needs and encouraging him to perform his duties, and by rituals to placate various deities. Harlan (1994) suggests the traditional view is that if the husband predeceases the woman she is culpable and may be accused of insufficient or insincere devotion. She can escape suspicion if she takes another vow (*vrata*) to die as a *sati* and become *Sativrata*. The period between deciding to die and the act itself allows a woman to become extremely powerful because she possesses special powers.

This is a moral ideal. Harlan (1994) points out that Rajputs understand the *sati* traditions to be theirs, although other castes and communities accept and follow their tradition. Mere self-destruction does not guarantee that one becomes *Sativrata*, which relies on selfless and pure motivation. For Rajput women, the decision to utter *vrata* of *sati* is selfless, spontaneous, and a direct reflex of her character. Being Rajput means knowing how to sacrifice; being predisposed to sacrifice makes Rajput women the best wives. Harlan (1994) proposes that this proof is necessary because the women's status is uncertain due to unpopular decisions she may have taken during her lifetime. The *Sativrata* may become angry and may curse, which is not a universal practice, but every *sativrata* makes her mark in a way, which protects her household. Brown (1994) accuses Harlan of misogyny on the basis that account is not taken of the role of Sati as mother, but only wife.

In the Hindu scripture *Mahabharata*, Madri, the favourite wife of Pandu, burnt herself with her husband's body because it is said that she was not sure that she could lead an ideal life. In *Virata-Parava*, Sairandhiri is ordered to be burnt with Kicaka and in *Mausala-Parva* four wives of Vasudeva, Devki, Bhadra, Rohini, and Madira, burnt themselves with him. The four wives of his adoptive son Krishna, Rukmini, Saibya, Haimavati, and Jambavati, burnt themselves along with Krishna's body, while other consorts such as Satyabhama went into the forest to meditate and toil. After the major war between the Pandavas and Kauravas in Kurukshetra, thousands of warriors died, but their wives did not commit the act of *sati*, although some are said to have drowned themselves.

Thakur (1962) suggests that the practice of *sati* may have been confined to the royal families and great warriors. It is possible that later *Puranas* may be projecting later customs of early history. It would appear that the burning of widows was a rare occurrence and that the people were neither very keen on observing the practice nor had any deep-rooted convictions about its absolute religious necessity. However, in medieval times the practice of *sati* appeared more prevalent. Radhakrishnan (1948) observes: 'In the matter of vegetarian food and the non-marriage of widows even the lowest classes imitate the highest. With the increase of confusion, instances of Sati also increased but all through protests were uttered.'

Bana, in his *Kadambari*, stated: 'This is a path followed by the illiterate, is a manifestation of infatuation, a course of ignorance, an act of fool-hardiness and short-sightedness stumbling through stupidity, that life is put an end to, when a parent, brother, sister, husband is dead . . . If it be properly considered, this suicide has a selfish object, because it is intended to obviate the unendurable sorrow of bereavement.' During the Middle Ages, the practice of *sati* continued across the country. In spite of several attempts made by the Mughal emperors Akbar and Jahangir to suppress it, Brahmin priests played an important part in the Sati rites. A woman who was about to practice *sati* was not allowed to be touched by a non-Hindu and people valued highly the blessing given by a Sati on her way to her death. The sacrifice was also seen as purifying the family of the father, the mother, and the husband. If the body of the husband had already been cremated, she took his sandals in her hands or some other article of his dress to tie to her and after purification ascended the pyre. Not only Mughals but later on the Sikhs also condemned the practice, but it was the British who managed to put an end to the ritual.

Mani (1989) argues that the legislative prohibition of *sati* was the culmination of a debate during which 8134 instances of *sati* were recorded, mainly though not exclusively among upper-caste Hindus, with 63% in the area around Calcutta city. Colonial rule, with its moral, civilising claims is said to have provided the context for a thorough re-evaluation of the Indian tradition along the lines of being more consonant with a 'modern' economy and India's incorporation into the capitalist world system. She suggests that even the anti-imperialists felt forced to acknowledge the 'positive' consequences of colonial rule on certain aspects of women's lives, if not in practice than at least at the level of ideas about 'women's rights'.

Raja Ram Mohun Roy, so-called father of the Bengal renaissance, worked with the British to abolish the practice of *sati*. Raja Budh Singh of Buneli took 84 *satis* with him and Ajit Singh of Jodhpur took 64. Raja of Idar took seven queens, two concubines, four female slaves and one manservant to the pyre. On a visit to England, Ram Mohun Roy complained to the Privy Council about their refusal to make *sati* illegal (Liddle & Joshi, 1986). When the Sati Abolition Law was passed in 1829, it made little difference as it did not apply to the independent states of the dominion of India. Daly (1978) citing Gage (1972) suggests that this was ironic as at the same time the Christian church was still burning women as witches late into the eighteenth century. Liddle and Joshi (1986) observe that although the British took credit for a progressive step in assisting women to their liberation, their motives remain ambiguous.

Nandy (1980) proposes that coercion in the cases of *sati* in the nineteenth century was common and subsequently (Nandy, 1994) recommended that suspicion as to coercion should be exercised in all cases of *sati*. Nandy eloquently questions the assumption on the part of decultured Indians that classical or mythological instances of *sati* degrade women. He argues that in the past *sati* was a rare, fearsome, but moving ritual that symbolised the reaffirmation of the purity, self-sacrifice, power, and dignity of women, and the superiority of the feminine principle in the cosmos. He goes on to urge scholars to differentiate between the event and its meaning within the cultural context. Embree (1994) interprets Nandy's outrage as a reflection that *sati* occurs because of attacks on traditional value systems by new forces from outside. Thus Nandy suggests that *sati* was a pathology of colonialism, not Hinduism (Embree, 1994).

Mani (1989) views the British abolition of the practice of *sati* as a colonial discourse where tradition was linked with scriptures simply because it suited the colonial masters. She argues that officers often saw the widow as a tender child and although the rates of *sati* varied across different geographical areas and castes, the colonial masters' ambivalent attitudes were responsible for their actions. Mani (1989) observes that the discourse on *sati* was a modern discourse on tradition. It exemplified late eighteenth century colonial discourses that elaborated notions of modernity against their own conceptions of tradition. Tradition in this discourse, according to Mani (1989), is posited as a timeless and structuring principle of Indian (read Hindu) society enacted in everyday lives of indigenous people. The widow was portrayed as either a heroine or an abject victim – thrown upon the heap. As a result she has to be salvaged from herself and the colonial masters see this as their (patriarchal) responsibility. Mani turns the argument on its head and believes that, rather than tradition being debated, it was the woman who became the site on which tradition was debated and reformulated.

References are available in plenty from the time of the earliest of the ancient texts to illustrate how women were denigrated and held worthy only of contempt: 'A man with a hundred tongues would die before finishing the task of lecturing upon the vices and defects of women, even if he were to do nothing else throughout a long life of a hundred years,' says the *Mahabharata*; to which the *Aunssasanaparva* adds: 'Women combine the wickedness of a razor's edge, poison, snake and fire.' Narasimhan (1998) goes on to point out that the *Ramayana* also lists 'falsehood, thoughtless action, trickery, folly, great greed, impurity and cruelty' as the 'natural faults of women'. Thus it is not entirely surprising that the male psyche continues to treat women in exactly the same way, even in the twenty-first century. Such oppression is bound to attack women's self-esteem in a manner which may be compared to chronic vulnerability and difficulty. Women and *shudra* (low caste) were often equated, the latter being the lowest caste. In addition, when menstruating the women became even lower and were not allowed in the kitchen to protect the purity of the food; this still happens today, in southern India.

Morally and intellectually women were held to be inferior and weak. They were not permitted to study the *Vedas*. Marriage and motherhood were the only goals. Marriage meant self-effacement in the services of the husband and subsequent family. Women were handed as property from father to husband. The notion of *pativrata* is drilled into the woman from birth – through societal rituals, mythology, attitudes, and religious observances. While men had various practices prescribed for ensuring their place in heaven, there were none for women because all she needed to merit ascent to heaven was devotion to her husband; a life spent in the service of the *patidev* (the husband who is god) could not be improved upon. The performance of domestic duties was 'equal to worshipping fire and attendance on the husband equalled the highest religious merit' (Narasimhan, 1998).

Thus with the woman's whole identity immersed in her wifely status, it is not surprising that with the death of her husband she lost her raison d'être. Widowhood was the worst calamity that could befall an individual. She simply 'disappeared' from the social scene and with shaven head had to go around begging. Often these women ended up at places of pilgrimage, away from the family. Such an obvious control of female sexuality and existence must have meant to the individual that death was a better option than living under such circumstances. Jain widows could and can become nuns and therefore have an option not to commit *sati*. The act of *sati* became much more rigid after the seventh century AD. Narasimhan (1998) describes the process of *niyoga*, which lasted up to third century AD, requiring widows to have sex without pleasure so that they could have sons.

Coomaraswamy (1957) argues that the 'oriental woman' should not be seen as passive and under the thumb of her husband, but being capable of fully asserting her freedom and femininity, because in this context love and marriage are not founded on passion as in the west ('accidents of sensibility'), but on 'the fulfillment of a traditional design'. The ego does not play a role in the realisation of self. The emphasis on spiritual freedom allows the individual to obtain liberation by *adhering* (emphasis mine) to the role that the group, society, and tradition have assigned to her. Sati in that sense is the perfect wife and essential being. Coomaraswamy could be considered to hold a very traditional male view, which reflects the attitudes of a patriarchal society. It was argued that the western woman has lost her femininity and power since the advent of the industrial resolution, whereas the oriental woman was 'older, purer and more specialised but certainly a universal type'. The woman of the industrial revolution, in an attempt to be more like the man, has strayed from that feminine ideal (Coomaraswamy, 1957). In recent times in India the dichotomy between westernised and traditional Indian woman has become of much more interest (Weinberger-Thomas, 2000). Male activists in modern-day India also like the idea of the subservient Indian woman who, in fulfilment of her *sati-dharma*, gladly mounts her husband's pyre. The expectation is virtually never explored from the point of the woman.

Weinberger-Thomas (2000) reports an interview with a woman who survived her own sacrifice through police intervention in 1988. In this interview the woman was unable to explain where the emotions and the idea of committing *sati* had arisen, saying that Lord Shiva had been responsible. Whether this was a post-hoc explanation because the act itself was illegal or whether it was a genuine act of devotion is difficult to ascertain. Whether in a psychiatric sense it was a possession trance or whether the woman had feelings of passivity is irrelevant because the act and the post-hoc explanation are both culturally coloured. Weinberger-Thomas (2000) also interviewed the son who lit the pyre, but obtained a similar explanation from him, which she attributes to the process of an unconscious strategy for ridding oneself of guilt feelings by couching them in acceptable and soothing terms within one's cultural idiom. In a series of interviews with relatives of various Satis, Weinberger-Thomas (2000) reported that all the stories appear to merge with one another and this objectification of the act and the actor produced changes both in physicality and spirituality in herself as well as those around her. There is an obvious explanation: widowhood in some communities is such an appalling state in which to live that giving up the body to escape and to gain 'immortality' as well as a better life in the next birth may appeal to individuals. Being a young widow further adds to the risk since pregnancy would cast an indelible stain on the husband's lineage. In a study from Gujarat in the 1920s, Stevenson (cited in Weinberger-Thomas, 2000) observes that widows were either poisoned or their clothes set on fire. Such crimes remained unpunished and even now often go undetected.

In recent years, *sati* has re-emerged in some parts of India. In a well-publicised case in Rajasthan in 1987, a young bride immolated herself on her husband's funeral pyre. This incident split the country in more ways than one. The young woman was seen as a goddess and men and women flocked to the site. Sangari and Vaid (1989) suggest that every successful immolation is always narrated as an act of pure volition on the part of the dead woman. Narasimhan (1998) points out there had been several incidents of *sati* in Central and North India but that this particular incident really shook the country. There was a clear split between politicians, who saw this is a religious event and action and an attack on religious values, and some women, especially in the cities, who saw it as an anti-feminist account which was used to hide the forced nature of the act. In India, such a process of immolation has been linked with dowry deaths, and in the UK as a potent means of suicide. When Soni-Raleigh et al. (1990) reported rates of completed suicide among Indian women they observed that even although social classes one and two were over-represented (the women were doctors or dentists), the commonest method of committing suicide was by setting oneself on fire.

## *JAUHAR*

*Jauhar* is the process of taking one's own life, committing suicide, fighting desperately to the death. When the Rajputs were attacked by an overwhelming force they sometimes slaughtered or burnt their wives and children on the field of battle. *Jauhar* was committed for the sake of the defence of the territory (and economic interests) and for the purity of the royal lineage, not for the chastity and wifely devotion implied in *sati*. *Jauhar* was a royal or noble prerogative: queens whose husbands were slain in battle had the prerogative to opt for collective suicide. It happened rarely and in exceptionally dangerous circumstances (Oldenburg, 1994). There are dissimilarities between *sati* and *jauhar*. The latter was committed without the body of the dead husband, only on uncertainty of the fate that awaited them, and was a practical solution to avoid rape, torture, or other ignominies. Oldenburg (1994) proposes that Brahmins borrowed the practice of *jauhar* from the Rajputs and modified the concept over time to suit their own sanskrit gender ideology of the good rather than the brave woman. She argues that conversion of Sati (pure wife) into the common name of rituals of *sati* may reflect a Brahminical wish to move into even higher echelons of society.

In making a distinction between *jauhar* and *sati*, it becomes clear that the former was a rite which, when performed, could make a whole tribe extinct within a few hours. Rajputs had the tradition that if their fort was about to be captured by the enemy then every female of the tribe would kill herself, either by self-immolation or by jumping into a well. Thakur (1962) suggests that this custom can be traced back some thousand years before the dawn of Christianity, although not in the form we know it. *Jauhar* was mass suicide and committed to avoid intolerable shame, and to escape rape and sexual dishonour.

Thakur (1962) reports that in the fourth century BC Alexander the Great invaded and defeated several tribes in North India. During the course of one such defeat in a single city some 20,000 males, females and children embraced the flames to escape captivity and dishonour at the hands of foreign enemies. Thakur (1962) cites the instance of Ala-ud-Din Khilji's invasion of Chittore in medieval times. A funeral pyre was lit within the great subterranean retreat in chambers impervious to the light of the day and several thousands of women committed *jauhar*. Similar events were reported in the sixteenth century, especially when Muslims or Mughal invaders attacked Rajasthan. The sites of these acts are worshipped even today. This rite has been reported to be carried out among other castes and in other parts of India as well.

The role of *sati* in a relationship with suicidal ideation has not been explored. Suicidal ideation must appear secondary to societal/kinship expectations if the woman is attempting to kill herself. The relationship between the goddess Sati and the act of *sati* is a complex one. It can be argued that the motivated death represents a sense of control and autonomy and faithfulness to her husband. The guilt and self-hatred inherent in such an act can lead to a sense of oblivion simply by eliminating oneself. The death of the husband may activate this guilt and self-abrogation where the female blames herself either for not performing her duties adequately and/or being punished for something she may have done in previous lifetime. Is the *sati* immolating herself in order to satisfy the demands of her own ego, asks Weinberger-Thomas (2000): 'Is the desire to abandon and burn her body reflective of narcissistic injury?' The interlocking systems of beliefs and symbols, individual and kinship, action and thought, have to be seen in the context of the broader cultural milieu and idioms expressed.

It is impossible to defend the practices of *sati* and *jauhar* in any way except to place them in the context of the society and culture that existed at the time. The perception of the self in the context of the family and giving oneself up for the greater good or cause for the society or family fits in with Durkheim's altruistic suicide. However, the argument here is that the family honour or impending dishonour plays a more important role than individual survival.

Furthermore, why should women have to sacrifice themselves because their males' honour depends upon it? The control, pillage, and rape of women of the vanquished tribes at the hands of the victor was one of the reasons expounded for the rites of *jauhar* especially. High rates of *sati* in Bengal, especially among Brahmins, suggest that although in many cases attempts were made to dissuade the widows, they went ahead with the practice nevertheless. Whether these rites remain in the universal unconscious in modern times so those women continue to commit suicide by self-immolation is for psychoanalysts to try and tease out. Suffice it to say that the religious orthodoxy still pays lip service to these acts and people flock to such sites to worship and seek blessings.

## PROTEST SUICIDE

Weinberger-Thomas (2000) has raised the question of the profile of groups like the Bhats and Charans from western India who have participated in protest suicides. Both groups were considered holy. The inspiration that was the source of their art was taken to be a sign of divine possession; a fact corroborated by their readiness to take their own lives. Bhats were well known and recognised as genealogists, and were the final authority on the subject of family trees. Capable of finding links between a given class or lineage and associated privileges, they were not only guardians of caste institutions but also craftsmen of social mobility. They made and unmade reputations.

The Charans would escort caravans and if these were attacked they threatened to shed their own blood by slashing their forearms with their daggers. The prestige of a Charan was judged by the number of scars. If the adversary did not yield, members of the clan would be put to death in increasingly macabre fashion. The main purpose was to place unbearable pressure on the opposing forces. The ghosts of the suicides would haunt the opposition. The children and elderly were sacrificed first, with priority given to girls and women imbued with a particular type of sanctity within the caste – their violent deaths transforming them into the goddess Devi. The Charans stood as sureties wherever a legal guarantee was required and the security was their body and their life. They collectively wounded, mutilated, and immolated themselves if the terms of the contract were not respected, if reparation was not made for a damage or offence, and whenever they themselves were victims of injustice or affront (Weinberger-Thomas, 2000).

Weinberger-Thomas goes on to suggest that the body of practices involving mutilation and voluntary death as a sign of protest bore the name of *tyog*. It was enshrined in the law in 1795 and 1799, but officially prohibited only in 1827. It did not totally disappear for another 70 years or so. The Charans would pierce their cheeks with a lancet and dance without displaying any sign of pain. They would cut their throats or open wounds, which would lead to bleeding from the wound until death. A Charan would set himself ablaze and dance before his adversaries until he collapsed in front of them in a heap of ashes. Weinberger-Thomas (2000, p. 61) reports that, in 1586, nearly 11,000 Charans whose villages had been confiscated sat before a temple blocking its entrance. At dawn a mass suicide took place in the temple.

## CONCLUSIONS

It is clear that members of every caste have made use of this approach and in due course the threat to harm oneself in public places had political connotations. Fasting to death and self-immolation became common threats to achieve political solutions. Thus the suicide act can be expiatory, devotional, a protest, or revenge.

CHAPTER EIGHT

# Attempted suicide in the Indian subcontinent

## INTRODUCTION

The rates of attempted suicide are difficult to obtain when the act is seen as illegal. Every effort will be made by the individual or his/her carers to hide the act, change its label (i.e. call it accidental rather than an intentional act) or undermine the seriousness of the intent. Survivors of suicide attempts, and family members, are often likely to be looked upon with suspicion and the associated stigma and the tainting of the family can have serious consequences on the individual's and family's standing in the community. Such fear and stigma can influence help seeking.

Trivedi (1997) in an editorial points out that under the terms of the Indian penal code, acts of suicide or any act towards the commission of such offence shall be punished with simple imprisonment for a term, which may extend to one year or with fine or both; thereby suggesting that the law esteems the life of an individual as not only valuable to them but also to the state. He then goes on to argue that as the essence of suicide is the intentional self-destruction of life, the courts have often employed the test of intention and tried to gather information to this extent before passing a judgement. If the attempt was 'accidental' or in an intoxicated state then it does not seem to count. This will also exclude slow death by alcoholic intoxication. Similarly, the status of political activities such as declared self-immolation and fast unto death as a form of political protest is unclear. As these may be seen as prolonged activities, theoretically at least they can be interrupted at any time.

Some of the attempters will suffer from psychiatric disorders, whereas others will simply respond to stress and stressful life events.

## INDIA

The exact rates of attempted suicide are difficult to ascertain. However, these cases have been reported from all over the subcontinent and some of the findings will be presented here. Venkoba Rao (1983) observed that in Madurai in South India, the number of cases of attempted suicide doubled between 1977 and 1978, having more than doubled previously between 1974 and 1977. He reported that the ratio of completed to attempted suicide ranged from 1:2 to 1:9. The gender distribution has leaned in favour of the male, although recently this has started to change. A significant number of cases were young and the precipitating causes were reported to be trivial in nature. In one of the earliest studies from Madurai, Venkoba Rao and Chennian (1972) found that 31% of attempters were students and more likely to be male. Of the 35 students studied, 27 made one attempt whereas 5 (14%) had attempted twice and 3 (7%) had attempted suicide four times. Of 35, 20 (55%) were a given clinical diagnosis of immature or hysterical personality, 8 (20%) had schizophrenia, and 3 (8%) were drug dependent. The absence of clinical depression was striking.

Lal and Sethi (1976) collected their data from a general hospital in North India in 1972, especially on cases of poisoning. They identified 133 cases presenting with attempted suicide. Males were more likely to present following the attempt than females. The peak age for both groups was between 21 and 30 and a significant majority of cases were below the age of 30 years. Insecticides and pesticides were the commonest substances used as a means to attempt suicide. A majority of the sample were illiterate or had education below school level, although it is not clear whether this means school completion or not attending school at all. Both sexes were equally likely to be married. The authors argue that their rates are less than those reported from the South Indian data, but the patterns of admission and access to services are not taken into account in this study. These authors suggest that high rates of attempts in males, who are more likely to be at better educational levels than females, indicate they are more at risk of self-harm. They suggest that as attempters are more likely to be married, there is an association between marriage and self-harm. However, without knowing the marital status of the base population, i.e. the denominator, it is impossible to be certain whether this is true. Furthermore, they did not ask the individuals about the causative or precipitating social factors to ascertain the causal link. However, the study – one of the first from North India – is remarkably similar to those from the south in findings on gender difference, age of vulnerable individuals, and the method itself. Venkoba Rao (1992) reported that the stigmatising nature of suicide influenced the financial status of the family as well as having emotional and social implications.

In the South Indian city of Madras (now called Chennai), Ponnudurai, Jeyakar, and Saraswathy (1986) studied 86 patients who had presented to the hospital with attempted suicide. Again, males were preponderant over females. The peak age was between 15 and 20 years. Nearly a quarter (23.2%) of the sample acknowledged harbouring suicidal ideation for quite some time prior to the actual attempt. A small proportion (4.6%) had prepared a suicide note. Among various causes reported, the most significant cause was quarrel with and resulting arguments and scolding by significant others. A further two females (5.2%) had decided to end their lives following family quarrels with their alcoholic fathers. Physical illness had contributed to 17.4% of suicidal attempts and marital problems to 14%. Another two females had attempted suicide after arguments with their alcoholic husbands. More than a quarter of males (27%) blamed their unemployment. Only 14% had been suffering from psychiatric disorders, which also included epilepsy. Of 42 individuals who were given a personality inventory, 45% scored high on extraversion and 95% scored low on the psychoticism scale.

Similar findings have been reported in North India. Sharma (1998) studied 75 cases over an 18-month period in the Himalayan state of Himachal Pradesh. Of these, 35 (46%) were male and 40 (54%) female. The peak age was between 15 and 24 and 85% cases were under the age of 34. A majority (68%) came from rural areas. One third (36%) reported quarrels with in-laws/spouse, parents or siblings, or failure in love as possible contributory causes. Nearly half (46%) were diagnosed as having a psychiatric disorder; the commonest being affective disorder, acute stress reaction, substance misuse, schizophrenia, or dissociative disorders. The increased rates among the females in this study were attributed by the author to social factors, including inadequate opportunities to express emotional conflicts and low social status given to the females in the family.

From a large industrial urban conurbation in Punjab, Narang, Mishra, and Mohan (2000) reported on 100 cases of attempted suicide out of a total of 208 who had presented to a general hospital. Of the 108 who had not been included, 28 had died and the rest were physically too ill to undergo detailed investigation. Of the 100 cases, 58 were male and 42 female. Only 27% were over the age of 30, females being slightly older when compared with males; females were either housewives or students. More than one third (35%) of the sample was attributed to come from low socioeconomic status. Females were more likely to be married than males. There were no details of all those who were not included – a majority in fact – and no social factors in causation were reported in the study so it is difficult to know what the exact role of factors such as conflict, arguments, alcohol was on the act itself.

Using data from admissions to an intensive care unit, Kumar (1998) reported on 100 consecutive suicide attempters. Nearly three quarters (17%) were below the age of 30 and two thirds were male. Again a majority were married (59%) and 48% were from a lower socioeconomic background. More than half (57%) had a family history of psychiatric morbidity with alcoholism, suicide, and depression, and 42% acknowledged having physical symptoms of which abdominal pain was the commonest. Interestingly, 41% gave a past history of psychiatric morbidity – depression and alcoholism being the commonest.

A vast majority (85%) had ingested poisonous substances, of which organophosphorus compounds were the commonest. Using the suicide intent questionnaire, the author found that the intent was mild in 19%, moderate in 49%, and severe in 32% of cases. A majority had a concurrent diagnosis of adjustment reaction.

Ten cases died within one week of admission. Positive family history of psychiatric morbidity was more common among males and physical ailments more common in females. Once again the higher rate in the married group is interpreted by the author as a causal association. The older subjects were marginally more likely to have positive family and a past history of psychiatric morbidity and have presence of physical illness. This study confirms some of the key findings earlier reported by Venkoba Rao and colleagues as discussed above. It is also a study of more serious attempters who had been admitted to an intensive care unit and had high mortality associated with it. It would have been interesting to see whether there was a history of repetition, which may have made a difference to the outcome.

In a recent study from Banglore in South India and its environs, Gururaj and Isaac (2001) reported that a total of 1260 cases of attempted suicide were identified over one year presenting to 12 hospitals which run services for accident and emergencies. Of all the cases, 671 were male (53%) and the rest female (47%). Those aged between 20 and 29 had the highest representation in the group (25%). Of all the subjects, 95% cases come from nuclear families, 78% were Hindus, 11% Muslims, and 11% Christians. Slightly less than half (49.6%) were married, although women were more likely (53.7% vs. 46.1%) to be married. Slightly more than half (51%) had a poor socioeconomic status. Of all suicide attempts, 91.5% males and 93.8% females had decided on the attempt by themselves and 6.9% males and 4.7% females had decided to make the attempt as a family.

A pact had been made by 1.9% of males and 1.5% of females. Males were also more likely to have attempted suicide previously (19.4% vs. 13.6% of females). A clinically recorded diagnosis was considered for arriving at the presence or absence of mental illness. Only 118 (9.8%) subjects were identified to be suffering from a mental illness – the commonest diagnoses given were depression (32%), schizophrenia (12%), alcoholism (11%), and the rest were unknown. Even more striking was the finding that only 9% were on any medication. Between 12 noon and midnight were the most likely times for the attempt to have taken place. Various causes of attempted suicide from this study are illustrated in Table 8.1.

Five major factors contributing to attempted suicide were family conflicts (38%), presence of an illness (16%), financial problems (9%), marriage-related problems (7%), and alcohol-related problems (6%).

A single cause of attempted suicide was observed in 34% male suicides and 51% of female suicides. A further two, three, four, and five factors were responsible for 35%, 26%, 3%, and 0.8% of male suicides and 25%, 18%, 3%, and 3% of female suicides, respectively. Interestingly, only 10.7% of the sample (where it was elicited) reported a stress of less than 30 days.

One third of the sample (males 34%; females 27%) reported motivating factors for attempt as a sudden act of frustration while nearly one quarter were unable to explain why it happened. This may reflect a genuine sense of bewilderment or it may be one way of ignoring what was likely to be an illegal act. Another quarter acknowledged that they wanted to draw attention to their plight to the people around and 14% genuinely wanted to end their life. These figures are deceptive because complete data are not available for a significant number of individuals.

Gururaj and Isaac (2001) conclude that rates of attempted suicide are likely to be higher in communities that are migrant (here they mean rural to urban settings), living in slums and adjoining areas, in unorganised labour industries, have alcohol as a major problem, and experience social disorganisation, high rates of crimes, violence, homelessness, and mental illness. The

Table 8.1
Causes of attempted suicide in the Bangalore study (after Guruaj & Isaac, 2001)

| | *Males (n = 495)* *n(%)* | *Females (n = 441)* *n(%)* | *Total (n = 936)* *n(%)* |
|---|---|---|---|
| Family problem | 168 (34) | 204 (46) | 372 (37) |
| Illness | 72 (14) | 83 (19) | 155 (16) |
| Financial problems | 70 (14) | 24 (5) | 94 (9) |
| Martial disharmony | 27 (5) | 39 (9) | 66 (7) |
| Alcohol | 47 (10) | 10 (2.3) | 57 (6) |
| Love disappointment | 18 (4) | 18 (4) | 36 (4) |
| Work related | 29 (6) | 4 (0.9) | 33 (3) |
| Death in the family | 9 (2) | 9 (2) | 18 (2) |
| School related | 8 (1.6) | 9 (2) | 17 (1.7) |
| Unemployment | 13 (3) | 1 (0.2) | 14 (1.5) |
| Fall in status | 3 (0.6) | 6 (1.4) | 9 (1) |
| Dowry problems | 2 (0.4) | 5 (1.1) | 7 (0.7) |
| Others | 29 (6) | 33 (6.5) | 66 (6.1) |

The percentage figure has been rounded up in some cases.

suicide process starts long before the actual act and passes through various stages of suicidal thoughts, ideas, behaviour, attempts, and completion of the act in a combination of various factors. Individual high risk factors that they identified include marital disharmony, disputes over property, income or dowry, family history of suicide or a known mental disorder, alcohol, recent migration, recent bereavement, inharmonious marriage, etc.

The commonest substances used for attempted suicide in all these studies were organophosphorous compounds in the shape of pesticides and herbicides. In the Bangalore study, for example, 70% of men and 49% women used it. Females were more likely to use drugs (26% vs. 15% males) and were also more likely to ingest kerosene (6.7% vs. 2.3%) or acid (6.7% vs. 2.3%) than males. In 60% males and 66% females the substances were ingested directly while 28% males and 18% females had taken them with food or alcohol.

In the study from Himachal Pradesh, 74% of the subjects had taken organophosphorous compounds, whereas only 6% used wrist cutting, jumping from a height or drowning (Sharma, 1998). In the Punjab study, 91% had ingested poison, of which 58% used insecticides or pesticides (Narang et al., 2000). Sato, Takeichi, and Hara (1993) reported from Japan that agricultural chemicals were the commonest means of attempting suicide. Similar findings have been reported from elsewhere in the Indian diaspora. The patterns suggest that ease of availability (of substances which can be lethal) and the impulsive nature of the act may prove to be a potentially fatal combination. In addition, access to over-the-counter medication will also increase the likelihood of the act succeeding. We shall now briefly look at the available data from other parts of the subcontinent before moving on to the diaspora.

## PAKISTAN

Although aspects of the Pakistani culture are similar to the culture of North India, the religion and tribal variations make direct comparisons quite difficult. The partition of India in 1947, when the British, left resulted in mass migration on an enormous scale, with Muslims leaving India and Hindus leaving Pakistan. The migratory patterns were forced and the result of religious differences. Significant killings occurred on both sides of the border. In modern-day Pakistan, a significant proportion of the population speak Punjabi. Like other developing countries, rapid urbanisation and the growth of shantytowns and slum dwellings has occurred, which has led to dissatisfaction and alienation. It is also clear that globalisation has contributed to a sense of alienation.

The attitudes of the population towards suicide in Pakistan are determined by law and religion. Ahmed (1983) observed that rates of attempted suicide in Karachi were 8.45/100,000 and 79% of subjects were in the age range 10 to 34 years. He found more females in his sample (54%) but Ashraf

(1964) reported that the male/female ratio in his sample was almost 7:1. Poisonous substances were the commonest methods employed. Family conflict with parents, in-laws, or spouses was the commonest precipitating factor in 41% cases; unhappy love affairs accounted for 46%; unemployment and financial problems accounted for 7% of cases (Jamil, Khan, Akhtar, & Sultana, 1977). Ahmed and Zuberi (1981) basing their findings on police records, reporting that men were 4.5 times more likely to attempt suicide and so confirming Ashraf's (1964) finding of a male:female ratio of 6.8:1. Domestic trouble was the commonest explanation for the act. However, the gender pattern began to change over the next 15 years or so. Jamil (1990), reporting on a 10-year study of cases of acute poisoning, observed that 53% were women. They were more likely (66% compared with 26% of men) to be married and the commonest explanation given was 'negligence by husband'. Ashraf (1964) also reported that 44% of attempts were caused by family problems, 8% due to unhappy love affairs, and 9% due to financial difficulties.

Khan and Reza (1998), in a study from the same part of Pakistan, reported that of 262 females and 185 males admitted to a private university hospital, three quarters were aged under 30. Females were younger than males and more likely to be married. These authors collected retrospective case-note data on patients admitted over a six-and-a-half year period. First-time suicidal acts were reported by 341 cases (76%), and 71 women (27%) and 35 men (19%) had engaged in one or more previous suicidal acts. Of the sample, 63% had completed at least six years of education compared with only 30% of the general population.

Self-poisoning using medication was the commonest act, seen in 74% of cases, and of the medication benzodiazepines were implicated in 83% cases and 21% cases used organophosphorous compounds. The commonest reason cited was conflict with in-laws, spouse, girlfriend/boyfriend, or family in 79.6% females and 57.5% of males. Males were more likely to report financial problems (16.7% compared with 1% of females), and psychiatric illness (18.9% compared with 11.4% females). Acute stress/situation reaction was the commonest psychiatric diagnosis, followed by affective disorder (in one third of both groups). The sample is atypical by virtue of a number of reasons – varying from educational status of the sample, the site of sample collection and the data being collected from case notes. However, like some other studies, the data confirm that younger married females are more at risk and the authors argue that the arranged nature of marriages may well contribute to stress and that suicide attempts may be seen as 'time out'.

## SRI LANKA

In Sri Lanka, two thirds of the population follows the Buddhist religion which, as noted in chapter 2, influences attitudes towards life and death.

The rates of completed suicide are extremely high in Sri Lanka and a number of reasons have been put forward to explain this. The educational status of these individuals is very high and it is likely that a sense of defeatism and lack of achievement may be a contributory factor. Traditional attitudes towards elders, the family and arranged marriage may well create a sense of alienation, with suicide or attempted suicide perhaps seen as an answer. Dissanayake and De Silva (1983) reported that 72% of all suicides occurred as a result of self-poisoning. They observed a higher number of young females in their sample, although this may have changed recently. Kerosene and copper sulphate were ingested by 35% of subjects.

In a study from northern Sri Lanka, Ganesavaran, Subramaniam, and Mahadeven (1984) reported that the commonest method was self-poisoning by agrochemicals and insecticides of the organophosphorous variety. They pointed to an earlier study where they had found that younger age groups were more likely to attempt suicide using agrochemicals or other substances. Of the sample, 81% were aged between 15 and 34 and were predominantly male.

Marecek (1998) observed that in parts of Sri Lanka the reported incidence of self-inflicted death had increased eightfold in the previous 50 years. In an attempt to probe the cultural dimensions of suicide, the author sets the scene for the investigation. She points out that steeped hierarchies are based on ascribed characteristics such as caste, class, generation, and gender and the aim is not to achieve social equality. The traditional emphasis on hierarchy has remained in the rural areas. She argues that there is no doubt that suicidal acts that do not end in death are common. Ganesvaran and Raja rajaswaran (1988) observed that for every completed suicide 14 cases of attempted suicide may be seen.

In the central town of Kandy, Kasturiaratchi, De Silva, and Ellawala (1996) reported that of a total 6086 cases admitted to the hospital for suicidal behaviour, 80% survived. Of the total, 68% were male and 60% of the suicide-related admissions involved young people aged between 16 and 25. In the younger age group the gender ratio was equal but the male/female ratio increased steadily with age. Again, ingesting poisonous substances and drug overdoses accounted for more than 80% of the suicide cases. Agrochemicals were the most common substances taken.

Marecek (1998) set out to investigate the local meanings of suicide as in Sri Lanka the act is not conceptualised as mental illness or deep-seated psychological disorder. She drew up a short vignette about an individual whose behaviour strongly suggested impending suicide. It described a 25-year-old individual who was experiencing lethargy, apathy, and loss of interest in friends and social activities. The vignette concluded by saying that the individual had recently purchased a bottle of insecticide. Three additional vignettes describing other kinds of disturbances in behaviour served as filler items. The gender of the actor in the vignette was altered across the respondents, as were the four vignettes. In all, 74 respondents participated (38 men and 36 women, aged 23–81 years). Each vignette was read aloud and the respondents were asked to elicit the likely causes of the behaviour, ideas about gender differences, and recommended ways family and friend could help such an individual. In explaining the cause, most responses attributed it to crisis, including interpersonal difficulty or disappointment in a love relationship. Failures in school, work, and family were also mentioned. Two thirds of the respondents did not regard the individual as mentally ill. There were no gender differences in explaining the causative factors, except for those which are gender specific such as pregnancy, rape, and early menopause.

Those who viewed the two sexes as equally at risk for suicide focused on the fundamental similarity between the two genders. In answering the question as to what to do in such circumstances, emotion-focused responses such as love and kindness, avoiding isolation, and diversions were the commonest. An equal number (35%) plumped for professional interventions such as western medicine, the mental health system, or religious intervention. Nearly 10% asked if the subject was married, and suggested that if they were not married, they must be made to marry. Interestingly, if the vignette actor was seen as female then more emotion-based interventions were offered. If the vignette actor was seen as male, more problem-focused interventions would be suggested. Compared with other methods of intervention, only a small proportion mentioned the mental health system. Although the method employed produced limited findings, it is an unusual study because it aims to understand the knowledge and attitudes of the general population rather than those who have attempted suicide.

## FOLLOW-UP AND REPETITION

The risk of repeating self-harm and subsequent outcome play an important role in managing patients who present with deliberate self-harm. The likelihood of succeeding inadvertently may well increase with repetition because the individual may learn the level of toxicity and also how many tablets or how much insecticide to drink. As noted by Maniam (1988), the success of the attempt also depends upon the distance from the nearest hospital and presence of others around the individual, apart from the actual dosage and type of substance ingested or other methods used. Follow-up studies of suicide mortality among patients who have already attempted suicide reveal a mortality of 1–2% during the first year after the suicide attempt (Batchelor & Napier, 1954; Greer & Bagley, 1971).

In a Danish study, Hanson and Wang (1984) reported that 3% of suicide attempters died by suicide during the three year after the suicide attempt.

Among those who had been admitted to an intensive care unit, the suicide rates on follow-up have been reported (Ettlinger, 1975) to be 12% in males and 11% in females – very similar to those reported by Kumar (1998). However, Ettlinger's follow-up was longer – 5–6 years – and Kumar's subjects had ingested more potentially lethal substances. The longer the follow-up, the higher the rates of suicide reported (Eisenthal, Fareberow, & Shneidman, 1966; Motto, 1965).

In Austria and Norway, suicide rates following an attempted suicide have been reported to be 0.05% and 2.6%, respectively – much lower rates than expected. Schneider (1954) observed that of patients who had attempted suicide, 10% committed suicide over a 10-year observation period, 11.8% over 18 years, and 13% over 28 years. Dahlgren (1977) also found that over a 0–12-year follow-up, 6% were likely to commit suicide, and 11% after 35 years.

Culberg, Wasserman, and Stefansson (1988) followed-up 163 individuals who had originally been admitted following attempted suicide. By virtue of being on a case register, patients could be followed up for 8 to 10 years. Six suicides were identified, along with four suspected suicides. The respective rates thus being 3.07% and 6.1% when both certain and suspected cause of suicide are identified. An additional 12 deaths not due to suicide were related to alcohol and accidents. When comparing suicide attempters with those who had succeeded in completing, the latter were more likely to have chronic alcohol or other associated addictive problems. There were a mean 3.5 suicide attempts before the eventual suicide. Although the authors suggest that several of the eventual suicides had depression, which combined with alcohol or other addictions may well have contributed to vulnerability, their diagnosis of depression is not clinically sound.

Myers (1988) also reported that the prediction of deliberate self-harm was linked with a number of factors – alcoholism, alcohol taken at the time of the attempt, and using violent means. Through standardised assessment tools he observed that, for female repeaters, past psychiatric history, repeated change of address, drug addiction, psychopathy, and absent fathers or mothers when the subjects were under age 10 were important, and that these factors could be used to differentiate between different grades of risk.

Bagley and Greer (1971) studied 204 patients over 1–2 years and reported that the presence of one or more of the variables (antisocial personality, organic brain disease, previous suicide attempt, widowed, separated or divorced, social class I–III) was likely to contribute to the possibility of repetition of the act.

Buglass and Horton (1974) found that sociopathy, alcohol abuse, previous psychiatric treatment whether inpatient or outpatient, previous attempt, and living alone were some of the significant factors in predicting the likelihood of repeating the attempt. Using the same scale, Garzotto, Siani, Tansella, and

Tansella (1976) in Verona found that four items were significantly associated with repetition in the Italian sample. These were previous attempts at self-harm, violence received, alcohol taken at the time of the act, and less than one year at the present address.

In a Belgian sample, Wilmotte, Charles, and Depauw (1983) reported that 8% of their sample had repeated suicide attempt within 7–17 months. They too found that alcohol, violence, and sociopathy contribute to the repetition of suicidal act. It is quite likely that some of the differences in these studies are linked with the sample selection, but the time periods during which they were carried out have changed as well. The gender differences remain important for the index act as well as repetition.

Very few studies have been carried out on repetition across other cultures. In one of the earliest studies in South India, Ponnudurai, Vivekananthan, Rajn, and Shivakumar (1991) undertook a follow-up of individuals. Of the total 86 subjects they were able to trace 51 subjects (59%), of whom one had died and 7 (41%) still harboured suicidal ideation. This is not dissimilar to the figure of 11.5% on follow-up reported from north India by Gupta and Singh (1981). Suicidal ideations were linked to alcohol abuse, family conflict and unemployment. Thus alcohol abuse becomes an important issue in the genesis and sustenance of the suicidal ideation. Similarly, family conflict where family is important will contribute to ongoing stress.

## METHODS

As mentioned earlier, methods used for attempted suicide depend upon the ease of availability of method. There are also quite clear cultural differences in the method chosen. The choice, combined with the impulsivity of the act, determines the potential outcome of the act. Methods can be culture specific or simply rely on ease of availability. In southern Trinidad, Hutchinson, Daisley, Simeon, Simmonds, Shetty, and Lynn (1999) have reported high levels of paraquat use. Nissen and Haggag (1998) reported on snow wandering in Arctic northern Norway. These authors hypothesise that the reasons for choosing to wander off into the snow as a method include black magic (highlighted by the term gaining) and depressed mood with delusions of guilt and suicidal thoughts so that the patient could freeze to death. In addition, possible dissociative states may play a role.

If the attempt is impulsive then whatever method is easily available will be chosen. Hawton et al. (1998) reported that farmers in England and Wales choose more dramatic means to commit suicide; they use firearms and hanging rather than ingestion of poisonous substances. Intent to die was expressed by only half the sample, they found in a study of psychological autopsy. Only 14% had given a history of previous suicide attempts. Those who committed suicide were also more likely to have lower levels of social support.

When jumping was used as a method, Kontaxakis, Markdis, Vaslamatzis, Ionnaides, and Stefanis (1988) reported that those using this method were more likely to be male, older, and to have serious somatic illness and a major psychiatric disorder. Thus correlation of a number of factors with male gender and more violent means can be seen.

Crome (1993) reported that the commonest drugs used in the UK for suicidal acts were older tricyclic antidepressants, which reflects their widespread use and higher levels of toxicity. In Kenya, organophosphorous compounds were reported to be the most common method in attempted suicide (Arap Mengech & Dhadphale, 1984) and only 8% used hanging as a means. These authors attribute this to the fact that most of their population was from the farming community and organophosphorous compounds were readily available for use as pesticides. Researchers in Hong Kong and Japan also found that the most common method of attempted suicide was ingestion of chemicals. Chiu (1989) reported from Hong Kong that between the 1954 data and the 1986 data the method used had changed and ingestion of hypnotics had gone up, as had use of domestic chemicals. Violent methods had reduced in frequency over the same period. Chiu suggests that reduced use of alcohol (compared with western methods) may well reflect the prevalent social norms.

## SELF-IMMOLATION

Although *sati* and *jauhar* have used self-immolation, this method is also used for political agitations. The act of self-immolation is more likely to be associated with completed suicide, although attempters may use this. However, very few studies have described self-immolation as a method in an attempt. Venkoba Rao et al. (1989) reported on 100 females who were admitted with burns to a general hospital in South India. Of these, 70% were reported to be suicidal, 25% reported the act to be an accident and 3% as homicidal, whereas in the rest no possible causation was reported. They included females aged 15 to 40 and admissions to the burns unit. Electric burns were excluded.

A psychological autopsy method was employed for the fatal cases. None of the subjects had left suicide notes. Again this may raise two possibilities: first, that committing something to paper may make them prone to legal action if they survived, or their family if they did not; second, there may be a likelihood that burning occurred due to poor amounts of dowry. It is also theoretically possible that due to illiteracy people may find it difficult to leave notes. Of all the cases, 47% were between age 20 and 29 and 30% were below 20, thus 77% were aged below 29. Three quarters were married. Thirteen subjects had been married for less than one year. Thirty-seven out of the sample had children. Seventy-eight subjects succumbed to their burns. Dying declarations (legal documentation) were available for 48 individuals and 31 declared their burns to be accidental. Out of these 31 accidents, 26 later told the researchers that their intent had been suicidal. Psychiatric disorders were diagnosed in 16 (22%) of subjects out of 70 who had declared that their burns were suicidal. The diagnoses included depression, paranoid schizophrenia, schizoaffective disorders or personality disorders. Another ten subjects reported physical illness, chronic abdominal pain, and menstrual problems. Of those who had interpersonal problems (36, i.e. 51%) alcohol, extra marital relationships, and adjustment problems with husband were common causes. Other family conflicts included problems with parents and in-laws and 8% acknowledged dowry-related problems. Eight out of the 70 (11%) had previously attempted suicide. Nearly a quarter (22%) reported a positive family history of psychiatric illness, suicide, and burns. This was seen in only 1 out of 25 accidental cases.

These authors conclude that marital problems were to the fore in more than half of cases and that alcohol too played an important role. They go on to argue that as Indian females are passive and submissive, and these traits are built into their psyche, consequently they find themselves unable adequately to deal with their negative feelings. They go on to suggest that if these females face family problems they feel helpless in the situation and one way out is by self-harm. The authors propose that specific psychological interventions which increase the self-esteem of young females may help to reduce the rates of self-harm.

Mahla, Bhargava, Dogra, and Shome (1992) studied the psychiatric status of attempted self-immolators in North India. Although they examined only four cases, these individuals had attempted self-immolation as a political protest. Three out of four were males and two were students, one was unemployed, and one was a mechanical worker. Three out of four had no manifest clinical problems on DSM-III-R diagnosis. The fourth individual had a dysthymic syndrome. Three were diagnosed as having a personality disorder on Axis II, one each of narcissistic, histrionic, and schizoid. Interestingly, all four had areas of major social dysfunctioning on Axis V. These authors conclude that a single sociopolitical event can cause individuals to come together to influence their actions. They suggest that three cases were of altruistic suicide and the fourth of anomie type. They observe that glorification of such acts may be a key reason for young people to be swayed to act out in this way. However, the interesting and unusual observation here is that three out of four had personality disorders, although only one had dysthymia. Thus a significant sociopolitical event can influence vulnerable individuals.

From newspaper reports, Bhugra (1991) reported that following a declaration by the incumbent Prime Minister of India to change the proportion of reserved jobs in favour of lower-caste applicants, students around the country started to protest. Following the self-immolation of a 20-year-old male student (who had forewarned his family that the students were going to stage a drama), several copy-cat immolations followed. In addition, students took overdoses, cut their throats, and ingested pesticides. During one week, 55 suicides and 23 suicide attempts were reported in the media, with ages ranging between 12 and 38 and men being predominant. In suicide notes left, the Prime Minister was blamed, as were other members of the government. This series could be seen as a reflection of the state of anomie instigated by political events, and the precipitant was not psychiatric but social. The first attempt was an outlet for suppressed frustration and anger where the individual chose to follow the most dramatic and public course of action to resolve his problems of identity by making a bid for glorious freedom (Kumar, 1990). Some of the subsequent suicides may have been purely for personal reasons, but the media coverage and political context may well have sanctified these acts.

## ORGANOPHOSPHOROUS COMPOUNDS

In all the studies cited so far in this chapter, the commonest method of self-harm is poisoning and organophosphorus compounds are most frequently used. These are employed extensively as pesticides and insecticides in domestic, agricultural, and industrial settings and are therefore easily and commonly available. In the Bangalore study discussed earlier there appeared to be an age-related pattern in the usage of organophosphorous compounds (see Table 8.2).

Females in different age groups were using different kinds of drugs, commonly psychiatric medications, sedatives, anxiolytics, and anti-epileptics. Males were more likely to use organophosphorous compounds. As noted earlier, Sato et al. (1993) also reported that in their sample in Japan agricultural chemicals were the commonest substance used and all these subjects were admitted to the hospital. These authors found that a peak occurred for

Table 8.2
Mode of poisoning (% rounded up)

| *Product* | *Male (n = 594)* *n (%)* | *Female (n = 465)* *n (%)* | *Total (n = 1059)* *n (%)* |
|---|---|---|---|
| Organophosphorus | 416 (70) | 237 (49) | 653 (62) |
| Drugs | 88 (15) | 146 (26) | 234 (10) |
| Seeds | 19 (3) | 25 (5) | 44 (4) |
| Kerosene | 14 (2) | 31 (7) | 45 (4) |
| Acid | 14 (2) | 31 (7) | 45 (4) |
| Not known | 34 (6) | 27 (6) | 61 (6) |

The percentage figure has been rounded up in some cases.

admissions in June and December each year. The mean overall age for males was 46.6 and for females 46.8 years. Unlike the Indian samples, they found that males in their fifties were the largest group. Not surprisingly, farming was the commonest occupation. The use of insecticides and pesticides indicates a major public health problem. Preventive strategies have to take into account all the ramifications of methods used by susceptible and vulnerable individuals.

## CONCLUSIONS

From this necessarily brief overview of the studies from Indian subcontinent, some common themes emerge. These include a preponderance of young males attempting suicide using organphosphorous compounds and the low rates of major psychiatric disorders and increased levels of social stressors, especially family conflict and marriage-related problems. Although there are serious problems with some of the studies, they suggest that social factors play an important role in the precipitation and perpetuation of suicidal ideation. Interestingly, where data are available from the Indian subcontinent it is likely that the rates of repetition are broadly similar across cultures, even if stressors are different. A common vulnerability is alcohol abuse, which may allow interventions to be focused on alcohol dependence and comorbid suicidal ideation. Violence and conflict related to alcohol abuse and other associated factors may play a significant role in the genesis of suicidal ideation and behaviour.

CHAPTER NINE

# Attempted suicide and the Indian diaspora

## INTRODUCTION

From the days of British colonialism, when the rulers encouraged people from the Indian subcontinent to move to islands and countries where the imperial power needed cheap labour, people have migrated. Some of the migration was due to the needs of the imperial power to run sugarcane plantations and factories, whereas others migrated voluntarily for economic, social, or educational betterment. To avoid persecution, large communities of people from the Indian subcontinent have settled in various parts of the world. These communities have put down roots and made their mark in more ways than one in Trinidad, Guyana, Mauritius, Fiji, the UK, and Canada. Serious overseas migration from the Indian subcontinent started in the nineteenth century.

European economic expansion from the fifteenth century onwards generated great interest among Europeans and non-Europeans alike. Europeans 'discovered' India, even though India had been exporting spices and other materials through the Middle East for centuries prior to this. Slavery and indentured labour were used to get cheap labour to carry out the dangerous and risky work. Coolie ships were engaged to carry indentured labour from India to the West Indies, Fiji, and other parts of the world. Trinidad received its first shipment of indentured Indians in 1845 and over the next two decades or so several more ships from Calcutta and Madras moored in Trinidad to deliver their loads. On arrival, migrants were noted to be in a depressed state and had dietary problems (Ramdin, 1994), but had not informed the ship's doctors of their ill health.

In his journal of one such voyage, Swinton (1859) observed that mortality was high. It was in the financial interest of the captain and the company that they deliver as many live coolies as possible because they were paid according to the number delivered alive to the new country. For example, one ship lost 86 out of 288 on board and as a result lost £1000. Although the captain had no voice in who was selected for travelling on his ship, their deaths caused financial difficulties for both captain and ship owners. Thus, historically, the memory of the experience of transition must mean that some migrants attempt to hang on to the culture they hail from much more rigidly and strongly than others. This cultural identity became crucial in settling down and making their mark. This chapter looks at rates of attempted suicide and possible causative and social characteristics among the Indian diaspora.

## TRINIDAD AND TOBAGO

Trinidad and Tobago are two islands in the Caribbean with an area of 1980 square miles containing two conflict-oriented ethnic subcultural groups – African–Trinidadians and Indo-Trinidadians. The rapid growth of the mining and sugarcane industries meant that the population rose accordingly. In Trinidad, Indo-Trinidadians are largely based in the agricultural midlands.

In one of the earliest studies from the islands Burke (1974) reported on clinical and social aspects of attempted suicide. He studied the case notes of all female patients admitted following self-poisoning and/or self-injury. Those patients who had two parents of East Indian origin formed the East Indian [sic] group: all others patients formed the African group. A total of 35 East Indian and 55 African cases were admitted – 17.8/100,000 and 15.5/100,000 were the rates for the two groups, respectively. One third of the patients could not be formally diagnosed.

The commonest psychiatric diagnosis was affective disorder: 54% in East Indians compared with 43% in Africans. Africans were five times more likely to have a diagnosis of personality disorder. Burke observed that psycho-neurotic disorders were more common among East Indians (three cases compared with only one African). Three quarters of Africans were aged below 24 compared with 43% of East Indians, whereas for over 25 the figures were 25% and 57%, respectively. Formal psychiatric diagnosis was linked with older age. As a means of attempt, East Indians were more likely to ingest chemical substances such as bleach, disinfectants, and insecticides than Africans, who were more likely to take tablets. An interpersonal dispute preceded the attempt equally frequently in both the groups. There remain several serious methodological problems in the study. First, the ascription of ethnic identity was not thorough enough. Second, the admission rates do not reflect the true incidence rates. The data are incomplete for causation and a number of other factors. The reflection that East Indian women are more likely to attempt suicide at an older age may reflect their changed circumstances and altered stresses.

Mahy (1993), in a review article, explained that attempted suicide in the 1960s appeared not to be a major problem in other English-speaking countries in the region (except Trinidad and Tobago). Mahy states that from his viewpoint, and after discussion with local psychiatrists, the cases of attempted suicide are few and far between in smaller islands. From this account it is usually a female in late adolescence or early adulthood who attempts suicide after having a dispute with the family or a loved one. Unlike Trinidad and Tobago, they would take tranquillisers and analgesics rather than household poisons.

Between 1963 and 1965 it was estimated that there were 184 annual attempted suicides in Trinidad, of which 48 were males and 126 were females. (Haynes, 1966). Five years later the figure had risen to 261, with 72 males and 189 females (Burke, 1974). From southern Trinidad, Mahy (1993) notes that 261 cases were reported to him from a catchment area of 300,000, with a higher representation of East Indians. The rates across different countries in the Caribbean are illustrated in Table 9.1.

Female:male ratios continue to be higher in the younger age groups. Since 1967–8, observations of high rates of attempted suicide among East Indians in Trinidad have been made. Similar observations in Guyana were attributed to exploitation, rejection, and shaming of young Indian females (McCandless, 1968). Maternal criticism and rejection were blamed for the impact on females (perhaps because Asian mothers are more lenient towards their sons). As the observation in Trinidad did not match this, Mahy (1993) argues that persons of East Indian descent broke away from their cultural habits much earlier in Trinidad than in Guyana. In both Guyana and Trinidad, once again pesticides, herbicides (organophosphorous compounds) are used for the attempt and completed suicide.

Hutchinson, Daisley, Simeon, Simmonds, Shetty, and Lynn (1999)

Table 9.1
Rates of attempted suicide/100,000
(from Mahy, 1993)

| *Country* | *Year* | *Rate* |
|---|---|---|
| Trinidad & Tobago | 1974 | 16.3 |
| Barbados | 1983 | 73 |
| Guyana | 1966 | 43 |
| Surinam | 1984 | 76 |
| Bermuda | 1983 | 98 |

reported that 81% of cases of suicide in one year had taken paraquat to kill themselves. Younger females aged 15–24 and older males aged 25–34 used paraquat. The commonest reason was family of origin dispute, followed by marital problems. Individuals of East Indian origin accounted for 89% of cases. In an earlier study again it had been reported by Hutchinson, Daisley, Simmonds, and Gordon (1991) that a vast majority of suicides were under the age of 35. In that study they reported that paraquat had been used in 75%. Paraquat thus becomes an agent of choice, suggesting an ease of access in agricultural families. The conflict between assimilation wished by the younger generation and relative social isolation in the older generation remains an important causative factor. In two case reports, Maharajh (1998) points out that religious and cultural factors appear to be contributing to suicidal behaviour and the change in normative beliefs may contribute to alienation. The girls committed suicide due to cultural conflict. Younger Indians, he argues, are caught in a borderline cultural state and under stress and duress ambivalent attitudes contribute to alienation and they then use the suicidal act for conflict resolution.

Parasram (1992) observed that absence of and/or denial of socialised power, prestige, and position to members of the Indian subculture are important contributory factors to suicide. Maharajh (1998) argues that in moving to a new environment the migrants had been 'denied rights to their beliefs' and first challenged and then devalued by British colonisers and subject to Christian indoctrination. These factors may have contributed to a further sense of not belonging. When the young wish to belong, their elders pull them up for doing so and try to control their behaviour.

## FIJI

Naidu (1980) observes that the Indian indentured labour system was introduced in Fiji by Sir Arthur Hamilton in 1879 in line with his native policy and his bid to establish Fiji as a viable economy. After occupation, the British annexed the island and the planters needed cheap labour, which came from Polynesia and then India. The first cargo of Indian immigrants reached Fiji in May 1879. Having abolished slavery in 1833, the British recruited Indians by fair means or foul (largely the latter) to supply cheap labour to Mauritius, British Guiana, Dutch Guiana, French Guiana, Trinidad and other Caribbean islands, Sri Lanka, Malaya, South Africa, and East Africa. The indenture system involved the movement of mainly Indian villagers to the plantations and processing plants in the sugar colonies.

Naidu (1980) illustrates five stages of the process: the upcountry sub-depots (for recruitment); the emigration depots (in the ports of embarkation); the passage overseas; the quarantine in the receiving colony; and finally the plantations or mills where the labourer was to spend five years serving his *girmit* (agreement). Upon completion of their contracts they were freed and could return to India by paying their own fares, or they could stay in Fiji and work on their own farms; or they could be re-indentured for another five years. After ten years working in Fiji they were entitled to a free passage to India. The regulations remained on paper only.

While talking about violence (to oneself or to others), Naidu (1980) illustrates that there was a tremendous amount of violence towards the labourers, not only physical and emotional abuse but economic abuse involving deduction of wages and imposition of fines. The same abuses must have been applicable to indentured labour across other colonies as well. Not surprisingly, the labour force would sometimes rebel and attack its leaders and overseers. Between 1885 and 1921, 206 male indentured labourers committed suicide, compared with 23 females, 65 free males, and 11 free females who did so. Sexual jealousies were common causes of suicide. Indentured labourers of South Indian origin were more likely to attempt and succeed in suicide than North Indians. Naidu (1980) attributes this to poor linguistic skills in Hindustani, which became the common language used on the plantations, thereby making communications more problematic for South Indians, resulting in them feeling more alienated and isolated. The extent of social adjustment required was greater, hence the stress was greater.

The migration and circumstances surrounding such migrations were additional factors, along with homesickness and nostalgia leading to feelings of alienation. Loss of 'ship brothers' to other plantations, ill treatment, alcohol usage, and societal circumstances may all have contributed to high rates of suicide. Similar situations must have existed in other sugar colonies and it is likely that similar stressors may well have produced similar responses of alienation, rejection, isolation, and abandonment. The use of force and power for capitalist purposes makes a mockery of individual aspirations and emotions, thereby making the option of suicide an attractive one.

Karim and Price (1973) reported that the rates of completed suicide among Indians in Fiji were 12 times that of native Fijians; among males these rates were 7 times but among females they were 33 times higher. The peak ages among females were 15 to 24 and 55 to 64, and all female suicides were due to hanging. Only 7 out of 90 had sought psychiatric treatment. The largest causation was due to personal, social, and economic problems. Quarrels within the family and failure at school were important factors. Rates in Fiji were reportedly higher than Australia, Denmark, England, Wales, Sweden, and the USA, but lower than Japan, Hungary, Austria, and Finland. The difference in rates among Indians and native Fijians are attributed by Karim and Price (1973) to rural residence, living in a more dependent culture with a sheltered, restricted, and isolated life, along with arranged marriages, family conflicts, etc.

Haynes (1987) described the suicidal rates in the rural Fijian province where 75% of the population was of Indian origin. In collecting the data, from police records, she found that only 3 out of 69 suicides were by non-Indians. Most of the suicides (83%) were of females under the age of 30. Although the numbers are too small for age-specific rates, there were a larger than expected number of Indian women aged 15 to 30 years. Haynes gave the rates of suicide for males aged 10 to 29 as 36.1/100,000, compared with 74.8/100,000 for females. Among the older groups, rates for males were 70.5/100,000 and for females 28.2/100,000. Thus younger females and older males were more likely to be at risk of suicide.

Haynes (1984) also reported that conflict within the family, especially between parents and children, and daughters-in-law and parents-in-law, appeared to be a major precipitating factor among female suicides. Childlessness was noted in some of the women which led to further taunting and conflict for failing to produce sons. Family conflicts also appeared as a possible cause in male suicides and some suicides were precipitated by shame, debt, and fear of disgrace and failure. Among older men, Haynes (1984) found that suicide was often precipitated by physical illness.

Between 1981 and 1985 a key change had occurred in the method of suicide and 177 cases were admitted with paraquat poisoning, of whom only 70 survived. Paraquat was introduced in Fiji only in 1972. Those who survived suicidal attempts may well have tried again but no data are available on repetition. Comparing Haynes's (1987) data with that of Ree (1971) and Karim and Price (1973), it would appear that changes in method and increase in numbers may have contributed to increased mortality.

Intention in cases of poisoning can only at best be surmised, whereas more violent means, such as hanging or shooting, leave little doubt as to the suicidal intent. Suicide and attempted suicide were arrestable offences at the time of Haynes's report. In a subsequent paper Haynes (1987) attempted to describe the historical aspects of society in Fiji. She quite rightly states that it is important to understand the reasons rather than relying on reducing the rates of suicide. Given the historical background of the arrival of the indentured labourers from India in 1879, high rates of suicide in Indian immigrants had been noted in the nineteenth century (Tinker, 1974). Rivalry, jealousy, nostalgia, and an intense desire to return to India were identified as key factors in the increased rates of suicide among Indian immigrants. High rates were reported at the first stage of recruitment (Andrews & Pearson, 1916). Many labourers did not really understand what the contract involved and were not prepared to travel abroad because crossing the seas meant that the individual had lost their caste and acts of repentance had to be carried out. Interviews with those who had experienced the indentured system showed that some were mainly seeking respite from problems in their village and looking for work in the city (Ali, 1979; Naidu, 1980) where they were either 'kidnapped' or lured to become indentured labour. On arrival at their destinations, more Indians committed suicide. Tinker (1974) explains that the gender role expectations also lead to stressors. Not only there were not enough women, but the owners used them for sexual exploitation. Male and female 'slaves' were not encouraged to live together.

As a last resort, the slave could commit suicide. Because he would not have other means of suicide, hanging and taking of poison through eating earth were common methods. With the emancipation of slaves a different set of problems emerged. In Mauritius, a significant proportion of the population was from South India. As Africa closed its doors, recruitment of indentured labour spread towards India. Tinker (1974) suggests that the actual functioning of the institution of slavery, indentured labour, and other forms of bondage which followed can be understood by reference to the plantation products and how this mode evolved. The production relied on using human beings as tools, with little or no concern for their psychological well-being. The indentured labour from North India was also influenced by overcrowding in agricultural districts as well as famines.

On the plantations, after a terrible voyage with little knowledge of the place of disembarkation, the labourers felt alienated. It was common for the emigrants to throw themselves overboard on the voyage. Depression during the first year or two of indenture caused many to decide to kill themselves. Suicide was also a feature of bad estates or periods in the different territories when conditions were equally stringent (Tinker, 1974). A large number of suicides in Mauritius were carried out by Indians gripped by nostalgia or an intense desire to return to India which they had no means of gratifying. Secret revengeful attacks on managers and owners may reflect the other side of suicidal thoughts and homicidal intent, as noted earlier.

Questions were asked in India about high rates of suicide in the Indian indentured labour force, but were met with silence from the British government. Poverty, inadequate housing and food, lack of female company, and separation from ship brothers leading to alienation are some of the factors that have been identified in relation to increased rates of suicide. Suicide figures were very high for Indians in Fiji when compared with rates in India itself. Haynes (1987) cites the work of Andrews and Pearson (1916) who gave the suicide rates for Madras presidency and United Provinces to be 4.6/100,000 and 5.4/100,000 compared with 64/100,000 for Natal and 78/100,000 in Fiji in 1903, going up to 83.1/100,000 in 1910. The high rates of suicide were attributed to all kinds of violence due to the indenture system. The altered male:female ratio of 3:1 was one possible cause, as well as loss of friends, illness, ill treatment, and hard work. All these factors contributed to suicidal ideation. Haynes (1987) suggests that it is likely that suicide and other forms of violence were under-reported or even unrecorded.

The workers feared reprisals if crimes such as suicide or attempted suicide were reported and had little faith in the prevalent system of justice. The stereotyping of the Indian labourer was almost always negative and the native people were also hostile.

Haynes (1987) suggests that rates of attempted suicide have been consistently high. In the early 1960s Indians constituted 90% of all suicides, whereas they comprise just over 50% of the population. In all these studies, high rates of suicide were found to be associated with Indian descent, Hindu faith, rural residence, young, females, joint family unit, an absence of diagnosed mental illness, and interpersonal conflict within the family. Hanging was the commonest method, followed by an increase in the use of paraquat (as noted above).

Among social responses, Haynes (1987) highlights the problems in social, legal, and healthcare policies. Increased rates of deaths due to paraquat have become more problematic and have increased the profile of suicide among the Indians in the public's mind. Media coverage that lists the names of all suicides and their underlying intentions have not deterred the potential suicide attempters. In addition to the influence of the media, Haynes (1987) argues that the effects of suicide on a small (integrated and close) community cannot be underestimated. She concludes that as Indians were accorded low status historically, their stereotyping and lack of assimilation may all have contributed to the increased rates. Furthermore, females within the Indian community are accorded lower status, as are the elderly, who may be seen as having lost their economic value, thereby contributing to a sense of rejection and alienation. In the past people attempted suicide by poisoning but survived and the availability of new toxins may have resulted in more fatalities. The question that needs to be addressed from a public health perspective is not how but why. Haynes (1987) argues for a multidisciplinary, culturally appropriate approach to develop preventive strategies.

## MALAYSIA

Teoh (1974) carried out a psychological post-mortem on 30 cases of completed suicide in Kuala Lumpur district. Analysing the data on completed suicide in 264 cases the author reported that the rates were 23.3/100,000 population for the Indian ethnic group compared with 1.1/100,000 in the Malay group. An earlier study by Hassan (1970) had demonstrated highest rates of suicide in the Chinese population, whereas Indian–Pakistani males had the second highest rates, and Malay females had the lowest rates. In the same study, Teoh (1974) analysed completed suicides from a district in Kuala Lumpur and showed that the Chinese had ten times the rates of Malays. Hanging was the commonest cause, followed by ingesting caustic soda, jumping, and taking insecticides. If all poisons were combined these caused one third of suicides of 30 cases that Teoh (1974) was able to study. Single, poor Chinese males constituted the largest group. There appeared to be two groups of suicidal behaviour and communication: those who spoke about the act and what they intended to do, and those who did not. The decision to kill oneself was taken a few days to few weeks prior to the actual act. After an intense struggle on an interpersonal and intrapersonal level, the subject suddenly developed a change of behaviour. The decision was often made after intense emotional turmoil and rejection by those around was often a key precipitating factor. The Indian community, Teoh argues, is less cohesive in Malaysia and this may well explain some variation in the rates.

The post-mortem study included 20 males and 10 females – 19 Chinese (11 males, 8 females), 10 Indians (9 males, 1 female), and only one Sikh. The Indians were younger than the Chinese. A vast majority 80% committed suicide at home. Teoh (1974) divides these into three categories: the young suicide; the physically ill suicide; the psychiatrically ill suicide. The young suicides ranged from 14 to 30 years old and had severe interpersonal relationship problems. Seven out of ten ingested caustic soda insecticide in the presence of a family member. The behavioural pattern was in the presence of others, during the daytime, and resembled introjected murder by placing maximum guilt on the bereaved. Four young girls killed themselves due to pressure for engagement and arranged marriage; thus using the suicidal act as a powerful way of communicating crisis. Six out of 30 (20%) had a past history of attempted suicide. All cases had communicated their desire to die and 37% of cues were directed at someone outside the family household. The decision to kill oneself was made after intense emotional turmoil. Tsoi (1974) observed that self-poisoning accounted for 94% of suicide attempts in Singapore and that the main cause for females was marital and domestic disharmony whereas for males it was poverty and mental illness.

Murugesan and Hock (1978) studied 96 attempts of deliberate self-harm in 94 individuals over a 10-month period. Indians were over-represented and females were three times more likely to attempt suicide than males. Nearly three quarters of the sample were aged 15 to 24 years. Ninety percent used self-poisoning, the commonest agent being insecticides. Other agents were tranquillisers, detergents, and weedkillers. Indians preferred using insecticides. The most frequent reason expressed was chronic domestic strife and conflicts over love affairs were common, especially with parents. Five Indian males were alcoholics. Indian females were more likely to deny suicidal intent. More than half (56%) decided on the day to commit the act. In 46% no psychiatric diagnosis was made and 15% had previously attempted suicide. Role conflict was a significant cause in the Indian group.

Maniam (1988), in an unusual study from the Highlands of Malaysia, reported interesting findings based on cultural and ethnic factors. He observed that in the district of Cameron Highland – a hill resort in Peninsular Malaysia that is virtually isolated from the rest of the country – 25%

population is of Indian descent. Collecting information from the register of suicides and parasuicides, he identified 100 suicides and 154 parasuicides over a ten-year period. Although due to the illegal nature of parasuicide (or suicidal attempt) this number may be an underestimate, he found that younger females (below the age of 30) had much higher rates of suicide – 68.4/100,000 compared with 13.4/100,000 for older females. Males under the age of 30 had a rate of 48/100,000 compared with 87.9/100,000 for males over the age of 30. The vast majority (86%) of all female suicides were under the age of 30. Although Indians formed 25% of the population, they constituted 81.1% of suicides and 78.4% of attempted suicide. Rates of attempted suicide were highest in the younger age group for both sexes.

Poisoning by weedkiller or insecticide was the most popular method for both suicides and parasuicides (89% of suicides, 66% of attempted suicides). Other substances used for attempted suicide included sleeping tablets, liniments, chlorox, and paracetamol. Age was not a factor for the choice of type of poison. In about 15% cases of suicide, paraquat was used. Three quarters of cases using paraquat were in the previous 5 years. Since emergency medical facilities and transport facilities to the nearest hospital were poor, a fatal outcome did not necessarily indicate an intent to die.

Although details of precipitating factors were recorded inadequately, interpersonal difficulties including marital quarrels and family conflicts figured prominently as factors, accounting for 64 of the 95 cases (67%) of attempted suicide. Mental illness was reported in only five cases of attempted suicide. Adherence to the caste system among Indians contributed to some problems with love relationships across caste barriers because of parental objections, which contributed to both attempted and completed suicide. The rates of suicide are much lower in Peninsular Malaysia – only 6.3/100,000, thus the rates among Indians of both attempted and completed suicide are extremely high. Local circumstances may explain some variation but not such a huge discrepancy. The peak for both suicide and attempted suicide appears in younger females. Maniam (1988) suggests that Hindu attitudes to suicide, which are ambivalent, may play a role in these high rates. Caste differences and pressures to have an arranged marriage are likely to produce a dichotomous thinking in the vulnerable, who may want to be assimilated and behave like the majority yet at the same time may be under extraordinary pressure to comply with rules and regulations of their own culture and community. Death is probably a better option than the shame and dishonour of elopement.

## UK

The migration to the UK from the Indian subcontinent and the Caribbean started in the late 1950s and reached its peak in the 1960s when a significant number of Asians were expelled from East Africa and came to settle in the UK. These large migrant groups from the Indian subcontinent and the Caribbean migrated broadly for the same reasons and at around the same time. However, the recruitment of the groups was different. The Caribbeans were encouraged to migrate to help the mother country and they also included women. For the Asians, however, men migrated first with a clear intention of returning to the country of origin. When the migration laws were about to be changed, they decided to bring their families over (see Rack, 1982). According to the methods of recruitment, Asian communities largely stayed together and decided to form strong community links, whereas African Caribbeans generally dispersed to different areas.

In one of the earliest studies looking at rates of attempted suicide among Asian immigrants to Birmingham, Burke (1976a) carried out an assessment of case notes. During a four-year period between 1 January 1969 and 31 December 1972, 4770 patients were admitted to inpatient units in Birmingham with iatrogenic, accidental, and self-induced poisoning, of whom 2695 had country of birth recorded. A random 10% sample from the rest was collected. Using place of birth as proxy for ethnicity, Burke (1976a) was able to identify 68 cases but then proceeded to exclude 16 cases of iatrogenic or accidental poisoning, studying the remaining 52. Of these 52 cases, 28 were female, 16 (57%) aged between 15–24, and 11 (39%) aged 25–44. Of the 24 males, 9 (37%) were aged 15–24 and 15 (63%) were aged 25–44 years of age.

Crude adjusted rates for young females (15–24) was 213/100,000 compared with 74 in males; for females aged 25–44 the rate was 96/100,000 compared with 70/100,000 for males of the same age. Few patients over the age of 44 reached the hospital. Most patients (64%) used psychotropic drugs and among 19 who used a domestic substance, 2 inhaled coal gas, 4 swallowed a household substance, 11 swallowed analgesic tablets, and 1 took other tablets. One female and seven males used alcohol at the same time. The commonest reason for both females and males was interpersonal dispute. Males (17%) acknowledged health problems as the cause of their attempt, but 28% females and 33% males were not able to give any reason. Formal psychiatric diagnosis was made in 17 cases (33%) of which 9 were female. Depression was diagnosed in 12 cases, schizophrenia in 2, personality disorder in 2, and psychoneuroses in one case.

Burke (1976a) remarks that the rate of attempted suicide among Asians is lower than expected. Bearing in mind the serious limitations of the study, which includes case-note data collection, place of birth as proxy for ethnicity (it is of course possible that some Asians may have been born in the UK, and some white Britishers born elsewhere, and the quality of case notes, these findings are of some interest. Inconsistency in data recording and the possibility that some overdoses may not have been admitted to the hospital make the findings difficult to interpret. The higher rates among younger Asian females are worth noting. Burke concludes that, after immigration, social stress may arise from altered interpersonal relationships. This stress on relationships may therefore lead to suicidal attempts.

Using the same data source, Burke (1976b) then looked at the rates of attempted suicide among West Indians in Birmingham and found that 60 cases (45 females, 15 males) had been admitted; he included 55 (41 females, 14 males) in the final data. He observes that again in this group that rates in females aged between 15 and 24 were five times that of the rates seen in the males. Two patients used coal gas and 53 took tablets (26 taking psychotropic medication and 25 using analgesics). Nine females were pregnant at the time and depression disorder was noted in 20 out of 22 cases in whom a psychiatric diagnosis has been made. Nearly three quarters reported a lovers' tiff to be a precipitating cause for the attempt. Bearing in mind the same serious methodological problems, it would appear that the rates of attempted suicide among West Indian migrants in this study were lower than those seen in British natives or black Americans, but higher than those in West Indian natives. Burke did not make a distinction and did not make it clear whether Indo-Trinidadians were included in this group.

Ten years later, in a prospective study where data were collected in a Birmingham hospital, Merrill and Owens (1986) provide a detailed and helpful picture of not only the rates but also the social and cultural factors contributing to these rates. The study was conducted over a three-year period from 1 January 1979 to 31 December 1981 on all patients presenting after deliberate self-poisoning. All patients (except 5% possible estimate) were admitted and if they were admitted more than once they were counted as one using the data from the first admission only.

Of the 975 white patients, those born in Northern Ireland or Eire were excluded. Asian patients included all originating from the Indian subcontinent plus those who had migrated from East Africa and constituted 196 in total. Detailed assessment was carried out by the researchers and marital problems and cultural conflict were identified using standardised questionnaire. The female:male ratio for Asians was 2.9:1 compared with 1.5:1 for the white group. Age distribution for both males and females in the Asian groups was much younger. Asian females reported more significant marital problems than their white counterparts. Rates of attempted suicide for Asian males were significantly lower than for UK-born males. However, there were no statistically significant differences between rates in Asian females and white females across different ages, although overall the Asian females were 1.5 times more likely than their white counterparts to attempt suicide. Asian females were more likely to reject arranged marriages and restrictive customs. Significantly lower numbers of Asian females aged below 35 were likely to be diagnosed as having a psychiatric diagnosis. As the authors acknowledge, the validity of some of the data, especially cultural and marital problems, is not strong enough. As all the assessors were white, it is difficult to know whether the information collected was good enough or robust enough.

The relative excess of marital problems in the Asian female group may reflect either a genuine problem or an ability to blame an external causative factor which is easily identifiable. Culture conflict was found in both male and females, but it is quite likely that gender roles may act as protective factors for the male, but expose the female to more vulnerability.

In comparing Asian, West Indian, Scottish, and Irish groups with English-born groups from the same data set, Merrill and Owens (1988) found that, bearing in mind the small numbers, the Scottish males between 25 and 34 and over 35 were significantly more likely to harm themselves. Asian males were significantly under-represented in the 25–34 and over 35 age groups, as well as overall. Although among the females aged 25–34 Irish females were significantly over-represented, over 35 Scottish females had significantly higher rates of attempted suicide. Merrill and Owens argue that the ease of migration may have led to higher distress because the less able are likely to migrate. This same principle could be applied to the Irish and Scottish. However, the robustness of migrant Asians and West Indians cannot explain all the changes. The authors argue that self-poisoning as a way of reacting to stress may be learnt from the host population and this may reflect on higher ability to learn as well as higher levels of stress. Interestingly, all four migrant groups had higher rates when compared with rates in their native countries.

Glover et al. (1989) reported their findings from an accident and emergency department in East London. All cases of self-poisoning aged 10–24 were identified. There were no differences in age groups 10–14 and 20–24. However, of the 156 women aged 15–19 who presented with self-poisoning, 25 (16%) were Asian compared with base population of 7% in this age range. Interestingly, these authors note that there were no reported suicides in the Asians aged 10–24 during the period under study.

## CONCLUSIONS

From an evaluation of data from different Indian diaspora around the world, it appears that young Asian females are at most risk of self-harm. Culture conflict, conflict with parents and the family, and social stresses appear to be important causative factors rather than psychiatric disorders. As Stock (2000) observes, race, gender, mass media, imitation, and opportunity to carry out attempted suicide, along with social construction of suicide rates and alcohol consumption, all contribute towards the rates of attempted suicide. Economic factors such as socioeconomic status and unemployment, and urbanisation and social integration at the social level, need to be considered when planning any studies to understand the causation and to put interventions into place.

CHAPTER TEN

# Rates of attempted suicide and social cultural factors in West London

## INTRODUCTION

In view of the literature reviewed a study was set up: first to establish rates of attempted suicide in the West London Borough of Ealing; second to ascertain if any social and cultural factors were responsible for the differential rates. In this chapter the key method of data collection and results are presented. There were three interlinked comparisons between the Asian attempters, the white attempters and community controls. The data from the two studies have been published elsewhere (Bhugra, Baldwin, Desai, & Jacob, 1999a; Bhugra et al., 1999b).

## METHOD

### Sample

As discussed in chapter 3, although there are problems in using the term 'deliberate self-harm', we have used it interchangeably with 'attempted suicide' because we were interested in studying suicidal behaviour. An act of suicide attempt was based on the patients' and health professionals' statements and information from the case notes. Acts which were called gestures, manipulative, or attention seeking were included. Heroin overdoses, alcohol abuse, and automobile accidents were not included.

Our definition of inclusion was based on Diekstra and Gulbinat (1993):

'suicidal gestures and manipulative attempts to serious but unsuccessful attempts to kill oneself – any act with nonfatal outcome that attempts to cause or actually causes self-harm or without intervention from others would have so or consists of ingesting a substance in excess of its generally recognised or prescribed therapeutic dose'. As Kreitman (1978) had previously recommended, habitual self-mutilation or alcohol abuse were not included in our consideration of parasuicide.

The patient sample was collected in the London Borough of Ealing, which has a large population of South Asian (Indian subcontinent) origin, and included all patients aged between 16 and 65 years who presented following deliberate self-harm to general medical, accident and emergency, or psychiatric services of local hospitals. We used a minimum six-month stay in the catchment area as one of the criteria for inclusion in the study. As previous investigations have suggested high rates of attempted suicide among Asian women, we decided to focus on this particular group. An equivalent number of white women (British or Irish) were also studied. The processes of acculturation into UK society were compared with those in an age-matched sample of South Asian women from a local GP surgery.

As far as possible, all patients were contacted whilst they were in hospital. With the cooperation of accident and emergency unit staff, every effort was made to interview patients prior to discharge. Those patients who had been discharged, or who discharged themselves, were contacted by letter, a subsequent letter being sent to arrange an interview at their home. If this letter did not elicit a response, direct contact at home was attempted on three separate occasions (at different times of the day and on different days), before giving up the attempt at contact. A similar method was employed in the control sample.

To determine the degree of 'leakage' of the sample (i.e. patient presentation to surrounding accident and emergency departments), all three hospitals in the surrounding geographical areas were monitored regularly to see whether people from the London Borough of Ealing catchment area had presented for treatment. These patients were not approached directly for interviews but information was collected from medical case notes, these then being traced through to ascertain whether the patients had any further contact with mental health services, in which case the psychiatric case notes were also obtained. Throughout the study, regular contact was maintained with local psychiatric services through visiting community mental health centres and psychiatric teams. In addition, three GPs practising in the area with the densest Asian population were selected randomly, and approached to ascertain the number of cases of attempted suicide they had seen. Lack of resources made it impossible to contact all the GPs in the catchment area to determine the overall incidence of suicidal behaviour. The rates of attempted suicide are based on the one-year period between 1 November 1994 and 31 October 1995.

## Ethnicity

Ethnicity for each patient was self-ascribed using the same approach as in OPCS population census categories. In cases where face-to-face contact had been refused, information on ethnicity was collected from medical case notes.

Where this information was not available (three cases) ethnicity was assumed by considering the patient's name, religion, place of birth, and first language, and in two cases (out of three) by parental origin. The data denominator for the population figures were collected from the OPCS data (OPCS, 1992). Although the problems in such an approach are recognised, this was the best option available at the time of the study because denominator identification was available only using this approach.

## Instruments

(a) Details of the act of self-harm itself were collected in a semi-structured descriptive interview (DACS) which focused on socio-demographic details, details of the present episode, precipitating factors, family situation, and previous medical and psychiatric histories. This descriptive questionnaire collects information in a semi-structured manner. It has 140 questions, which gain qualitative information especially to deal with the act.

(b) 28-item General Health Questionnaire, GHQ-28 (Goldberg, 1972): all women were given the GHQ-28 in Hindi or English, depending upon their choice of language. Both versions have been validated in Asian women (Gautam, Nijhawan, & Kamal, 1987; Jacob, Bhugra, & Mann, 1997). Clinical interviews included the Clinical Interview Schedule (Revised) (CIS-R) (Lewis, Pelosi, Araya, & Dunn, 1992) which has also been validated in these two languages (Jacob et al., 1997).

(c) Life Events Inventory (LEI) (Cochrane & Robertson, 1973): this questionnaire has been previously validated in the Asian group (Bhugra, Baldwin, & Desai, 1997b). This gathers information on significant life events the individual may well have experienced prior to the act. As we were also interested in measuring *racial* life events, we modified the inventory by adding extra questions to determine whether the life events were influenced by racial or cultural differences. The LEI itself is subgrouped into life events related to employment, education, finance, health, bereavement, change of residence, marital, familial, assault, legal, and other miscellaneous factors.

(d) Asian Cultural Identity Schedule: this schedule has been specifically designed to establish the cultural identity of Asian sample. The schedule is an interview with the individual and consists of 140

> questions, which cover domains of religion, marriage, language, entertainment, dietary habits, attitudes to the community, cultural, etc. (Bhugra, Desai, & Baldwin, 1999c). In addition, the validation and relationship with deliberate self-harm are discussed elsewhere (Bhugra, Bhui, Desai, Singh, & Baldwin, 1999d). The schedule is reprinted in Appendix I.

White women were interviewed using the DACS, GHQ-28, CIS-R and LEI. Asian women were interviewed using the DACS, GHQ-28, CIS-R and modified LEI. The control group of Asian women from the GP surgery were interviewed using the same instruments except for the details of attempted suicide, although enquiries were made into any history of self-harm.

## Inception rates

### *Sample*

A total of 434 patients presented following suicidal behaviour to medical, accident and emergency departments, or psychiatric services. Of the total, 45 (10%) had presented to one of the neighbouring three hospitals.

The group of South Asian patients included all those whose origins were within the Indian subcontinent (including India, Pakistan, Bangladesh, and Sri Lanka). Patients described as 'black' include those of African–Caribbean or African origin (born in the UK, Caribbean, or Africa), and were combined as one group. Those who had identified themselves as 'mixed race' were included in the 'other' category. Among the total group, 41% were Christian and 41% either gave no religion or stated they had no religion. Of the rest, 8% were Sikh and 8% Hindu or Muslim.

In the South Asian sample there was a relative preponderance of women (57%). In the white sample this figure was 50%. Women formed over 70% of the sample in the remaining ethnic groups. The majority of the total sample (77%) was single, separated, widowed, or divorced. Among the South Asian women, 44% were married, the rest being single, separated, or divorced. The mean age of the total sample was 31 years (SD 10.85 years). Rates of attempted suicide calculated from the base population are shown in Table 10.1.

There is a significant difference in the age distribution of self-harm among South Asian men and women above and below 30 years (see Table 10.1). The greatest differences are in the group aged 16–19 years, where rates in South Asian women are 17 times that in men. Fewer South Asian women over the age of 30 years attempted self-harm, and there were no women in their fifties, this finding being similar to other groups. White and South Asian men show a more equal distribution of rates.

Table 10.1
Rates of attempted suicide

| *Ethnic group* | *Population* | *Number of suicide attempts* | *Rate/10,000/year* | *95% Confidence intervals* |
|---|---|---|---|---|
| South Asian women | 17,322 | 65 | 37.7 | 29.02–47.1 |
| White women | 63,258 | 65 | 23.3 | 19.7–27.4 |
| Black women | 7089 | 17 | 23.9 | 13.9–38.7 |
| Other | 5641 | 17 | 30.1 | 17.6–48.2 |
| South Asian men | 17,196 | 25 | 13.0 | 8.9–20.8 |
| White men | 61,248 | 151 | 24.6 | 20.9–28.7 |
| Black men | 6191 | 7 | 11.3 | 4.6–23.2 |
| Other | 5741 | 5 | 8.7 | 2.8–20.3 |

The vast majority of episodes of attempted suicide (87.5%) were through the ingestion of a poisonous substance. Of those, 1.2% (5) involved the use of non-ingestible substances such as bleach, nail polish remover, or Tippex™. Self-laceration was reported in 8.5% (37 cases), and 2.5% (11 cases) used more than one method, usually a combination of self-laceration and poisoning. Six cases (1.4%) involved other methods, which included self-strangulation, jumping from heights, attempted drowning, and jumping in front of a moving vehicle. There were no significant differences in the methods used across sex or ethnic group (see Table 10.2).

There were 86 repeat episodes, made by 48 patients within the same year. The vast majority (80%) of the 'repeaters' were white. Most of the repeat attempts were by overdose. Of the 48 patients, there were 26 women (3 Asian, 22 white, 1 black) and 22 men (1 Asian, 17 white, 1 black, 3 'others'). Of the 86 repeat attempts, 73 (85%) were by self-poisoning, 8 (9%) by self-laceration, 3 by other methods, and 2 by more than one method.

The rates of attempted suicide among various ethnic groups were presented in the previous section. Asian women may be especially prone to experiencing cultural conflict, which includes dealing with changes in family

Table 10.2
Method of attempted suicide

| | *White women n (%)* | *Asian women; n (%)* |
|---|---|---|
| *Overdose* | 39 (85%) | 25 (86%) |
| *Self-laceration* | 2 (4%) | 1 (3%) |
| *Other* | 2 (4%) | 1 (3%) |
| *More than one* | 1 (2%) | 1 (3%) |
| *Non-ingestible* | 2 (4%) | 1 (3%) |
| *Total* | 46 | 29 |

expectations regarding social behaviour. This section describes possible links between cultural identity conflicts and attempted suicide: first by comparing South Asian suicide attempt patients with patients of similar origin attending a GP surgery; second by comparing the characteristics of South Asian and white patients who had recently attempted suicide.

## Comparison across groups

Previous studies of attempted suicide have suggested that cultural factors play a significant role. In order to measure elements of culture conflict two intergroup comparisons were carried out. In the first, 27 South Asian women who had presented to hospital services following attempted suicide were matched with a group of similar-age South Asian women attending the GP surgery for other reasons. When compared to GP attenders, those who had attempted suicide were more likely to have a history of previous suicidal behaviour, to have a psychiatric diagnosis, and to be unemployed. Their parents were more likely to have arrived in the UK at an older age. In addition, those who attempted suicide were more likely to have been in an inter-racial relationship and to have changed religions.

In the second intergroup comparison, the characteristics of South Asian and white suicide attempt patients were examined. White women were more likely to have mental illness, and were more likely to use alcohol as part of the method of attempted suicide. By contrast, Asian women were more likely to have suffered significant life events in the year prior to the attempt, took fewer tablets, and expressed greater regret at not succeeding in the attempt. Although numbers are small, social support appears to play an important role in protecting against the development of suicidal behaviour.

### *First control group*

The first control group consisted of 27 South Asian women attending GP surgery (called GP Asian group) on different days. On varying days of the week the researcher approached Asian females attending one GP surgery (with 98% of registered patients of Asian origin) and women in the age groups between 18 and 64 were asked to take part in the interview. The GP receptionist (well known to the patients in the local community) was instrumental in helping recruit patients. No controls refused to take part. The controls were age matched with attempters (within one year either side). As mentioned earlier, during an extensive interview they were asked about details of any previous suicide attempts, and assessed further through use of the GHQ-28 (Goldberg, 1972), CIS-R (Lewis et al., 1992), and a modified version of the LEI (Cochrane & Robertson, 1973).

In addition, they were interviewed using the Cultural Identity Schedule

(Bhugra et al., 1997d), which measures cultural identity in areas of religion, education, family decisions and behaviour, social expectations and behaviour, entertainment, links with relatives here and abroad, and dietary and shopping habits. Only those subjects who were able to complete the Cultural Identity Schedule are described in detail in this section.

### *Second control group*

As part of the second intergroup comparison, interviews were conducted with white women who had presented to the team with overdose or attempted self-harm within the same week. For case-control purposes, we had wanted to recruit two white women for every Asian woman who had attempted suicide, but were only able to obtain complete data on 46 white attempters. After recruiting one Asian attempter, two sequential white attempters were approached for recruitment. The refusal rates were acceptably low (8 individuals out of 54 refused or did not persist with the interview).

Complete data were collected on 46 white attempters. These will be presented here. The data were analysed using Mantel–Haenszel test and Fisher's exact text was employed if indicated. Where $\chi^2$ values have not been given, Fisher's exact 2-tailed test was carried out.

Refusers from both white and Asian groups were brutally frank in their reasons for refusing to take part in the study. Even with a female Asian interviewer fluent in three regional languages, reasons for refusal included distrust of the investigator and of the system and establishment in general. More specifically, either the attempters or key family members were keen not to be reminded of their act, which was often reported as sinful or shameful. As the family had come together to support the individual or couple, any outside 'interference' was resented. On comparing the refusers and completers, no differences emerged on religion or social class.

Three attempts at direct personal contact were made after two letters or telephone calls. On several occasions, husbands or parents refused access to the individual. Home visits were made (following a contact by letter) on at least three different days at different times of the day.

## RESULTS

### 1. Comparison of Asian attempters with Asian GP attenders

A total of 64 South Asian women attempted suicide and presented to medical services. Due to a range of problems and family concerns, only 30 women agreed to be interviewed, and 27 completed all sections of the interviews. There were no age or social class differences between those agreeing to the interview and those refusing it.

Of the refusers for whom information was available, 12 had presented with an attempt following a family argument and did not want to be reminded of this further. In three cases the reasons were not clear and four were said to be 'depressed'. Others had left the catchment area and were either abroad or could not be traced. Two women refused because the researcher was unable to offer financial incentives. Amongst those who were contacted repeatedly, most responded by saying that they wished to forget the incident and did not wish to be reminded of it by speaking

### *General Practice Sample*

The age range was 16–64 years, the mean age being 29 years (SD 13). Nearly half (44%) were married, there being no significant difference in marital status between the two groups. Nearly half (48%) of the GP sample were employed, compared to 26% in the suicide attempt group, this difference not being statistically significant. Table 10.3 gives details of the employment status of the two groups.

When social class was defined according to employment, more patients in the control group were from classes II and III, but again this difference was not statistically significant. Most of the GP sample were either in employment or studying, although no statistically significant differences emerged.

### *Accommodation*

In both Asian groups a majority were (76%) reported to be living in owned accommodation. None of the patients in the two samples lived on their own.

One third (32%) lived with their partners, and 39% lived in the parental household; 15% of the women lived in an extended family household. There

Table 10.3
Employment status and social class (unemployment vs the rest ($\chi^2$ 3.75, $p = .05$))

| *Social class/employment status* | *Self-harm patients (%)* *(n = 27)* | *Control (%)* *(n = 27)* |
|---|---|---|
| Employed | 7 (26%) | 10 (48%) |
| I | 0 | 0 |
| II | 1 (4) | 2 (7) |
| III | 1 (4) | 5 (18) |
| IV | 5 (19) | 2 (7) |
| V | 0 | 1 (4) |
| Students | 4 (15) | 8 (30) |
| Retired | 2 (7) | 2 (7) |
| Unemployed | 14 (52) | 7 (26) |

were no differences in either the type of accommodation or the household structures of the two groups.

### Psychiatric history

The two groups differed significantly with respect to psychiatric history. Only one patient (3%) from the GP group had a psychiatric history compared to 16 (59%) in the patient group ($\chi$-square 9.247, $p$ = .0023). Only one subject from the GP group gave a history of attempted suicide (compared to a history of previous deliberate self-harm in 44% of the attempter group). Of the attempters, 12 (44%) had a history of physical disorder in the past (compared with 2.7% of GP sample; $p = .0001$).

The mean GHQ-28 score for the suicide attempt group was 15.5 (9.9), compared to 6.4 (1.7) for the controls (independent samples $t$-test $t$ value = 3.31, df 36.80, 2-tail significance 0.002). The mean CIS-R score was 23.2 (10.8) for the patients and 7.2 (7.6) for controls ($t$ value 0.22, df 51, 2-tail significance 0.000). There was no relationship between GHQ or CIS-R scores and place of birth. Those who had attempted suicide were more likely to have a past psychiatric history (37%) and a history of previous self-harm (48%), whereas among the GP group only one patient had past psychiatric history and one past self-harm.

### Place of birth

A third of the attempters and 48% of the groups were born in the UK. In the attempters group, 52% were born in Asia and 15% in East Africa, compared to 44% and 7%, respectively, in the GP group. Of those born outside the UK, the majority were born in India. The average age of arrival in this country was 18.7 years (ranging from 6 months to 47 years), there being no significant differences between the two groups.

### Parental origin

Parental origins were checked in both groups; one patient did not know her parents' origin. More than three quarters of fathers came from India, 13% from East Africa, and 4% from Pakistan. More parents arrived at a younger age (below 30 years) in the control group than in the self-harm group.

### Cultural factors

Various factors in the Cultural Identity Schedule showed a significant difference. We shall present only these differences in detail:

(a) *Arranged marriage*. When asked to define 'arranged marriage', it was defined by virtually everyone as when parents, family, or someone in the community arranges a match. Of the GP group, 24 (88%) considered arranged marriage to be a good idea, compared to only 9 (30%) from the attempters – a further 18 (70%) in the latter group were either against the concept, or ambivalent about it ($\chi^2 = 17.207$ df = 1, $p = .00003$).

(b) *Age of marriage*. Both samples believed that women should be married in their early twenties, and men only a few years later in their mid-twenties. In the attempter sample, nearly half (43%) felt cohabitation to be acceptable compared with only 8 (30%) in the GP group, this difference just failing to reach significance. The vast majority did not believe in having children before marriage, for practical reasons, reporting fears that the man may leave or the family environment may not be stable for the upbringing of the children.

(c) *Inter-racial relationships*. Whereas six of the attempters (22%) group described a relationship (romantic/sexual) with a white person, none of the control group did (2-tailed test $p = .022$). However, among both groups, more subjects were agreeable to the idea of their children or siblings having such relationships. As one respondent in the attempter sample put it, 'I cannot even consider marrying a white man because it would hurt my parents deeply, but my children can do so because I will accept it.'

(d) *Religious affiliations and practice*. In the patient sample 12 (44%) were Sikh, 11 (41%) Hindus, and 3 (11%) Muslim; one women described herself as having no religion. In the GP group, the numbers were 16 (59%), 8 (29%), 2 (7%), and 1 (4%), respectively. Two patients from the self-harm group had changed their religions – one because of marrying into a different religion. A further two women in this group were thinking of changing religion, whereas no one from the GP group had done so; again, because of the small numbers, differences did not reach statistical significance.

(e) *Gender roles*. All but three respondents (88%) in the attempter sample believed that all tasks should be shared between a couple, but actually these were shared in only one quarter of respondents. The attempters were less likely to keep in contact with relatives abroad (only 20 did so), compared with all the GP attenders (2-tailed $p = .010$).

(f) *Life events*. There were no differences between the two groups in the number of life events experienced over the previous year. However, a significant higher number of miscellaneous events (loss of valuable object, family arguments, separation) were experienced by the self-harm group ($t$ value 2.92, df 41, 2-tail significance = 0.006). Amongst those born in the UK, legal events ($t$ value 2.17, df 41, 2-tail significance = 0.036) and events related to education ($t$ value 2.87, df 41, 2-tail significance = 0.006) were more likely to have occurred, and the number of events related to relationships with the opposite sex (non-marital) was significantly higher in those born in the UK ($t$ value 2.40, df 41, 2-tail significance = 0.021) (see Table 10.4).

Table 10.4
Racial life events

| | *Asian attempters (%)* | *Asian GP attenders (%)* |
|---|---|---|
| Racial | 5 (23) | 3 (19) |
| Cultural | 1 (4.5) | 1 (4.8) |
| None | 16 (72) | 16 (76) |

(g) *Problems.* The vast majority (80%) in both samples believed that people of Asian background faced difficulties in the UK, although there were no intergroup differences. The problems highlighted concerned housing, financial difficulties, language problems, and differences with children who are growing up here. Nearly three quarters of the total sample acknowledged that racism had played no role in the life events they had experienced. In the attempters, only 17% felt they had been affected by racism. Two subjects in the attempter sample believed that their experiences occurred because of the conflict in cultures they faced, such as differing expectations between their family and community and that of the dominant western society.

## 2. Comparison of Asian and white suicide attempters

Apart from religious differences and place of birth, the demographic characteristics of the two groups were broadly similar. Out of 27 Asians, 10 were born in the UK, 16 in the Indian subcontinent, and 1 in East Africa. Of the white sample, 37 were born in the UK, 5 in Ireland, and 4 in the rest of Europe. Among the white women, 16 (35%) were single, divorced, or separated, compared to 16 (55%) of Asian women.

### *Attempt*

When asked whether they regretted that the suicide attempt had not succeeded 17 (36%) of white women and 18 (62%) of Asian women expressed regret. Among the group of 47 white women, 29 had wanted to die (62%) compared to 86% of 29 Asians ($p < .010$). Approximately one quarter of both groups (white women 23.9%, Asian women 27.6%) had taken an overdose of paracetamol, and another quarter (23.9% and 13.8%, respectively) had taken a mixture of tablets. White women generally took more tablets than Asian women (mean 37.9 compared to 21.7, 2-tail significance $p = .016$).

Eight white women (17%) and 4 Asian women (13%) had written their wills whilst preparing for the attempt, and 10 white women (23%) and 9 Asian women (31%) had written a suicide note. Twenty-five (55%) of the white attempters (out of 46) who had been interviewed and 14 (52%) Asian attempters had a past history of attempted suicide.

When asked whether the respondent thought that the number of tablets taken would be fatal, 58% of the total sample believed so, there being no significant differences between the two groups. Asian women were more likely to live in owner-occupied accommodation (68%) than white women (38%) ($p = .00893$). All Asian women lived with someone. White women were more likely to have used alcohol in their attempt (33 out of 46: 72%), than Asian women (4 out of 29: 13%), (Pearson co-efficient 23.89346, $p < .00001$).

### *Psychiatric disorder*

Of white attempters, 24 (52%) were depressed, compared to 8 (27.6%) Asian attempters. Four white women four (9%) and 4 Asian women (14%) had an adjustment reaction. Nearly one fifth of the white women had a drug or alcohol problem compared to only one Asian woman (3%). Six white women (11%) and 14 Asian women (48%) had no psychiatric disorder.

Psychiatric disorder was significantly more common in white women ($p = .001$). At clinical interview (CIS-R), 17 out of 47 white women (36%) and 7 out of 29 Asian women (24%) had depression, another 6 (20%) and 14 (58%) having other psychiatric disorders. Twenty-four white women (51%) and eight (27%) Asian women had no psychiatric disorder ($p < .00029$).

### *Life events*

When the presence of life events prior to the attempt was compared across the two groups, significant differences emerged in two categories only. Asians were more likely to have had health-related life events (43%) than 17% whites ($\chi^2$ 11.089, $p = .0008$). Asian women were also more likely to have experienced life events related to the opposite sex (22% compared with 4% white attempters: 2-tail test = 0.036).

## INTERPRETATION OF FINDINGS

Two caveats need to be emphasised before we interpret our findings. First, for the Asian attempters the attrition rates are very high. Although the refusers gave a variety of reasons for refusing further contact or interview, there is a theoretical possibility that their circumstances or family ties may well be such that the degree of conflict and resulting chronic difficulties are high, thereby affecting the rates. They may not want an outsider to know this. It is possible that financial inducements might have made some difference.

As the basic demographic details between refusers and completers are not dissimilar, it is likely that some generalisations can be made. The data from the case notes were not always reliable enough to get details of life events, type of marriage (mixed or not), or previous psychiatric history. This remains a key weakness of the study. Second, the heterogeneity of the three groups – Asian attempters, Asian attenders and whites – must be borne in mind, when interpreting these comparisons, even though these have been used here as if they were homogeneous groups with similar experiences.

Two key problems in method must be addressed. First, although every effort was made to track all self-harmers, either through case notes and/or direct personal contact, these rates cannot and should not be seen as true incidence rates but contact with services thus as inception rates. Second, the problems of defining ethnicity and the heterogeneity of the groups must be remembered while interpreting these findings.

## Rates

The rates in South Asian women were 1.5 times higher than those in white women. When age is taken into account these differences become more prominent, especially in the group aged between 16 and 24 years. This supports the findings of Merrill and Owens (1986), who had suggested that younger Asian women were more prone to attempt suicide. In their later study (Merrill & Owens, 1988) they reported that older men and women were generally underrepresented in groups of patients who had attempted suicide, another finding similar to ours. However, although they demonstrated that younger women in Asian and West Indian groups had similar rates of attempted suicide, we have been unable to replicate this finding.

The rate of attempted suicide in those below 30 years belonging to the 'other' category of women (refugees and those from other cultures including people of Spanish, Polish, and other continental European origins) is broadly similar to that in the South Asian female category. These groups need to be studied in more detail in future studies.

Rates among black men and women over the age of 30 years are much lower than those reported in the US samples, where peak rates in black males occur between 25 and 30 and it has been suggested that blacks age quickly and lose hope (Sudak et al., 1984). It would be interesting to determine whether these differences represent a 'growing out' of distress, or whether this group begins to use some other methods of expressing distress.

Presentations by men following attempted suicide were less frequent, and men were also less likely to repeat acts of self-harm than women. Black men had the lowest rates – another finding seen in other studies (Mahy, 1993). Over the age of 34 years, there are no black men in our sample, the incidence being broadly similar to that in other men.

It would appear that in certain ethnic minority groups, attempted suicide is a gender-related phenomenon. Diekstra and Gulbinat (1993) had reported that female:male ratios varied between 1.4 and 4.0 across several countries. They argued that as criteria for reporting parasuicide vary considerably, there is evidently a clear relationship between method (not just medical seriousness) and probability of hospital referral of parasuicide cases. Thus it becomes difficult to obtain 'true' incidence of rates.

## Methods

The relative availability of means also plays an important role in the method of attempted suicide. In rural or agrarian societies, agricultural poisons are used more often. As drugs are easily available over the counter in India and Pakistan, this has been the commonest method in those countries.

There are no significant differences on the basis of gender or ethnicity, but ingestion of poisons is the commonest method. In countries where males are more likely to attempt suicide, other methods, like ingesting battery acid (Wilson & Wormald, 1995 from South Africa) and agrochemicals (Adityanjee, 1986 from India; Marecek, 1998 from Sri Lanka), or more violent methods may be used. There were no episodes of attempted self-immolation (which has been reported to be one of the commonest causes of suicide in this group), this being similar to findings reported by Burke (1976a) and Merrill and Owens (1986). These rates suggest that younger Asian women are vulnerable to increased rates of deliberate self-harm.

The group of repeaters is interesting. The commonest group is that of white women using poisoning as a means of repeating the attempt. Unfortunately, as we did not get details of the previous attempts and precipitating life events, this remains a weakness of the present study. We recommend that use of qualitative data is encouraged in future studies to understand the needs and patterns of usage in this vulnerable group.

## Previous history

More of the patients in the attempted suicide group had made a previous suicide attempt, and had previous medical or psychiatric illness. Despite the small numbers, this observation is striking and supports findings from the Indian subcontinent suggesting that repeat attempts are linked with various kinds of psychosocial distress (Venkoba Rao & Cheinnian, 1972).

Our findings are in marked contrast to previous work in Birmingham, which found that previous psychiatric history, psychiatric illness, personality disorder, or previous suicide attempts were less likely in a sample of suicide attempt patients (Merrill & Owens, 1986). In our control group, only one person had taken an overdose, probably because of conflict within the family (parental unwillingness to accept her choice of husband). The conflict with the family as a precipitant and life event in Asian females is a remarkable and important finding and deserves to be studied further. These repetitions suggest that continuing conflict within the family needs to be understood and managed within the gender and cultural boundaries so that repetitions can be reduced. Steele (1977) had argued that white attempters were more likely to modify behaviour or induce guilt in others, which may explain some of the reasoning for differential rates of repetition. However, as we did not set out to study repeaters it is difficult to make any general observation here.

Prior to writing, these findings were presented to Asian females in the community. Their overwhelming recommendations were that families needed to be educated, not the individuals. This may reflect the fact that, in the sociocentric context, the individual is seen as part of the kinship.

## Religious difference

Most attempters were involved in religious activity on a regular basis. Sikhs formed the largest religious group. This probably reflects the local population, although it has been argued that the ambivalent attitude of the Hindu religion towards suicide (where some kinds of suicide are acknowledged and others are not) may account for some of the increased rates of self-harm (Maniam, 1988).

Another interesting finding in our attempters sample was either a recent change in religion (two cases) or current thoughts of doing so (two further cases). This may stem from a need for acceptance in the new relationship, but would increase alienation from the family and previous support systems. It may also be an attempt also to increase social support in those under extreme psychological pressure.

## Arranged marriage

Although one fifth felt arranged marriage was not a beneficial institution, the attempter group appeared somewhat ambivalent and one third would like their relatives to have arranged marriage. These mixed feelings may reflect changing mores or indicate an uncertainty about an institution supported by the culture against which they might wish to rebel. The description of arranged marriage as outlined by our respondents is not a static one – an element of choice by the partners has become an important component. Furthermore, some of the women acknowledged that the couple should be allowed to get to know each other for some time before marriage. The reported differences between the two groups could reflect the greater turmoil that the self-harm group had experienced.

As Khan and Reza (1998) reported from Pakistan, arranged marriages have stresses of their own. Newly married couples (even in the UK) may share the house with the groom's family, having little or no space of their own. Under such conditions the cultural expectation is that the bride will make all the compromises, thereby contributing to the stress. In our interview we did not ask about the duration of marriage, which may well affect the social functioning.

Inability to have children or a comfortable sexual life in situations where privacy is at a premium are likely to make the individual feel even more alienated, especially if the family expects the newlyweds to have children as soon as possible. These systematic social, economic, and cultural pressures are more likely to affect the females than their male counterparts and deserve to be studied further.

## Inter-racial relationships

Although there were no statistically significant differences between the two Asian groups in their relationships (romantic or sexual) with white men, patients in the self-harm group had experienced more of such relationships. This may reflect personality traits of extraversion and curiosity, or the subjects may have generally experienced pressure on themselves and distress as a consequence. Because there were no educational or socioeconomic differences between the two groups, it seems possible that the reasons are more likely to be intrapersonal. Similar findings in the Indian diaspora in Trinidad have led to suggestions that inter-racial relationships, love affairs, and marriages play an important role in precipitating suicide attempts (Mahy, 1993).

In spite of the small numbers, social support or lack of support appear to play an important role in the development of psychosocial distress, which can lead to acts of self-harm. Changing religion may be a possible warning sign of future suicidal behaviour. In addition, a past medical or psychiatric history indicates an increased likelihood of repetition of self-harm.

## Asian and white attempters

Although numbers are small, comparison of the Asian group with the sample of white women produces some interesting differences. For example, in comparison to the Asians, white attempters were more likely to have used alcohol and Asian attempters had lower rates of alcohol dependence. Rates of alcohol dependence are low in Asian women (Cochrane, 1999). Although Sikhism as a religion is not entirely anti-alcohol, it does not encourage women to drink. As we did not include a measure of assessment of alcohol abuse we are unable to comment on the levels of problem drinking or alcohol dependence in the two groups.

The socio-demographic characteristics of the groups were broadly similar, although clinical characteristics varied significantly. Suicide intent and a regret that an attempt did not succeed was more common in the Asian sample. Asian women were more likely to regret that they had failed because they did not know how many tablets to take. White women took more tablets in overdose, and although there were no differences between the groups in preparing for the attempt (i.e. writing a will or suicide note) ingestion of fewer tablets was a feature within the Asian sample.

Unlike previous reports, both samples showed a significant proportion of major or minor psychiatric disorder. Asian attempters were also more likely to have had health-related life events, which suggests the possibility of arranging preventative strategies through early diagnosis, use of telephone helplines, and early and assertive psychiatric management (see chapter 13).

Unlike previous reports from the UK, but confirming some US observations, a significant proportion of our sample had previously attempted suicide. Longitudinal studies in this group of patients may give a clue to the contributing factors and suicidal intent. Two possible factors to emerge from interview of the respondents were a sense of a desperate need for something to be done and a simultaneous reluctance to give information about a private and deliberate act. Those who agreed to the interview process were more likely to be inpatients. Once they had been discharged from hospital, repeated contacts with a female Asian researcher who spoke their language and understood their culture were usually unsuccessful. We suggest that future researchers in this field give further thought to the method of recruiting subjects.

Perceptions of racial harassment and reporting of racial life events suggest that in the Asian group racial harassment, although present, was not a markedly significant factor. Significant life events in Asian attempters were to do with relationship difficulties, suggesting that pressures because of family and relationships and resulting conflict are important precipitants in deliberate self-harm in this group.

We believe that even though we have used the term ‘white’ and ‘Asian’, these terms are sometimes ambiguous. Within the ‘white’ category we have included British, Irish, and continental Europeans for the sake of simplicity, but the uniqueness of these cultures has to be understood when assessing the impact of culture on acts of deliberate self-harm.

## CONCLUSIONS

It is evident that rates of attempted suicide are much higher in Asian females than in Asian males and white women. Some of the possible reasons for these elevated rates include social and cultural stresses. Interestingly, racial pressures and harassment were not increased in the two Asian groups but inter-racial relationships and a level of less traditional views were common in the Asian attempters. More attention must be paid to better recruitment and future research must be multicentred and include numbers of Asians belonging to different religions to ascertain the role of religion.

CHAPTER ELEVEN

# Rates of attempted suicide in adolescents in West London

## INTRODUCTION

The rates of self-harm in adolescents have increased in recent years to such a degree that it has been called an epidemic (Hawton, 1986). There is clinical evidence to suggest that children and adolescents who have attempted suicide are more likely to have a family history of alcoholism and more overt or aggressive behaviour (Cohen-Sandler, Berman, & King, 1982). Previous work suggests that problems within the family, especially with parents or boyfriend/girlfriend, and problems at school are important precipitating factors in the attempt among adolescents (Hawton, O'Grady, Osborn, & Cole, 1982b). Anger and feelings of loneliness and of being unwanted are commonly reported. It has been suggested that attempted suicide is an attempt to alleviate or demonstrate this distress (Hawton, Cole, O'Grady, & Osborn, 1982a).

Many attempts are linked with underlying family difficulties and previous contact with social services or health-care agencies have been reported to be common (Clarke, 1988). Parents are often reported to be cold, uncommunicative, and unable to tolerate change or crisis, and are commonly perceived by their children as being hostile or indifferent (Garfinkel, Froese, & Hood, 1982; Taylor & Stansfeld, 1984). Hawton et al. (1982b) reported that four fifths of adolescents who had attempted suicide reported an inability to discuss their problems with their father and nearly half had this problem with their mother.

The data available for attempted suicide among ethnic minority adolescents is limited. Biswas (1990), in a retrospective study, reported that Asian females were more likely to describe their attempt as accidental and lesser numbers in this group were in social care. McGibben, Ballard, Handy, Mohan, and Silveira (1992) reported that mean annual rates of hospital admissions were broadly similar between Asian and Caucasian adolescents, with an excess of girls in both groups. In an earlier study from the same city (Coventry), Handy et al. (1991) identified intergenerational, cultural conflicts as major precipitating factors.

Kingsbury (1994), in a study of 50 adolescents, of whom 13 were Asian and the rest white, reported that Asians were more socially isolated and, despite having low levels of suicide intent, were reporting higher rates of depression, hopelessness, long premeditation time, and previous overdosage. He argued that suicidal intent should not be a key assessment feature. Lockhart (1998) reported from Scotland that 93% of cases had presented having taken an overdose in the first audit cycle and 87% in the second audit sample and as expected females were more likely to attempt self-harm. Nasr, Vostanis, and Winkley (1997) found that in their sample in Birmingham all attempts at self-harm were due to drug overdose and 5% were repeaters within a 6-month follow-up period. However, they do not make any distinction in their ethnic groups. Goddard, Subotsky, and Fombonne (1996) showed that the rates of referral among black adolescents for deliberate self-harm were in proportion to the community composition. The socio-demographic variables across black and white adolescents were similar, except that social stress was reported in the black group.

In this study we have used the terms 'deliberate self-harm' and 'attempted suicide' interchangeably. The terms denote any act that could be construed as an attempt to harm oneself. We set out to study the socio-demographic characteristics of all adolescents who had presented to the child and adolescent assessment service and to determine whether there were any clear ethnic differences. As several studies (Lewinshon et al., 1994; Morrissey et al., 1995) have suggested, some risk factors like previous history, conduct disorder, and substance misuse are linked with self-harm, it was decided to study these.

## CASE-NOTE STUDY

### Method

All cases of deliberate self-harm presenting to the child and adolescent team for assessment were identified over a 3-year period. Their notes were studied and information obtained on basic socio-demographic details, including ethnicity. The details of the act of deliberate self-harm and any precipitating factors identified by the clinicians assessing the circumstances surrounding the actual event were clarified as far as possible from the case notes.

The ethnicity of individuals was either self-ascribed or as described by their parents. Only two groups of whites and Asians were included in the study. Asians here include those whose parents were born or came from the Indian subcontinent; thus South Asians are being termed Asians.

A standardised proforma was used to obtain details of precipitating factors, which were divided into broad areas of arguments with family, relationship difficulties, problems at school, unfavourable home environment, and problems like avoiding court cases. In addition, details on parental relationship and past history of physical and/or sexual abuse were collected. Predisposing factors were identified, especially in relationships with peers as well as family.

## Results

Ninety-nine cases of attempted suicide were identified and their case notes studied. Of these, 76 (77%) were white and 23 (23%) Asian. Of the 76 white, 13 (17%) were male and the rest female (a ratio of 1:4.8). Among the Asian groups 2 (0.8%) were male and the rest female (a ratio of 1:10.5). The age distribution across the two groups is shown in Table 11.1. The local services deal with adolescents only up to the age of 16. The data are presented according to ethnicity not gender.

The nature of self-harm was impulsive in 35 (46%) whites and planned in 10 (13%), whereas in the rest it was not clear. Among the Asians it was impulsive in 8 (35%), planned in 4 cases (1.7%), and no information was available for the rest. Of the 76 whites, 23 (30%) gave a previous history of deliberate self-harm, as did 6 Asians (26%). Only 2 whites had prepared a suicide note. Fourteen whites (18%) and 2 Asians (8%) acknowledged that their attempt was directed at someone. Sixteen whites (21%), compared with 6 Asians (26%), wanted to die, whereas 8 whites (10%) and 6 Asians (26%) did not want to die and this information was not available for the rest. Sixteen whites (21%) and 5 Asians (22%) had subsequently made deliberate efforts

Table 11.1
Age distribution in the two groups (%)

| | *White* $n = 76$ | *Asian* $n = 23$ |
|---|---|---|
| <10 years | 2 (2.6%) | 0 |
| 11–13 years | 19 (25%) | 7 (30%) |
| 14–15 years | 52 (68%) | 13 (56%) |
| >15 years | 3 (4%) | 3 (13%) |

to avoid detection. Twenty-one whites (27%) and 5 Asians (22%) regretted having made the attempt. Eighteen whites (23%) were in social services care and another 2 were adopted, whereas 5 Asians (22%) were in social services care.

The commonest method was taking an overdose in 67 (88%) in the white group, 5 cases (6%) used cutting, 3 (4%) used hanging or strangling, and one individual drank bleach. Among all cases that took an overdose the commonest drug used was paracetamol either alone (22 whites and 6 Asians) or in a combination (13 and 3 cases, respectively). Other tablets or combinations were used in the rest who took overdoses.

The precipitating factors as outlined by the individuals or their informants are illustrated in Table 11.2. These are the factors that led to the attempt and need to be differentiated from ongoing stresses.

Eleven whites (14%) and 5 Asians (22%) acknowledged bullying problems at school. Among the white group, in 38 cases parents were separated compared with 1 Asian. Only 12 white parents were married and 14 were cohabiting after separation. Eight whites (10%) and 3 Asians (13%) reported physical abuse, and 14 whites (18%) and 7 Asians (30%) reported sexual abuse. In 18 cases (14 whites 18%, 4 Asians 2%), conduct or behavioural problems were reported. Six respondents (3 in each group) admitted to using illicit substances.

Predisposing factors are illustrated in Table 11.3. These are the factors that have generally been ongoing. They suggest that an unfavorable home environment was an important factor. However, not all cases identified predisposing factors, hence the numbers do not match up.

Table 11.2
Precipitating factors (total exceeds number of multiple problems)

| | *White* $n = 76$ | *Asian* $n = 23$ |
|---|---|---|
| *Arguments:* | | |
| Family | 25 (32%) | 7(30%) |
| Friends | 2 (3%) | 1 (4%) |
| Others | 1 (1.3%) | 0 |
| *Relationship problems:* | | |
| With parents | 4 (5%) | 0 |
| With peers | 2 (3%) | 0 |
| With girlfriend/boyfriend | 8 (10%) | 0 |
| *Unfavourable home environment:* | 8 (10%) | 1 (4%) |
| Culture conflict | 0 | 4(17%) |
| School problems | 40 (53%) | 7(30%) |
| Avoiding court | 3 (4%) | 0 |

Table 11.3
Predisposing factors

| | *White* *n* = 76 | *Asian* *n* = 23 |
|---|---|---|
| *Relationships:* | | |
| Parents | 15 (20%) | 1 (4%) |
| Sibling | 5 (6%) | 0 |
| Others | 1 (1.3%) | 1 (4%) |
| *Unfavourable home environment:* | | |
| Parent's problems | 5 (6%) | 0 |
| Violence | 4 (5%) | 1 (4%) |
| Parental mental illness | 5 (6%) | 0 |
| Physical abuse | 6 (8%) | 1 (4%) |
| Sexual abuse | 6 (8%) | 6 (23%) |
| Alcohol in parents | 6 (8%) | 2 (8%) |
| Culture conflict | 2 (2.5%) | 10 (43%) |
| *School:* | | |
| General problems | 6 (8%) | 8 (35%) |
| Bullying | 1 (1.3%) | 3 (13%) |

## Discussion

Several caveats need to be borne in mind when interpreting the results of this study. First, it is a retrospective case-note study and, like all case studies, there are limitations in the quantity and quality of the data available. Second, the numbers are still small, especially in the Asian group, hence generalisations are fraught with difficulties. Third, the heterogeneity of the two groups must be borne in mind when interpreting the data.

Age distribution of the sample confirms findings by other authors. The marked increase at the age of 14 highlights the impact of puberty itself. It is also likely that this is the age where individuation starts to develop and stresses at home and inhibitions start to play an important role. This needs to be studied in prospective studies.

### *Nature of attempt*

The commonest method reported in the total sample was that of taking an overdose – only a small number attempted cutting. The observation that a vast majority of the sample across the two groups took paracetamol, either alone or in combination, confirms findings reported by Lockhart (1998) as well as Nasr et al. (1997). It make sense that individuals will use the means which are easily available, especially if the act is impulsive, so analgesics become a prime candidates for use in drug overdoses. Any preventive strategies must therefore include reducing the access and also adding compounds like methionine to paracetamol to reduce its toxicity.

### *Unfavorable family environment*

The gender differences are not surprising but the high number of reported parental separations, especially in the white groups, emerged as a surprising finding. In some cases, abuse of alcohol by one of the parents or by one of the siblings was an important factor. Repeated physical or sexual abuse at home, combined with difficulties at school and poor peer relationships, appear to be contributing to the pressures these subjects are under, and taking an overdose gives them 'time out', albeit only for a while. Two subjects mentioned racial harassment. In one case, it was an Asian female who did not want to tell her parents about it, as she wanted 'to protect them'. Another subject felt that her mother was being abused by the higher classes by virtue of her position as a domestic helper, and felt that the whole of her community was being exploited.

Two possible explanations can be offered for the sex differences in rates in Asians, which is more marked than the whites. First, the gender role expectations of the family and the community are quite different when comparing Asian boys with Asian girls. Girls may be seen as a burden on the family, and the family's views on their behaviour are likely to be stricter. They are expected to behave more traditionally and share the responsibility of housework, yet at school they are expected to be like their peers. This conflict, combined with abuse, poor interpersonal relationships, and family conflict, may create for them an intolerable situation with overdose being one means of escape.

Second, if they are spending time at home while avoiding school, they are more likely to become aware of any parental marital conflict. However, as it is difficult to measure the cultural and marital conflict in retrospective data, prospective studies are planned to address these issues.

### *Problems at school*

Of the two key areas in which a teenager is expected to function, it is not surprising that problems at school affect both precipitation and predisposition to attempt deliberate self-harm. More than half of whites and one third of Asians reported problems at school as precipitating factors and 9% whites and 48% Asians as predisposing factors. Either way, problems at school (which include academic problems, bullying, peer problems, etc.) can contribute to a sense of hopelessness and helplessness which needs to be studied in prospective studies. These, combined with problems at home, mean that vulnerable adolescents may not have any other prospective escape bar taking an overdose and 'time out'. As Nasr et al. (1997) found, family arguments and school-related stressors accounted for 64% of cases and the findings of the present study tend to confirm this. McGibben et al. (1992) had observed that there were significantly more hospital admissions during school terms than holidays, suggesting that school can act as a stressor.

These findings in relation to ethnicity suggest that, like those reported by Goddard et al. (1996), ethnicity per se is not a key factor in the rates of deliberate self-harm in adolescents, and neither is suicidal intent (Kingsbury, 1994). The incidence rates are impossible to calculate from the case-note data.

The general feeling from the cases is one of despair with themselves, with their families, and feeling abandoned by their families and their schools. Descriptive studies are needed to identify various explanations, causes of overdose, and the act itself in order to put preventive strategies in place. It would appear from our study that schools, parents, and health professionals need to work very closely together to determine the causes. Factors which affect repetitions of overdose, once identified, can be used to reduce attempts, and the youth can take other less life-threatening options to express their distress rather than this potentially fatal one. The differences according to ethnicity are not marked, but the family stresses, physical and sexual abuse, and problems at school must be highlighted in order to plan appropriate interventions.

## STUDY OF RATES OF ATTEMPTED SUICIDE BY ADOLESCENTS

The findings from the study of rates of attempted suicide in adolescents and possible causative factors are described below.

### Method

The sample from which the data are reported was collected over one calendar year (1997–8) in the London Borough of Ealing.

### Sample

1. All adolescents presenting to the accident and emergency centre with overdose and deliberate self-harm were seen by a paediatrician and then referred to a child psychiatry service. Over a 1-year period all cases were identified.
2. All cases were contacted. Those cases who refused to take part in the study were included as parent/child case-note data. Cases who agreed to take part were interviewed.

### Controls

Controls consisted of any adolescent matched for age, sex, and ethnicity who presented to the accident and emergency centre for reasons other than deliberate self-harm within 1 week of the case presenting for deliberate self-harm.

## Measurements

1. Semi-structured interview concerning details surrounding the attempt (DACS-A).
2. Cultural Identity Schedule (details elsewhere in this volume).
3. Life Events Inventory (Robertson & Cochrane, 1993), including racial life events).

Some of the findings have been reported (Bhugra, Thompson, Singh, & Fellow-Smith, 2003).

## Results

Total sample size was 76. Of these, 29 were from identified case notes. For the purpose of the analyses, case-note data were combined with non-case-note data. All analyses were carried out between white and Asian adolescents. A breakdown of the sample is given in Table 11.4. Variables from the DACS-A were categorised into the following domains: social problems (Table 11.5), home life problems (Table 11.6), school problems (Table 11.7), emotional problems, precipitating factors, and characteristics of the deliberate self-harm.

Table 11.4
Sample inception rates by age group for the Borough of Ealing

| *Age (years)* | *White male* | | | *White female* | | | *Asian male* | | | *Asian female* | | |
|---|---|---|---|---|---|---|---|---|---|---|---|---|
| | *n* | *BP* | *R (CI 95%)* | *n* | *BP* | *R (CI 95%)* | *n* | *BP* | *R (CI 95%)* | *n* | *BP* | *R (CI 95%)* |
| 10–14 | 3 | 4084 | 7.3 (0.01–0.21) | 20 | 3859 | 51 (0.03–0.79) | 3 | 2187 | 9 (0.02–0.2) | 6 | 2737 | 21 (0.08–0.04) |
| 15 | 5 | 796 | 62 (0.02–0.14) | 7 | 1579 | 44 (0.07–2.8) | 0 | | | 6 | 472 | 127 (0.460–2.7) |
| 16–17 | 0 | | | 3 | 3015 | 9 (0.02–0.29) | 0 | | | 0 | | |

Key: *n*, number; *BP*, base population; *R*, rates; *Cl*, confidence intervals.

### *Social problems*

Prevalence of adjustment problems was highest in females: 15 white females (39.4%) and 7 Asian females (58.3%) reported adjustment problems, compared to only 1 white male and 1 Asian male. The same was true for alcohol use. No males reported using alcohol whereas 11 of their female counterparts reported using alcohol, 8 white females (21.05%) and 3 Asian females (25%). Ten white females (26%) were involved in a court case, compared to 1 white male (12.5%) and 2 Asian females (16.6%). This is partly reflected in criminal activity. No Asians were involved in criminal activity

Table 11.5
Social problem variables

| *Variable* | *White female n = 38 (%)* | *White male n = 8 (%)* | *Asian female n = 12 (%)* | *Asian male n = 3 (%)* |
|---|---|---|---|---|
| Adjustment problems | 15 (39.4) | 1 (12.5) | 7 (58.3) | 1 (33.3) |
| Alcohol use | 8 (21.05) | 0 | 3 (25.0) | 0 |
| Court case | 10 (26.31) | 1 (12. 5) | 2 (16.6) | 0 |
| Criminal activity | 5 (13.15) | 1 (12.5) | 0 | 0 |
| Drug use | 9 (23.68) | 2 (25.0) | 3 (25.0) | 2 (66.6) |
| Bad friends | 4 (10.52) | 2 (25.0) | 2 (16.6) | 2 (66.6) |
| Harassed | 5 (13.15) | 1 (12.5) | 0 | 0 |
| Peer problems | 18 (47.36) | 3 (37.5) | 5 (41.66) | 3 (100) |
| Relationship problems | 23 (60.5) | 6 (75.0) | 9 (75.0) | 3 (100) |
| Sexually active | 3 (7.89) | 0 | 1 (8.3) | 0 |
| Violent outburst | 11 (28.94) | 2 (25.0) | 1 (12.5) | 1 (33.3) |

whilst 5 white females (13.5%) and 1 white male (12.5%) were. Prevalence of drug use was fairly similar between groups. No Asian adolescents reported being harassed, whilst 5 white females (13%) and 1 white male (12.5%) did. Peer problems were common in both white and Asian adolescents, 18 white females (47%), 3 white males (37.5%), 5 Asian females (42%), and 3 Asian males (100%). Relationship problems were also common in all groups. Only females reported being sexually active: 3 white females (8%) and 1 Asian female (8.3%). All four females were aged 15.

### *Home life problems*

Absconding from home was reported by 21% of females, compared to 2% of males. By ethnicity, this is accounted for by 9 white females (24%) and 4 Asian females (33%). Behaviour problems were reported in 30% of adolescents. Communication problems were reported by 52% of the sample. The distribution by ethnicity and sex can be seen in Table 11.6.

Both Asian males and females reported being compared to other children more than their white counterparts, whilst conduct problems were highest in white males (25%) and Asian females (25%). As expected, cultural conflict was highest in Asian adolescents, being reported by 7 (58%) of Asian females and 1 (33%) of Asian males. In all these cases, parental country of birth was India. Parental history of suicide and physical harm was present in 13% of cases, parental history of suicide was highest for Asian females (3 = 25%).

Intergenerational clashes were more common in Asian adolescents (59% females, 67% males) than white adolescents (32% females, 25% males). Six white females (11%) reported being sexually abused.

School problems were reported in 45% of cases, although these seemed to be marginally higher in Asian adolescents. The prevalence of bullying was similar

Table 11.6
Home life problems

| *Variable* | *White female n = 38 (%)* | *White male n = 8 (%)* | *Asian female n = 12 (%)* | *Asian male n = 3 (%)* |
|---|---|---|---|---|
| Absconds | 9 (23.68) | 1 (12.5) | 4 (33.3) | 0 |
| Behaviour problems | 10 (26.3) | 2 (25.0) | 4 (33.3) | 2 (66.6) |
| Communication problems | 18 (47.3) | 4 (50.0) | 8 (66.6) | 2 (66.6) |
| Compared to other children | 2 (5.2) | 0 | 4 (33.3) | 1 (33.3) |
| Conduct problems | 5 (13.15) | 2 (25.0) | 3 (25.0) | 0 |
| Cultural conflict | 1 (2.6) | 0 | 7 (58.0) | 1 (33.3) |
| Finance problems | 6 (15.7) | 2 (25.0) | 5 (41.6) | 2 (66.6) |
| Parental history of suicide | 4 (10.52) | 1 (12.5) | 3 (25.0) | 0 |
| Parental history of physical illness | 4 (10.52) | 2 (25.0) | 1 (8.3) | 1 (33.3) |
| Intergene rational clashes | 12 (31.5) | 2 (25.0) | 7 (58.8) | 2 (66.6) |
| High parental expectations | 4 (10.52) | 1 (1.6) | 2 (3.27) | 1 (33.3) |
| Sexual abuse | 6 (15.78) | 0 | 0 | 0 |

for all groups, which might suggest bullying occurred for reasons other than ethnicity in the present sample. The highest levels of truancy were reported in Asian males (2 = 66%) and Asian females (3 = 25%) (see Table 11.7).

Table 11.7
School problems

| *Variable* | *White female n = 38 (%)* | *White male n = 8 (%)* | *Asian female n = 12 (%)* | *Asian male n = 3 (%)* |
|---|---|---|---|---|
| Academic problems | 19 (50) | 3 (37.5) | 4 (66.6)* | 2 (66.6) |
| Bullied | 12 (31.5) | 2 (25.0) | 1 (12.5)* | 1 (33.3) |
| Likes school | 6 (15.7) | 1 (12.5) | 2 (25.0)* | 1 (33.3) |
| Special needs | 8 (21.05) | 2 (25.0) | 0 | 0 |
| Likes teacher | 0 | 0 | 4 (33.3) | 0 |
| Truants | 6 (15.7) | 1 (12.5) | 3 (25.0) | 2 (66.6) |

* More than one response means that numbers are higher than would be expected.

### *Deliberate self-harm characteristics*

Overdose was the most popular method of self-harm, accounting for 66% of all cases, followed by overdose and cutting, accounting for 15% of all cases. Paracetamol was the most common tablet taken: 28 adolescents (45%) took paracetamol, whilst 9 of these adolescents (14%) took paracetamol with other tablets. Of the sample, 26 took 20 tablets or more. Overdose was impulsive in 42% of cases and planned in 16% of cases, no information was available for the remaining cases. No Asians reported having regrets about the deliberate self-harm, whilst 25 white females (66%) and 3 white males (37.5%) regretted having made the attempt. Of the sample, 54% were deemed to be at risk of future self-harm, and this was highest in Asian females (10 = 83%) (see Table 11.8).

Of all the precipitating factors listed in Table 11.9, having a disagreement with parents was the most common factor. Of the sample, 29%, reported that having a disagreement with their parents was a precipitating factor to the act of deliberate self-harm. Of white females 2 (5%), 1 white male (12%) and 1 Asian male (33%) reported having an argument with a friend or sibling (16%). Breaking up with a boyfriend was reported to be a precipitating factor by 6 white females and 1 Asian female (8%). No males (white or Asian) reported breaking up with a girlfriend to be a precipitating factor to deliberate self-harm. Prevalence of alcohol problems at home was low. Of the total sample, one Asian female reported parental alcohol problems to be a precipitating factor. Separation anxiety was reported by 2 white females (5.2% and 2 white males (25%).

Table 11.8
Deliberate self-harm characteristics

| *Variable* | *White female n = 38 (%)* | *White male n = 8 (%)* | *Asian female n = 12 (%)* | *Asian male n = 3 (%)* |
|---|---|---|---|---|
| Overdose | 26 (68) | 5 (62.5) | 11 (91.6) | 2 (66.6) |
| Overdose and cutting | 7 (18.4) | 1 (12.5) | 1 (8.3) | 0 |
| Cutting | 3 (7.8) | 2 (25.0) | 0 | 0 |
| Overdose and alcohol | 2 (5.2) | 0 | 0 | 0 |
| Impulsive | 24 (63.1) | 5 (62.5) | 9 (75) | 3 (100) |
| Planned | 9 (23.68) | 0 | 0 | 0 |
| Regrets | 25 (65.7) | 3 (37.5) | 0 | 0 |
| Note left | 3 (7.8) | 0 | 0 | 0 |
| Future risk of self-harm | 16 (42.1) | 5 (62.5) | 10 (83.3) | 2 (66.6) |

Table 11.9
Causation

| *Variable* | *White female n = 38 (%)* | *White male n = 8 (%)* | *Asian female n = 12 (%)* | *Asian male n = 3 (%)* |
|---|---|---|---|---|
| Argument with parents | 10 (26.3) | 3 (37.5) | 3 (25) | 2 (66.6) |
| Argument with friends | 3 (7.8) | 0 | 0 | 0 |
| Fight with friend/sibling | 2 (5.2) | 1 (12.5) | 0 | 1 (33.3) |
| Break up with girl-boyfriend | 6 (15.78) | 0 | 1 (8.3) | 0 |
| School problems | 2 (5.2) | 0 | 1 (8.3) | 0 |
| Exam pressure | 2 (5.2) | 0 | 1 (8.3) | 1 (33.3) |
| Disciplinary action in school | 0 | 1 (12.5) | 0 | 0 |
| Alcohol problems at home | 0 | 0 | 1 (8.3) | 0 |
| Separation anxiety | 2 (5.2) | 2 (25) | 0 | 0 |

### *Emotional problems*

Eating disorders were reported only by females, 7 white (19%) and 2 Asian (17%). Females also reported having lower self-esteem then males: 23 white females (61%) and 5 Asian females (42%) compared to 2 white males (25%) and no Asian males. Feelings of isolation were reported in 36 (59%) of cases. (see Table 11.10).

A large proportion of the sample reported some form of depression. Of the sample, 18% were clinically depressed, whilst 21% were experiencing temporary depression. Thus if these two categories are collapsed, 39% of the sample had some form of depression. This depression was most common in females (white and Asian). Ten white females (26%) and 1 Asian female (8%) were clinically depressed, whereas no males (white or Asian) were clinically depressed.

Anxiety was less common. Only 7 adolescents (8%) reported suffering from anxiety. However, a higher percentage of males reported suffering from anxiety than females.

The prevalence of phobias was low. Only 1 adolescent reported having a phobia (unspecified). Of the sample, 11.5% (7 adolescents) reported suicidal ideation. This is accounted for by 4 white females (10.5%), 2 white males (25%), and 1 Asian male (33%). No Asian females reported suicidal ideation. Rapid mood changes were reported by 2 white females, and 2 white females reported hearing voices (Table 11.11).

Table 11.10
Self-described emotional problems

| *Variable* | *White female n = 38 (%)* | *White male n = 8 (%)* | *Asian female n = 12 (%)* | *Asian male n = 3 (%)* |
|---|---|---|---|---|
| Eating disorder | 7 (18.42) | 0 | 2 (16.6) | 0 |
| Low self-esteem | 23 (60.5) | 2 (25) | 5 (41.6) | 0 |
| Feelings of isolation | 22 (58.0) | 3 (37.5) | 8 (66.6) | 3 (100) |

Table 11.11
Self-described mental illness

| *Mental illness* | *White female n = 38 (%)* | *White male n = 8 (%)* | *Asian female n = 12 (%)* | *Asian male n = 3 (%)* |
|---|---|---|---|---|
| Clinically depressed | 10 (26.3) | 0 | 1 (8.3) | 0 |
| Temporary depression | 6 (15.7) | 3 (37.5) | 1 (8.3) | 3 (100) |
| Anxiety | 3 (7.8) | 1 (12.5) | 0 | 1 (33.3) |
| Phobia | 1 (2.6) | 0 | 0 | 0 |
| Suicidal ideation | 4 (10.5) | 2 (25) | 0 | 1 (33.3) |
| Rapid mood changes | 2 (5.2) | 0 | 0 | 0 |
| Hearing voices | 2 (5.2) | 0 | 0 | 0 |

## INFERENTIAL ANALYSIS

A linear logistic model was performed to examine the effects of ethnicity and gender on the proportion of the sample experiencing behavioural problems. These data are presented in Table 11.12. Significant differences were found for both cultural conflict and low self-esteem. A greater proportion of Asian females and white females were experiencing low self-esteem than their male counterparts ($\chi^2$ square probability = 7.82, $p < .05$, df = 3). Asian male and females were also more likely to report cultural conflicts than white male and females ($\chi^2$ square probability = 7.82, $p < .05$, df = 3. Detailed data on cultural identity are presented in chapter 12.

It is worth noting that when parents and their children were compared, interesting differences emerged. Table 11.13 illustrates differences between case child and case parent. Children were found to be less traditional in spoken language (i.e. they spoke English), were against arranged marriages, made their own decisions, and decided their own and food habits.

When control children were compared with their parents, not surprisingly they too were less traditional in language and food, but were as traditional on arranged marriages (Table 11.14).

On comparing two sets of parents, the parents of cases of deliberate self-harm appeared to be more traditional in a number of parameters, but this reached statistical significance only as regards aspirations where parents of cases had lower levels of aspirations (Table 11.15).

On comparing the two groups of children, it emerged that children who had self-harmed were more traditional in food habits and also keen to work with white people (Table 11.16).

Table 11.12
Output of linear logistic model

| *Tested variable* | *White* | | | | *Asian* | | | | $\chi^2$ *p. 7.82 (p < .05) df = 3* |
|---|---|---|---|---|---|---|---|---|---|
| | *Male* | | *Female* | | *Male* | | *Female* | | |
| Bullied | 2/4 | 0.500 | 19/31 | 0.1629 | 2/3 | 0.667 | 5/6 | 0.8333 | 1.5306 |
| Abscond | 7/8 | 0.875 | 29/38 | 0.7632 | 3/3 | 1.000 | 8/12 | 0.667 | 2.811 |
| Communication problems | 4/8 | 0.500 | 20/38 | 0.5263 | 1/3 | 0.333 | 4/12 | 0.333 | 1.6567 |
| Cultural conflict | 8/8 | 1.000 | 37/38 | 0.9737 | 2/3 | 0.6667 | 5/12 | 0.1416 | 21.679 |
| Eating disorder | 8/8 | 1.000 | 31/38 | 0.8158 | 3/3 | 1.000 | 10/12 | 0.8333 | 3.9272 |
| Low self-esteem | 6/8 | 0.7500 | 11/34 | 0.3235 | 3/3 | 1.000 | 7/12 | 0.5833 | 10.757 |
| Feelings of isolation | 5/8 | 0.6250 | 16/38 | 0.4211 | 0/3 | 0.000 | 4/12 | 0.333 | 4.9803 |
| Adjustment problems | 7/8 | 0.8750 | 23/38 | 0.6053 | 2/3 | 0.6667 | 5/12 | 0.4167 | 4.6417 |
| Drug use | 6/8 | 0.7500 | 29/38 | 0.7632 | 1/3 | 0.333 | 9/12 | 0.7500 | 2.2883 |
| Peer problems | 5/8 | 0.6250 | 18/36 | 0.500 | 0/3 | 0.000 | 6/11 | 0.5455 | 4.7533 |
| Relationship | 2/8 | 0.2500 | 15/38 | 0.3497 | 0/3 | 0.000 | 3/12 | 0.2500 | 3.7087 |

Table 11.13
Case child by case parent (Wilcoxon Rank sum W test)

| *Variable* | *Case child Mean* | *Case parent Mean* | *2-tailed P p < .05* |
|---|---|---|---|
| Religion | 11.50 | 11.50 | 1.000 |
| Language | 7.73 | 15.27 | 0.0035* |
| Marriage | 7.59 | 15.41 | 0.0014* |
| Lwhitper | 8.95 | 14.05 | 0.0452* |
| Decision | 7.59 | 15.41 | 0.0024* |
| Joindecn | 12.91 | 10.09 | 0.2639 |
| Mardecn | 9.50 | 13.50 | 0.0317* |
| Work | 8.68 | 14.32 | 0.0353* |
| Childbeh | 12.18 | 10.82 | 0.6091 |
| Socontac | 13.77 | 9.23 | 0.0789 |
| Emphouse | 9.45 | 13.55 | 0.1186 |
| leisure | 7.86 | 15.14 | 0.073 |
| Foodshop | 8.05 | 14.95 | 0.0072* |
| Aspire | 11.45 | 11.45 | 0.9724 |

* Significant.

Table 11.14
Control child by control parent (Wilcoxon Rank sum W test)

| *Variable* | *Control child Mean* | *Control parent Mean* | *2-tailed P p < .05* |
|---|---|---|---|
| Religion | 11.50 | 11.50 | 1.000 |
| Language | 7.68 | 15.32 | 0.0039* |
| Marriage | 10.27 | 12.73 | 0.3175 |
| Lwhitper | 8.86 | 14.14 | 0.0208* |
| Decision | 8.41 | 14.59 | 0.0119* |
| Joindecn | 15.00 | 8.00 | 0.0021* |
| Mardecn | 11.45 | 11.55 | 0.9475 |
| Work | 9.41 | 13.59 | 0.1031 |
| Childbeh | 10.77 | 12.23 | 0.5775 |
| Socontac | 10.77 | 12.23 | 0.5720 |
| Em house | 8.91 | 14.09 | 0.0462* |
| leisure | 9.27 | 13.73 | 0.1013 |
| Foodshop | 8.50 | 14.50 | 0.0166* |
| Aspire | 9.14 | 13.86 | 0.678 |

* Significant.

* Religion, religious activity; Language, primary language and where spoken; Marriage, views about arranged marriage; Lwhiteper, relationship with white persons; Decision, who makes the decisions/should do so in the family; Joindecn, joint decisions made by parents; Mardecn, decisions regarding marriage; Work, work colleagues, place of work; Childbeh, behaviour/tolerance of children's behaviour; Socontac, social contact with others of the same ethnicity; Emhouse, employment outside the house; Leisure, leisure activities; Foodshop, type of diet, place of shopping; Aspire, aspirations.

Table 11.15
Case parent by control parent (Kruskal-Wallis 1-way ANOVA, df = 1)

| *Variable* | *Case parent Mean* | *Control parent Mean* | *2-tailed P p < .05* |
|---|---|---|---|
| Religion | 11.50 | 11.50 | 1.000 |
| Language | 12.55 | 10.45 | 0.3799 |
| Marriage | 12.14 | 10.86 | 0.5309 |
| Lwhitper | 10.41 | 12.59 | 0.2410 |
| Decision | 13.41 | 9.59 | 0.1572 |
| Joindecn | 13.50 | 9.50 | 0.317 |
| Mardecn | 12.95 | 10.05 | 0.1521 |
| Work | 12.05 | 10.95 | 0.6644 |
| Childbeh | 9.41 | 13.59 | 0.1042 |
| Socontac | 9.86 | 13.14 | 0.2080 |
| Em house | 11.23 | 11.77 | 0.8367 |
| leisure | 10.14 | 12.86 | 0.3145 |
| Foodshop | 11.45 | 11.45 | 0.9611 |
| Aspire | 8.86 | 14.14 | 0.0465* |

* Significant.

Table 11.16
Control child by case child (Kruskal-Wallis 1–way ANOVA, df = 3)

| *Variable* | *Control child Mean* | *Case child Mean* | *2-tailed P p < .05* |
|---|---|---|---|
| Religion | 17.05 | 20.50 | 0.247 |
| Language | 19.91 | 19.33 | 0.8715 |
| Marriage | 20.18 | 19.22 | 0.7749 |
| Lwhitper | 27.64 | 16.19 | 0.0018* |
| Decision | 23.77 | 17.76 | 0.1161 |
| Joindecn | | | |
| Mardecn | | | |
| Work | 28.05 | 16.02 | 0.0016* |
| Childbeh | 23.91 | 17.70 | 0.1069 |
| Socontac | 17.55 | 20.30 | 0.4783 |
| Em house | 21.86 | 18.54 | 0.3792 |
| leisure | 23.82 | 17.74 | 0.1205 |
| Foodshop | 24.50 | 17.46 | 0.0491* |
| Aspire | 16.73 | 20.63 | 0.3105 |

* Religion, religious activity; Language, primary language and where spoken; Marriage, views about arranged marriage; Lwhiteper, relationship with white persons; Decision, who makes the decisions/should do so in the family; Joindecn, joint decisions made by parents; Mardecn, decisions regarding marriage; Work, work colleagues, place of work; Childbeh, behaviour/tolerance of children's behaviour; Socontac, social contact with others of the same ethnicity; Emhouse, employment outside the house; Leisure, leisure activities; Foodshop, type of diet, place of shopping; Aspire, aspirations.

## Results

To summarise, significant differences in views between case children and case parents were found for the following domains: language, marriage, relationships with white persons, decision making, marriage decision, food habits, food shopping, shopping, and work. In all instances, the differences were represented by case parents holding more traditional views than their children.

For control children and control parent comparisons, significant differences in views were found for the following domains: language, relationships with white persons, decision making, joint decision making, employment outside the house and food shopping. Again, the differences in views are represented by parents holding more traditional views than their children. Comparing the differences in views between case child/case parent and control child/control parent, differences in views for the following domains arise: case children and case parents differ in their view of marriage, whereas control children and control parents do not; case parents and control parents only differed on one domain of aspiration, with control parents holding more traditional views than case parents; case child and case parent only differed on work and food shopping.

## INTERPRETATIONS

There are several limitations that should be acknowledged before drawing conclusions from the data. First, the sample size is small, a disproportionately large percentage of which is accounted for by white females, whilst a disproportionately small percentage is accounted for by Asian males. Particular attention should be paid to this when comparing percentages between groups.

Second, part of the data is derived from case notes, and thus the validity of this data is called into question. Various studies have suggested that there are differential levels of suicides between Asian and whites. Soni-Raleigh and Balarajan (1992) found that rates of suicide were low among Asian males and significantly higher in Asian females. Maniam (1998) also found that rates of suicide were highest in Asian females. Merrill and Owens (1986) found that Asian females are over-represented in self-poisoning amongst females at all ages. However, the inception rates for these data set do not lend support to these assertions in full. There is no evidence to suggest that rates of suicide are highest in adolescent Asian females. In the present sample, rates of deliberate self-harm were higher in Asian females than in both white males and Asian males, but the highest rates of deliberate self-harm were accounted for by white females in all age groups except the 16–17-year age group, where rates of deliberate self-harm were marginally higher in Asian females. These data tend to lend support to findings by Goddard et al. (1996) that referral rates of deliberate self-harm in ethnic groups are in proportion to the community composition.

In relation to social problems, the data lend support to the suggestion that a variety of youth deviant behaviours are associated with deliberate self-harm behaviours. However, peer problems and relationship problems were a common experience across all groups, as was drug use. Adolescents in the sample were involved in criminal activity, used alcohol and drugs, kept bad company, were sexually active, and had peer and adjustment problems. However, there were no significant differences between these groups with respect to these variables. There was no evidence to suggest that among parasuicide individuals boys show more deviant behaviour (Gasquet & Choquet, 1993). In the present sample it would appear that females, in particular white females, had a higher prevalence of deviant behaviours. Adjustment problems were more common in Asian females than in their white counterparts. Only females (white and Asians) reported using alcohol and being sexually active. This is the obverse to findings that suggest boys involved in parasuicide are more sexually active than girls.

Problems at school were also reported to be precipitating factors. Although academic problems were reported by 45% of the sample, whether this was a precipitating factor of the deliberate self-harm cannot be concluded from these cross-sectional data. However, other problems at school, examination pressure, and disciplinary action at school were highlighted by some children as being a contributory cause to the act of deliberate self-harm. The prevalence of bullying was broadly similar across all groups. This might suggest, in the present sample at least, that bullying occurred for reasons other than ethnicity. Only white adolescents (male and female) had special needs in school. The majority of children in all groups reported that they did not like school, which is partly reflected in the levels of truancy across the groups. A higher percentage of both Asian males and females reported truancy more than whites.

Emotional problems were present in many adolescents. Females reported having lower self-esteem than males, and this is partly reflected in the fact that only females reported having eating disorders (although it is noted that eating disorders are more common in females than males). Feelings of isolation and rejection were also reportedly common. Depression, both clinical and temporary, was common, with 39% of all adolescents suffering from some form of depression. There was no evidence to suggest that Asians were more likely to suffer from depression than white males (Kingsbury, 1994), and that almost all involved in parasuicide are depressed (Taiminen, 1995). However, the high prevalence of feelings of isolation and depression is in line with findings by Roberts et al. (1995) that loneliness increases the risk of depression; low self-esteem might further contribute to it.

Having an argument with someone was a common precipitating factor to deliberate self-harm. Disagreement with friends was most common for females, particularly with boyfriends. However, the most common precipitating factor was having an argument with parents. A total of 29% reported that having an argument with their parents was a precipitating factor to the deliberate self-harm. Further analysis of the source of these arguments can be gained from looking at home life problems and 23% reported absconding from home as a result of problems there.

Behaviour problems were reported by 30% of adolescents, whilst 52% of the sample reported communication problems. Other problems at home seem to be particularly relevant to Asians alone in that it may be that the nature of Asian adolescents' deliberate self-harm attempts is qualitatively different from that of whites. Is it possible that a different set of variables, which are culturally specific to Asians, may be operating as risk factors to deliberate self-harm intention? Both Asian males and females reported being compared to other children more than their white counterparts. This often suggests parental dissatisfaction with a child's attainments. This is particularly true for Asian males. A higher percentage of Asian males reported high parental expectations than Asian females, which suggests a greater pressure to succeed is placed on Asian males, and could be a specific cause of deliberate self-harm; 33% of Asian males reported high parental expectations, compared to only 12% of white males. Yet the levels of aspiration do not confirm this. A greater percentage of both Asian males and females reported intergenerational clashes than their white counterparts, and were also significantly more likely to report cultural conflict. However, what do intergenerational clashes and cultural conflict relate to and what are their effects? Each of the 15 variables from the acculturation (see chapter 12) represents a set of views and traditions that are specific to some Asian families. From looking at the comparisons between case parents/control parents and case children/control children, an indication of the sources of conflict leading to deliberate self-harm can be gained.

Significant differences in views between case children and case parents were found for the following domains: language, marriage, relationships with white persons, decision making, marriage decision, food shopping, food habits, and work. The difference in views was represented by case parents holding more traditional views than their children. Thus these domains can be seen as a source of cultural conflict between child and parent. However, they cannot be attributed as a cause of deliberate self-harm alone, as the same conflicts exist in other Asian families, as shown by the control child/control parent comparisons. For control children and control parent comparisons, significant differences in views were found for the following domains: language, relationships with white persons, decision making, joint decision making, employment, and food habits. Again, the difference in views is represented by parents holding more traditional views than their children.

## CONCLUSIONS

Comparing the differences in views between case child/case parent and control child/control parent, differences in views for the following domains arise. Case children and case parents differ in their view of marriage, whereas control children and control parents do not. This could suggest two possibilities. First, control children and control parents do not differ in their view of marriage because control parents hold less traditional views about marriage. As a result there is likely to be less conflict between child and parent. However, this assertion is not supported by the results of the case parent/control parent comparison. There were no significant differences in views on marriage between case parents and control parents, although an analysis of the means does reveal that case parents hold slightly more traditional views on marriage than control parents. The second possibility, as the case parent/control parent comparison would suggest, is that they do not differ in their view of marriage, but control parents are more permissive and less likely to enforce this view on their children, thus reducing conflict and the likelihood of deliberate self-harm.

Case children and case parents do not differ in their view on employment, whereas control children and control parents do, with control parents holding more traditional views. Case parents and control parents differed in only one domain: aspirations. Control parents held more traditional views than case parents. Case children and control children differed in their view of work. Case children hold more traditional views on work than control children. When analysed in the light of the case child/case parent analysis, this is particularly interesting as case children hold less traditional views than their parents. Case parents hold more traditional views than control parents. It may be that case children receive a mixed message about work from their parents. Whilst holding less traditional views than their parents, they actually hold more traditional views than their control counterparts as a result.

CHAPTER TWELVE

# Cultural identity and deliberate self-harm

## INTRODUCTION

With migration of groups across the globe, it is inevitable that cultures too come into closer contact and influence each other. Acculturation is the process whereby different cultures represented by different individuals come into contact. It needs to be differentiated from culture change and assimilation. Acculturative changes may be influenced by direct or indirect exposure. The process involves two groups and generally the nondominant group changes its patterns more easily than the dominant group. The contact and change may be difficult, reactive, or conflictual.

Cultural identity can be defined as that part of an individual's psyche which identifies with his/her culture. This identity is not static and the changes occur when an individual from one culture is placed in, or faced with, another culture for a significant period of time. Under these circumstances some aspects of cultural identity are more prone to change than the others. The process of acculturation comprehends those phenomena which result when groups of individuals with different cultures come into continuous first-hand contact, with subsequent changes in the original culture patterns of either or both groups (Redfield, Linton, & Herskovits, 1936, pp. 149–52). Acculturation has also been defined as a cultural change that is initiated by the conjunction of two or more autonomous cultural systems.

Acculturative changes may be the consequences of direct cultural transmissions. It may be derived from noncultural causes such as ecological or demographic modification induced by an impinging culture. It may be delayed, as with internal adjustments following upon the acceptance of alien traits or patterns, or it may be a reactive adaptation of traditional modes of life (SSRC, 1954, p. 974). Berry (1990) suggests that this process must be seen at both individual and population levels. Graves (1967) recommends using the term 'psychological acculturation' for the changes in individual experiences following close contact with other cultures.

Following contact, conflict may or may not occur. This may lead to adaptation, which will reduce or stabilise conflict. The nature, purpose, duration, and permanence of the contact will determine the response. Most adaptation is likely if the nature of the contact is prolonged and its purpose is trade, education, or communication. The contact can be both at the individual and group levels. The acculturation process may lead to withdrawal, reaction, or adjustment. Of these responses adjustment is positive and the other two are negative. A positive response can lead to assimilation (relinquishing culture identity) and integration (retaining cultural identity). The processes of acculturation may be slow or rapid. Rejection and deculturation may make the individuals more isolated. The acculturation of the group may develop at a different pace than that of the individual. Favouring assimilation is positively related to the degree of contact already experienced, but so too is favouring rejection. Younger, better educated, and more exposed people are likely to assimilate more quickly.

In measuring psychological functioning, six different aspects must be remembered. These are language, cognitive style, personality, identity, attitudes, and acculturative stress. Stopes-Roe and Cochrane (1987) suggest that processes of assimilation vary across generations. They observe that second and consequent generations of ethnic minority groups may enjoy the same life style and follow the same customs in dress, food, recreation, and so on as the host (dominant) society and be involved in secondary group contacts through work and education, but may still maintain a primary group selectivity and a strong ethnic identification. Assimilation may be cultural and social (i.e. external) or interdependent (i.e. internal). Gordon (1964) argues that cultural or behavioural, structural or social, identificational or personal assimilation has to be seen as both interlinked and separate. It is, of course, entirely possible that individuals may preserve a traditional life style more or less intact and yet assimilate into secondary groups. Stopes-Roe and Cochrane (1987) were able to demonstrate in their sample of Asians in Birmingham that generation had an extremely strong effect on cultural and identificational assimilation. Questions covered areas such as food, drink, dress, language, and mass media, and the effects of these on language and country of residence plans for future living; feeling of home, identity and difference; religion; endogamous marriage; and value of customs and their preservation. Structural assimilation covers work/education, neighbours, and other social groups. The motivation to assimilate is also likely to vary according to generation and religion.

Cultural identity is a crucial part of any individual's self and disturbances in cultural identity have been associated with increased psychological distress (Bhugra et al., 1999c). Cultural identity consists of several important components including religion, religious rites and rituals, leisure activities, languages spoken, primacy of places where these languages are spoken, aspirations, functioning and importance of family, dietary habits, shopping for items of food, and feelings regarding contact with others of the same ethnic grouping.

A number of acculturation questionnaires have been used for measuring cultural identity and acculturation in a number of ethnic groups and clinical settings [Stopes-Roe & Cochrane (1987) on Birmingham Asians; Mavreas, Bebbington, & Greely (1988) on Londoners and Greek Cypriots; Cheung (1995) on Vietnamese in New Zealand; Ghubash (1993) on women in Dubai]. These questionnaires focus on individuals and often do not take into account the relationship between individuals in the minority group and the wider society. In this chapter we describe the development and validation of the Asian Cultural Identity Schedule (ACIS) (see Appendix I.)

## DEVELOPMENT OF THE ASIAN CULTURAL IDENTITY SCHEDULE (ACIS)

### Method

An 'Asian' is defined as someone who comes from or who has family links with the Indian subcontinent, which includes including countries of India, Pakistan, Nepal, Sri Lanka, and Bangladesh. The terms 'Asians' and 'South Asians' are used interchangeably. The Asian Cultural Identity Schedule (ACIS) was developed following discussions with a number of community leaders in the South Asian community in the London borough of Ealing. The questionnaire was piloted on 12 Asian medical students who were asked the questions twice with a 6-week interval in between. Modifications were made in order to simplify and make clear the intention of each question.

The following areas of cultural identity were considered important: religion, language, marriage, living with a white person, decision making in the home, joint decision making, marital decision making, work, children's behaviour, social contact, employment outside the house, leisure, food shopping, and aspirations. Clearly the schedule taps attitudes to these arenas rather than reflecting actual behaviour.

### Sample

As described in previous chapters, for adult females, all Asian cases who presented to the A&E department with deliberate self-harm (DSH) were approached over a 1-year period. Deliberate self-harm was defined as suicidal gestures and attempts to kill oneself – with any act of nonfatal outcome that attempts to cause or actually causes self-harm, or which would have done so without the intervention of others, or which consists of ingesting a substance in excess of the generally recognised or prescribed therapeutic dose (Bhugra et al., 1999a). These were then watched for age and sex with GP surgery attenders in a general practice in the catchment area. Twenty-seven patients and twenty-seven controls completed the study (Bhugra et al., 1999a).

Over a 1-year period, all Asian adolescents presenting with deliberate self-harm were approached. Over the same period, Asian adolescents attending the A&E department without deliberate self-harm were selected as controls. Mothers of the patients and controls were interviewed and asked to fill in the Cultural Identity Schedule. Eleven adolescents with DSH and eleven controls, and the same number of mothers for patients and controls, were included. Thus 54 Asian women who attempted self-harm (27 cases, 27 controls), and 22 adolescents (11 cases, 11 controls) and their parents (11 cases, 11 controls) completed the ACIS (Table 12.1).

Table 12.1
Demographic characteristics of three study samples

| | | *DSH cases n (%)* | *DSH controls n (%)* | *AD cases n (%)* | *AD controls n (%)* | *ADP cases n (%)* | *ADP controls n (%)* |
|---|---|---|---|---|---|---|---|
| *Gender* | Male | – | – | 3 (27) | 3 (27) | 3 (27) | 3 (27) |
| | Female | 27 (100) | 27 (100) | 8 (73) | 8 (73) | 8 (73) | 8 (73) |
| *Age in* | 1–20 | 9 (38) | 7 (26) | 11 (100) | 11 (100) | – | – |
| ;groups | 21–29 | 6 (27) | 8 (30) | – | – | – | – |
| | 30–39 | 7 (26) | 8 (30) | – | – | 4 (36) | – |
| | 40+ | 5 (19) | 4 (15) | – | – | 7 (64) | 11 (100) |
| *Religion* | Catholic | – | – | 2 (18) | 1 (9) | 2 (18) | 1 (10) |
| | Muslim | 3 (12) | 2 (8) | 3 (27) | 1 (9) | 3 (27) | 1 (10) |
| | Hindu | 11 (42) | 8 (31) | 3 (27) | 2 (18) | 4 (36) | 3 (30) |
| | Sikh | 12 (46) | 16 (61) | 3 (27) | 6 (55) | 2 (18) | 5 (50) |
| | Pentecostal | – | – | – | 1 (9) | – | – |
| *Ethnicity* | British | 2 (7) | – | 2 (18) | 1 (9) | – | – |
| | British Asian | 8 (30) | 13 (48) | 8 (73) | 6 (55) | 5 (45) | 2 (18) |
| | Asian | 4 (15) | 2 (7) | 1 (9) | 1 (9) | 1 (9) | 3 (27) |
| | Indian | 10 (37) | 10 (37) | – | 3 (27) | 5 (45) | 6 (55) |
| | Other | 3 (11) | 2 (7) | – | – | – | – |

AD, adolescent self-harmers; ADP, parents of adolescents; DSH, deliberate self-harm.

### *Questionnaire*

The questionnaire contains questions on various aspects of culture. The eight areas of cultural identity were:

- *religion:* frequency of attendance at religious meetings, in all seven questions
- *languages spoken:* eight questions
- *marriage and family:* age of marriage; best age to get married for men and for women; arranged marriage; same for boys/girls; living with partner before marriage; having children before marriage; mixed race relationships; responsibility for looking after children; decision making in the family – who should and who does on a number of parameters, e.g. children, household purchases, holidays; whether one or both parents should work; questions on behaviour of Asian children and reasons for this; school curriculum and inclusion of cultural matters; behaviour of Asian parents towards their children compared with white parents; child care and support; contact with relatives abroad, in all, 52 questions
- *employment and housing:* preference for working and living with same ethnic group and reasons, 9 questions
- *leisure:* time alone or with family, magazine and papers read, preferred language, portrayal of Asians in the media, Hindi films seen, memberships of clubs, music, etc., 25 questions
- *food and shopping:* dietary habits, food preferences, 9 questions
- *aspirations:* who is admired, in what field and whether they are white or Asian and in which field – politics, sport, music, religion, etc., 3 questions
- *self attitudes:* use of and views on skin lightening products, retirement plans and possible return to the subcontinent, 10 questions.

## Statistical analysis

The Likert scale score from 1 and 6 was examined for each item and, following discussion among a panel of experts, a consensus was reached about recoding these into dichotomous variables (0 or 1). The dichotomous variable indicated either a more English view (score = 0) or a traditional 'Indian subcontinent' view (score = 1). The mean and median scores were calculated for each of the groups. We made six comparisons:

- Adolescent cases and controls were compared.
- The parents of adolescent cases and those of controls were compared.
- Cases amongst the Asian women who attempted DSH were compared with controls.
- Adolescent cases were compared to their parents.
- Adolescent controls were compared to their parents.

- Asian women who attempted DSH were compared with the parents of control subjects from the adolescent sample.

In view of the non-normal distributions and the relatedness of the samples (matching at recruitment and same family origins of child and parent), the Wilcoxon signed rank test was used to compare the distributions of any one item between any two subsamples.

Only in one instance, for independent samples, was the Kruskal-Wallis analysis of variance test applied. This was for the comparison of the scores for the control sample for the 'Deliberate Self-harm Among Women' study, with the scores of the parents of the control group of 'Deliberate Self-harming Adolescents'.

Thus the study affords the opportunity to examine how case/control status and how adolescent/parent status are associated with acculturation items. We examine the face and content validity of the ACIS and consider the implications of the findings for the better understanding of deliberate self-harm behaviour as a function of acculturative stress associated with identity development. This affords a unique opportunity to investigate discordance in identity items between adolescents and their parents, and adolescent cases and their parents, in comparison to the discordance between adolescent controls and their parents, and whether Asian women controls differ from parental controls.

## Results

The demographic characteristics of each of the samples are set out in Table 12.1. This clearly illustrates the different age and gender structures of each study sample. The data showing the median and mean scores within each of the study groups are set out in Table 12.2.

1. On comparing adolescent cases and controls, there were no statistically significant differences for any of the item scores.
2. On comparing the parents of adolescent cases and those of controls, there were no statistically significant differences for any of the items.
3. For the item on 'Social Contact', the mean score among women who attempted deliberate self-harm was lower (less traditional) than amongst women in the control group ($Z = -2.03$, $p = .04$). Women who attempted deliberate self-harm were less traditional (lower score) on the 'Aspirations' item than control women ($Z = -2.63$, $p = .01$). There were no other differences between these groups on any of the items.
4. Compared to their parents, adolescents who attempt deliberate self-harm show less traditional 'Language Preferences' ($Z = -0.27$, $p = .007$), 'Marriage Preferences' ($Z = -2.48$, $p = .01$), attitudes to 'Living With a White Person' ($Z = 2.08$, $p = .04$), attitudes to 'Decision Making' ($Z = 2.54$, $p = .01$), attitudes towards 'Work' ($Z = -0.72$, $p = .01$), 'Leisure' ($Z = -2.69$, $p = .007$), and 'Food Shopping'

Table 12.2
Comparisons of acculturation items scores for cases and controls

| *Items* | | *DSH Case* | *DSH Control* | *AD Case* | *AD Control* | *ADP Case* | *ADP Control* |
|---|---|---|---|---|---|---|---|
| *Religion* | Mean | 1.00 | 1.00 | 0.82 | 0.82 | 0.82 | 0.82 |
| | Median | – | – | 1.00 | 1.00 | 1.00 | 1.00 |
| *Language* | Mean | 0.58 | 0.59 | 0.35 | 0.31 | 0.67 | 0.58 |
| | Median | 0.6 | 0.6 | 0.4 | 0.4 | 0.6 | 0.6 |
| *Marriage* | Mean | 0.7 | 0.82 | 0.51 | 0.69 | 0.91 | 0.82 |
| | Median | 0.8 | 1.0 | 0.4 | 0.8 | 1.0 | 1.00 |
| *Lwhitper* | Mean | 0.66 | 0.79 | 0.75 | 0.78 | 0.91 | 0.98 |
| | Median | 0.6 | 0.8 | 0.8 | 0.8 | 1.0 | 1.0 |
| *Decision* | Mean | 0.44 | 0.41 | 0.38 | 0.35 | 0.67 | 0.53 |
| | Median | 0.5 | 0.3 | 0.33 | 0.33 | 0.67 | 0.5 |
| *Work* | Mean | 0.440 | 0.46 | 0.5 | 0.56 | 0.68 | 0.65 |
| | Median | 5 | 0.5 | 0.5 | 0.5 | 0.67 | 0.67 |
| *Childbeh* | Mean | 0.61 | 0.57 | 0.53 | 0.6 | 0.47 | 0.66 |
| | Median | 0.5 | 0.5 | 0.6 | 0.6 | 0.6 | 0.6 |
| *Socontac* | Mean | 0.6 | 0.74 | 0.73 | 0.67 | 0.59 | 0.7 |
| | Median | 0.75 | 0.75 | 0.67 | 0.67 | 0.67 | 0.67 |
| *Emphouse* | Mean | 0.34 | 0.32 | 0.18 | 0.18 | 0.36 | 0.36 |
| | Median | 0.25 | 0.25 | 0.25 | 0.25 | 0.25 | 0.5 |
| *Leisure* | Mean | 0.58 | 0.68 | 0.46 | 0.61 | 0.72 | 0.78 |
| | Median | 0.6 | 0.7 | 0.5 | 0.5 | 0.7 | 0.8 |
| *Foodshop* | Mean | 0.76 | 0.84 | 0.69 | 0.76 | 0.93 | 0.95 |
| | Median | 0.8 | 0.8 | 0.8 | 0.8 | 1.0 | 1.0 |
| *Aspire* | Mean | 0.33 | 0.52 | 0.25 | 0.3 | 0.27 | 0.48 |
| | Median | 0.33 | 0.67 | 0.25 | 0.25 | 0.25 | 0.5 |

Deliberate self-harm sample of women
[Z] Adolescents who have attempted deliberate self-harm
[3] Parents of adolescents who have attempted deliberate self-harm
Religion, religious activity; Language, primary language and where spoken; Marriage, views about arranged marriage, Lwhiteper, relationship with white persons; Decision, who makes the decisions/should do so in the family; Joindecn, joint decisions made by parents; Mardecn, decisions regarding marriage; Work, work colleagues, place of work; Childbeh, behaviour/tolerance of children's behaviour; Socontac, social contact with others of the same ethnicity; Emhouse, employment outside the house, Leisure, leisure activities; Foodshop, type of diet, place of shopping; Aspire, aspirations.

($Z = -2.20$, $p = .03$). As expected, adolescents did not show more traditional attitudes on any of the items.

5. Compared to their parents, adolescent controls showed less traditional attitudes to 'Language' ($Z = 2.57$, $p = .01$), 'Living With a White Person' ($Z = -2.23$, $p = .03$), 'Decision Making' ($Z = -1.98$, $p = .05$), 'Leisure' ($Z = -2.10$, $p = .04$), 'Food Shopping' ($Z = -1.98$, $p = .05$) and 'Aspirations' ($Z = -1.99$, $p = .05$).

Thus, for the adolescent deliberate self-harm sample there are differences in the parent/child comparisons, which are unique to cases or to controls on three items: marriage, work, and aspirations. Adolescents who attempt deliberate self-harm show less traditional attitudes to marriage and work than their parents, in the absence of such differences in the control subjects. Adolescents who attempt self-harm do not differ from their parents in their aspirations, whereas those in the control group have less traditional aspirations than their parents. This is explained by the parents of adolescents who attempt self-harm having similar 'Aspiration' scores as their children whereas the parents of the control group adolescents have higher scores reflecting more traditional aspirations.

Less traditional attitudes to marriage and work than parents may be risk factors for deliberate self-harm amongst adolescents. Furthermore, where parental aspirations have modified and are as untraditional as their children's, this may act as a risk factor. Equal degrees of parent–child acculturation may be a risk factor for deliberate self-harm for children.

6. Asian women who attempted DSH were compared with the parents of control subjects from the adolescent sample. Women who attempt deliberate self-harm are less traditional than parents of control group adolescents on domains of 'Living With a White Person' ($\chi^2 = 9.78$, df = 3, $p = .002$), 'Work' ($\chi^2 = 9.91$, df = 5, $p = .002$) and 'Food Shopping ($\chi^2 = 3.87$, df = 2, $p = .05$). They are more traditional than control women on the domain of 'Religion' ($\chi^2 = 5.05$, df = 1, $p = .02$).

It is instructive to examine the domains for which adolescent/parent differences are unique to adolescents who attempted DSH. It seems reasonable to consider that identity shifts in these domains (work and aspirations) are strongly associated with DSH behaviour, but a casual association cannot be verified in this study. Indeed, the small sample sizes mean that any data are considered tentatively as a guide to future areas of research work where substantial studies can be established. A second set of differences between adolescents and parents are common to adolescent cases and controls. These are for language, living with a white person, leisure, decision making, and food shopping. Hence these can be attributed to 'benign' acculturative differences, although almost certainly their presence is unlikely to be free of family distress. Finally, in a comparison of women who attempt deliberate self-harm and control women, less traditional attitudes to food shopping, work, and living with a white person may be risk factors along with more traditional attitudes to religion than control subjects. One might interpret that parents per se are likely to be older and more traditional, as the DSH women samples are generally younger than the parental sample. Alternatively, one might conclude that traditional religious views are more common among Asian women and that the parental control group contains some men.

## Discussion

Several caveats must be borne in mind while interpreting the results of this study. First, although we have used the word Asian, the heterogeneity of such a group must be taken into account. Second, although data collection was carried out by two researchers, no formal assessment of inter-rate reliability was carried out. Third, the samples were recruited from those seeking help for attempted suicide or attending hospitals or general practices for health-related problems. Furthermore, parents of the child are from the same 'family unit', thereby raising the possibility that cultural identity may be influenced by similar factors.

The questionnaire succeeds in illustrating the role of acculturation and culture identity in deliberate self-harm, in demonstrating less traditional values in the attempter cases compared with controls for some domains and vice versa. Furthermore, it appears to demonstrate expected generational differences in terms of traditionalism versus modernism, thereby suggesting that it can be used in measuring traditional values in this group.

The key areas that showed significant findings are related to the following areas: religion, language, inter-racial relationships, decision making in the household, social contact including employment outside the home, and aspirations. As Stopes-Roe and Cochrane (1987) demonstrated, the process of assimilation, identificational assimilation especially with regard to religion, suggests that ethnic identity becomes an attempt to maintain some permanence. They found that Hindus and Sikhs were more likely to be assimilated, which is indicated in the present study as well. Often, religion and its practice are the most significant aspects of an individual's ethnic and cultural identity and are most likely to be retained after language, leisure activities, and dietary habits have changed. Some of this may be linked with the type of religion practised and rituals associated with it, whereas other changes may be related to social and peer acceptance if one attends places of worship.

Decision making in the household is traditionally associated with elders, especially males, making decisions on a number of issues within the household. In Asian families the fact that decisions are still made by the older males suggests that traditionalist views still prevail. Decisions linked with inter-racial relationships provide a high degree of reliance on traditionalist views. Stopes-Roe and Cochrane (1987) propose that there are three types of assimilation – cultural, identificational, and structural. My argument is that cultural assimilation is the first step in assimilation followed by structural assimilation and the least resistance to change would appear to be identificational. Thus the most significant and generational differences in the present study are linked with identificational assimilation such as arranged marriages, religion, ethnic customs, and language.

Among minority ethnic communities hailing from the Indian subcontinent, conditions of employment and housing are important features. These may reflect structural assimilation and it is likely that the groups in the present study are in the midst of such an assimilating change. The degree of acculturation and ethnic identity has been shown to be related using the present questionnaire. The generational differences and psychopathology suggest that older females and parents of adolescent attempters and adolescent controls are likely to be influenced by the process of acculturation, which needs to be measured accurately in order to determine stress and psychological stressors.

A close association between traditionalism and attempted suicide confirms the findings previously reported by Merrill and Owens (1986). Subjects depending upon their psychotherapy and generational status differed significantly in their responses. Thus the older generation is more likely to be traditional and stressed (as evinced by the psychopathology) and the most acculturated (least traditional) are likely to be young and students. Several explanations can be put forward to account for this relationship between age, traditionalism, and psychopathology. Older females are more likely to be stressed, especially if they hold unconventional views such as accepting mixed-race relationships. They are more likely to caught between the 'older' first generation immigrants who are in a transitional state between the cultural values of their parents and the dominant society and will not appear well rooted to them. The values of second-generation individuals differ significantly from those of the dominant society (Yamamoto, 1968). Thus role expectations are different in the home when compared with those in society. It is likely that these attitudes will differ markedly in males, who may hang on to more traditional values, especially if any changes threaten their position. It is also possible that men may change their cultural and structural values more quickly than women – an area that deserves to be studied further.

## CONCLUSIONS

Cultural identity for Asians can be measured using the Asian Cultural Identity Schedule, which contains sections on cultural, structural, and interaction assimilation. It is recommended that the questionnaire be used for measuring cultural identity and gender differences. It is important to emphasise that cultural identity is not static. It is fluid and will continue to evolve and the individual's perceptions of their own cultural identity will change according to a number of factors, including exposure to other cultures and experiences within specific cultural settings. The concept of self is extremely useful in the way an individual perceives his/her psychological well-being. The process of acculturation will influence the individual in a number of ways – it may change attitudes and/or behaviour. A number of facets of the self exist and only some can be measured by any questionnaire. Clinicians need to be aware of the concept of acculturation, as well as the component of cultural identity, in order to understand the psychopathology and to plan interventions.

CHAPTER THIRTEEN

# Prevention strategies and community involvement

## INTRODUCTION

In view of the high rates of attempted suicide in South Asian women, especially under the age of 30, whereas rates of attempted suicide in Asian adolescents are no different than their white counterparts, it was decided to undertake a series of studies asking members of the South Asian community their views on the act of attempted suicide and possible collaborative factors. These followed on from a series of focus groups held by an Indian psychologist fluent in Hindi, Punjabi, and English. The findings from the focus groups, development of the educational material, and its pilot testing are described in this chapter. The educational material should make it possible for increased recognition, help seeking, and acceptance of treatment for depression and suicidality in Asian women living in Britain.

## AIMS OF THE STUDY

1. To produce educational material that could reduce rates of attempted suicide in Asian women by increasing their recognition of depression and other suicide risk factors, and by increasing their likelihood of seeking help early for depression and suicidality.
2. To pilot-test the educational material as part of forming a preventive strategy to reduce rates of depression and suicide attempts in Asian women.

3. To increase community awareness of risk factors for depression and suicide in Asian women and to increase knowledge of available sources of help.
4. To train staff at accident and emergency departments to be aware of key risk factors which lead to attempted suicide in Asian women.

## OVERVIEW OF STUDY METHODOLOGY

Ethical approval was obtained for the study. The study was primarily based in the Ealing area of London because of its large Asian population. The study was done in three phases.

### Phase 1

Timeline: September 1998 to April 1999. Actions included:

- Community liaison work and participant observation with GP surgeries and Asian community organisations to engage them in the study, to identify concerns and opinions about how depression and suicidality in Asian women can be effectively addressed, and to create the basis for subject recruitment for Phase 3 of the study.
- Recruitment of Asian women from the community for focus groups.
- Completion of Asian women focus groups. The groups were a preliminary source of community opinions on causes of suicide attempts and identified factors relevant to developing an acceptable and appropriate educational pamphlet.

### Phase 2

Timeline: February 1999 to April 1999. Actions included:

- Development of the pilot pamphlet which provided educational information on depression and suicidality in Asian women and advice on seeking help.
- A directory of local services was created and included in the pamphlet.

### Phase 3

Timeline: April 1999 to July 1999. Actions included:

- 180 Asian women were recruited from GP surgeries and Asian community organisations for pilot testing of the educational pamphlet.

- The educational pamphlet was tested for acceptability, appropriateness, feasibility, and effect on knowledge and help-seeking attitudes of Asian women regarding depression and suicidality.
- The staff at participating GP surgeries, Asian community organisations, and the deliberate self-harm nurse at Ealing Hospital were familiarised with the pamphlet and its contents, including the directory of local services.

### After the study ended

Data collection and community training aspects of the study were covered under the 9-month period funded by the Department of Health. The subsequent qualitative and quantitative data analysis and writing of results took place during the following year. The findings have been published elsewhere (Bhugra & Hicks, 2004; Hicks & Bhugra, 2003).

## PHASE 1: FOCUS GROUP STUDY

### Goals of Asian women's focus groups

- To gather preliminary, in-depth, descriptive data on causes of attempted suicide and conceptualisations of suicide and its risk factors from the perspective of Asian women living in the community.
- For perspectives and themes from focus groups to provide preliminary data and a guide for developing the educational pamphlet to be relevant, appropriate, and acceptable for use in the Asian community.
- For Asian women of diverse backgrounds to be included in groups so that perspectives from different subpopulations would be represented. This would be important in order to gather a wide range of information on risks and causes of suicide in Asian women, and for later development of a pamphlet useful for as large an Asian population as possible.

### Methods for focus groups

The focus group method was chosen for preliminary, in-depth investigation of community opinions about causes and conceptualisations of suicide attempts in British Asian women. The primary purpose for using the focus groups was to aid the development of an educational pamphlet for depression and suicide prevention in British Asian women.

Such in-depth pilot data on community opinions was necessary to develop and present an educational pamphlet in a way that would be acceptable and appropriate for its target population. In addition, the feasibility of focus groups in Punjabi-speaking British Asian women had already been demonstrated (Bhugra, Baldwin, & Desai, 1997a, 1997b). Finally, the focus group method allows intensive and flexible exploration of a topic, which is useful for exploring important themes and perspectives within the nonpatient community population of interest, in order to supplement data obtained from clinical populations of Asian suicide attempters.

## Preliminary community fieldwork

Centres and organisations of cultural and social importance in the Asian community were identified. The project link worker liaised with leaders in the Hindu and Muslim Asian communities and with key individuals at important Asian community sites, including Muslim mosques, Hindu temples, Sikh gurudwaras, cultural centres, and Asian counselling, health, and advice centres. This built upon previous ethnographic fieldwork done by the project link worker during her work with London Asians in the same geographical area over the previous three years. Community liaison contacts, fieldwork, and focus group recruitment took place from September 1998 to January 1999. In the process of community contacts and fieldwork, the following project goals were met:

1. A written and verbal introduction of the study and its goals was given to key members of the Asian community.
2. The project engaged community members to establish a collaborative working relationship and to gather their opinions and concerns about depression and suicide in Asian women.
3. The community contacts formed the basis for recruitment of women to participate in the focus groups and for establishing convenient community sites for focus group meetings.
4. These contacts also enabled the later recruitment of community-based subjects for pilot testing the pamphlet in Phase 3 of the study.

## Focus group recruitment

A convenience sample of South Asian women was recruited from the community contacts and organisations described above. For the purposes of this study, 'South Asian' refers to those whose ethnic background originates from the Indian subcontinent. When recruitment was done through a community organisation, the relevant office staff or trust committee was informed about the objectives and methods of the study, their opinions and concerns discussed, and their approval obtained. Indian Muslim women were also recruited by referral through key contacts in their community. The groups included Asian women of diverse backgrounds regarding age, first- and second-generation immigration history, immigration status, acculturation level, religion, and education.

When women were invited to participate in the study, informed consent was obtained by explaining the goals and nature of the study, and that confidentiality would be maintained regardless of their decision to participate. Focus group meetings were held in the community for the convenience and comfort of participants. Sites included Hindu temples, Sikh gurudwaras, health service offices, and women's homes. Focus groups were held between January and April 1999. The duration of focus group discussions was generally around 45 to 50 minutes based on the preference of participants, who were generally very busy. Focus groups were led by an Asian female psychologist. Groups were held in Hindi, English or Punjabi.

In order to facilitate a focused discussion of causes and factors in suicide attempts by Asian women, participants were asked at the beginning of the group to consider the following three questions, which were also listed in a handout:

1. How do you perceive cases of attempted suicide – its situations, issues and solutions?
2. What do you think might be causes and factors for attempted suicide?
3. What do you think are solutions for this problem and how can we prevent it?

To further stimulate discussion, participants were also presented with a typical case scenario based on previous findings of factors in attempted suicide in British Asian women (Bhugra et al., 1997b, 1999a, 1999b) and asked for their reactions and comments:

> A girl from India was married to a boy who was born and brought up here (in the UK). They started having conflict. From the beginning, the in-laws always supported the husband. The in-laws started creating all sorts of problems for her. Her husband was involved with another girl. All her relatives were in India. She had no support from her relatives. She had no friends here. Ultimately, one day she decided to take 20 paracetamol and she took the overdose. She was then taken to hospital for treatment.

The focus group leader used a semi-structured method, in that she guided discussion only as much as necessary to ensure that the three research topics were addressed and that all group members were allowed to contribute. Spontaneous discussion was encouraged on the main topic of suicide and attempted suicide in British Asian women. As much as possible, the natural course of the group discussion was allowed to develop. Data were recorded in written fieldnotes in Hindi and English by the focus group leader both during and immediately after the meetings. These fieldnotes consisted of direct, unedited quotations of comments made during the meetings, characteristics of the speakers, observations, and preliminary interpretations of recurring themes in the groups. She then translated the quotations into written English for analysis. Audiotaping focus group discussions is useful for recording reliably verbatim, extended quotations and the flow of conversation, but the method is limited by difficulty in identifying individual speakers within the group. Although audiotapes would have been a useful supplement to written fieldnotes, the cost of transcribing and translating audiotapes would have made the their use prohibitive. Also, in view of the primary goal of this project's use of focus groups – to aid in developing an educational pamphlet – written fieldnotes were considered more appropriate to record and analyse relevant main themes and issues.

## Analysis of qualitative focus group data

Quotations from focus groups were read and reviewed multiple times by members of the research team, both independently and together, to identify recurrent themes that emerged in discussions. Quotes were coded for thematic content. They were then organised into categories pertaining to major identified themes and to aims of the project. Coding of qualitative data is part of the process of data analysis and organisation. It is a method which informs further more abstract theoretical analysis and is frequently used in anthropological and sociological research analysis (e.g. Strauss & Corbin, 1990). Preliminary interpretations were discussed and noted to provide clarification and background for women's comments, and were based on observations of the groups and on previous ethnographic experience in the community. Further theoretical analysis and interpretation was based in part on participant observation and personal ethnographic experience in the London Asian community, and on analysis of relevant literature found in medical anthropology.

## Results of focus groups

### *Characteristics of focus groups*

The total number of focus group participants was 43. All were women residing in the London area whose ethnicity was identified as 'Asian' by themselves and the project link worker. They formed ten focus groups. Participants represented a diversity of Hindu, Muslim, and Sikh religious communities, Indian and Pakistani backgrounds, a wide range of ages, and a variety of acculturation and immigration backgrounds. Education levels of the participants ranged from primary school to professional degrees. Occupations included housewives, students, and professionals. Income levels ranged from lower middle class to upper middle class, but were predominantly at the middle and upper range, possibly due to the inclusion of key informants who tended to be professionals, and possibly due to self-selection by those who are more comfortable voicing their opinions in groups and taking part in studies. Older participants had migrated from India, Pakistan, and Africa. Younger women were born in the UK or had immigrated at an early age.

This diversity of characteristics in British Asian women was purposely sought in forming the focus groups in keeping with the exploratory nature of this project, in which a wide scope was desired to include as many suicide factors as possible, and to allow for different perspectives about possible suicide factors, as well as exploring whether there may be different patterns of opinions between groups. Some focus groups consisted of laypersons and some of a mixture of laypersons and key informants. A key informant for the purposes of this study was someone with wide and expert knowledge of the circumstances of British Asian women due to her provision of volunteer or professional services to large numbers of Asian women, or her being in a leadership position in the community.

A breakdown of characteristics of the 43 participants and 10 focus groups is as follows:

- *Hindu women:* 19 Hindu women formed 4 focus groups. The groups consisted of laypersons from a Hindu temple (6), a group of layperson relatives (3), a group of laypersons and key informants from a mental health services office (6), and a group of laypersons and key informants from a GP surgery (4). There were 6 women aged 40 or younger and 13 over 40.
- *Muslim women:* 9 Muslim women formed 3 focus groups. One group was a mixture of laypersons and key informants (4), a second was a pair of neighbours, including one key informant (2), and a third was of layperson relatives (3). Ages ranged from 23 to 74 years, with an average of 27 years.
- *Sikh women:* 15 Sikh women formed 3 focus groups. One group consisted of laypersons and key informants from a gurudwara (9), another of laypersons from a second gurudwara (4), and the other of related key informants (2). Ages ranged from 19 to 67 years, with an average of 39 years.

## Suicide attempts in Asian women: A summary of contexts and causes according to Asian women focus groups

From the focus groups, a number of factors and situations could be identified that were repeatedly described as important contributors to suicide attempts in Asian women. These factors were widely described and accepted by participants, with negligible variation in opinion based on religion, age, or education.

A summary is presented here of what were considered proximal causes and important distal contributors to suicide attempts in Asian women. Example quotations are provided to illustrate the identified themes. A more in-depth and anthropological analysis of the qualitative data formed by the full body of quotations is currently being written for publication.

## Proximal causes of suicide attempts: Scenarios

Four main types of scenario were recounted repeatedly in the focus groups as examples of situations leading directly to suicide attempts in Asian women:

- isolalation
- in-laws
- marriage problems
- dowry.

### *Isolation after immigration to the UK*

A frequent scenario was that young female immigrants from India find themselves 'trapped' in difficult social situations upon arrival and are more vulnerable than women who are raised here. They are considered isolated and vulnerable due to being separated from supportive natal family members and community ties. They have multiple pressures to accept the conditions of living with a new spouse and in-laws (e.g. financial and moral). They generally lack English skills. The risk factor of social isolation after immigration was considered to be significantly compounded by marital conflict arising from a mismatch between husband and wife, e.g. 'a well-educated girl from India gets married to an uneducated boy (from Britain)'.

Another compounding factor can be if the new immigrant wife has high unmet expectations of her new life in Britain which are disappointed and not ameliorated by having entered marriage with a satisfactory partner:

> She is protected. The [husband's] family has somebody do things for her, so she doesn't [have contact outside her husband's family]. They come from another

> country. Their own family is far away. She's lost all links. She does not have anybody of her own to support her. She is not accepted. It is very difficult. There is nobody to understand her.

> When they come here from a village in India or Pakistan, they are not educated, are isolated, don't know the language, don't know the system. No friends. She is all alone. She has to adjust to everyone. She can't understand the English language. And on top of that is she has marital conflict [and it can lead to suicide].

### *In-law problems compounded by poor support or mistreatment by husband*

This factor was considered very important. In-laws were mentioned frequently and played an important role in multiple themes. They were considered to be a more common proximal factor for suicide for women in Asia:

> The girl [a new immigrant from Pakistan] got married. The first few months were OK. She and her husband lived with his mother . . . The mother dominated her son. The husband would fight with the girl and beat her. He threatened to leave her. He said 'I am not interested in this girl. She should be sent back.' She contacted the [Muslim charity]. She was desperate and about to commit suicide. The main cause was in-laws' pressure. The [Muslim charity] helped her and sorted her problem out.

> You try to please the in-laws. Even if they are very unreasonable and demanding. You have to be lucky – then you are appreciated. You work like a donkey. Attempting suicide is a distress in quietness.

### *Marriage problems*

Infidelity, battering, and bearing the burden of the husband's problems were frequently mentioned as leading to suicidality in Asian wives. A critical co-factor seemed to be lack of support from other family members and society:

> When she gets married, then the husband gives you so much trouble. And you are not able to tell your parents. If there is some problem, anyway, you do not want to tell your parents because you want to spare them the hurt or worry or the situation that you cannot do anything. Girls are in the situation where they try 'Let's forget everything and take an overdose'. I think man is the cause of everything.

> 90% of the cases [suicide attempts] are because of men, unhappy marriages, too much interference by in-laws, and the stress of in-laws.

> A girl attempted suicide because of alcoholism by her husband. Her husband would try to assert his authority [physically]. He took drugs, too.

### *Dowry*

Verbal and emotional torture by the in-laws for dowry was considered to be a proximal cause of suicide attempts. Dowry problems in general were considered a distal, predisposing contributor and were mentioned to a moderate degree. It was considered to be more of a problem for women living in Asia than for Asian women living in the UK:

> Depending on whether she has got a dowry or not, and the financial background of the girl's family, the daughter-in-law can be miserable. Mostly, the taunting and torture comes from the mother-in-law and sister-in-laws.

> Dowry – to try to please the in-laws of the daughter. [If] they treat her badly, how damaging it is for a young woman! Eventually they turn her into a bundle of frustration. And if the husband is not supportive, then she does not know where to go.

> The girl doesn't bring any dowry. She is tortured until the day she gets fed up and she does it [attempts suicide].

## Themes

The four most commonly mentioned types of scenarios and anecdotes in focus groups are described above. However, the bulk of focus group content consisted of discussions and commentary about suicide attempts and distress, and what factors are important in making life difficult or better for Asian women. Using the coding and thematic analysis already outlined, the following major themes were delineated for suicide attempts in Asian women, which can also be seen to emerge within, and in the first case coincide with, the four types of scenarios.

### *Theme: Being 'trapped'*

A woman becomes socially isolated and 'trapped' by a combination of control by the new in-law family and loss of support from her natal family and community after immigration. This was considered to be both a proximal and distal cause of suicide attempts:

> In India, [parents] just see the boy and get their daughter married to him. They don't know anything about the boy, his family, his financial condition, whether he already has a wife. They just see the boy in India and get the daughter married to him. If somebody tells them 'This boy is already married' they just

think the person is trying to cut off the marriage negotiations. And when she comes here, she finds that he's already married, or not earning, or they're incompatible. And she can't go back. And she attempts suicide. These are the kinds of girls who get trapped.

Women get trapped in the family. It does cause stress. Especially an Asian woman who is from India, with the language barrier, no family of her own, no one to talk to.

They [in-laws] measure her amount of contact. People monitor how much she has contact with her family members. How much she talked on the phone. She is discriminated against, definitely. It is businesslike. It is all measured.

### *Theme: Being unable to tell others – 'Attempting suicide is a distress in quietness'*

The situations described above are clearly causes of distress in Asian women. However, the social situation itself is not the only source of suicidality. *Being unable to tell anyone of her distress* emerged as another major theme of suicidality in Asian women:

If there is communication between husband and wife and you are able to tell your husband 'This is what I do not like of you' then there is a strong bond. And if a woman is unable to communicate to your children or to your husband, then she has to die.

There are a number of reasons that an Asian women might not be able to tell others of her feelings and situation. The *social isolation* already described, which is sometimes enforced upon women, can lead to a lack of confidants within the woman's social world. Language barriers isolate her further.

Telling of marital or family problems can lead to the woman and her family being *stigmatised* by the Asian community:

It is a big problem for Asian women – social stigma. There is a big stigma. You are not supposed to talk about your family. You are not supposed to talk about your emotions. Your are supposed to keep quiet and have control over yourself. A lot of Asian women do not express themselves. That kind of stress builds up. Then she attempts suicide. She should be outwardly normal. Indian ladies are supposed to be very strong. They pretend that they are very strong.

There is shame in admitting that anything is wrong. [Such women] they will not even talk to their parents. She feels that they will be stigmatised that their daughter is not happy and she thinks 'Why trouble my parents?'.

If children are having drug and alcohol problems. It is shameful. Or if there is an unwanted pregnancy. It's a matter of family prestige, and the woman might attempt suicide . . . Men impose upon the wife not to acknowledge or address such problems, do not talk, deny. It is not a question of educated or uneducated. The rules are almost the same for the educated and uneducated.

[Mentioned as a direct cause of suicide] Unmarried mothers and pregnancies. An Asian girl is condemned for her whole life. The whole community will outcast her. They will go for an abortion quietly. There is no parental support and all this stigma is there.

Linked to the stigma described above, there can be *cultural expectations of women to contain their thoughts*. Women should not speak out within the family or about the family. If the expectation is present in the family that the woman should not question her situation, then questioning can be unhelpful or can even place her in a worse situation:

Women are more worried about stigma. Cannot discuss with anyone. Cannot speak out. You are brainwashed by your parents. Those values are still there. Parents say 'You must obey your husband and in-laws.

A girl was married to a cousin of hers. He hit her and would go out and sleep around. When she tried to explain to her parents, her mother said 'He is a man'. They did not want to know. They were worried about what people will say.

This is common – We do not openly speak about whatever we feel, whatever we go through.

Keep quiet and listen to everyone.

It's when she has no power of saying, and the burden of the work. This creates a feeling of insecurity – 'What am I living for?'

In my view, in the majority of the families, when women are living in joint families and the husband's family has more hold on decision-making, and she has no say, then there is attempted suicide.

The wife is not supposed to ask [the husband] 'What have you done?' If she asks [him], then she is beaten up. We sit in the cell. The cell becomes very big and you commit suicide.

### *Theme: Limited options for leaving a distressing situation – 'No way out'*

Based on comments by focus group participants, the options for many Asian women to change or leave a distressing situation are highly limited. Having limited or no options can itself be a direct contributor to suicide attempts. The main social dilemma referred to by women was of having no perceived options to staying in a bad marriage. She might not be able to leave due to lack of money, having small children, lack of support by her parents, having nowhere else to go, social stigma, identity being linked to the husband, or lack of knowledge of how to live independently:

> When women do not want to take divorce, they can attempt suicide. Especially when the woman is in a vulnerable position – a housewife, with no financial independence. You feel your role is through your husband, to a large extent. And you are more vulnerable when you have children.
>
> Our life is full of hypocrisy. The parents always say 'Go back to your husband'.
>
> There is the stigma of divorce. There is that you do not know the system – 'Where will I go?' she wonders.
>
> If a British girl is chucked out of the house, she knows where to go. She will stay a bit longer, but there is a limit. Ultimately she will draw the line. Going back to Indian girls [from or living in India], there is no line. The girl's parents lay down the rules. There is no option for girls. They will say 'That was your decision' [to leave your husband]. So doors are closed for her.
>
> Asians reject a single [divorced] woman. She is not respected.

## Distal contributors and contexts for suicide attempts by Asian women

Very briefly, the following themes arose in focus groups as contextual stressors for Asian women, which can form distal, background contributors to more direct causes of suicide attempts:

1. Asian women carry the burden of exemplifying the ideals of Asian culture, of keeping Asian culture pure and 'present' for the family.
2. Asian women are the 'bearers of blame' for family problems.
3. Husbands and in-laws may expect her to be highly educated and to earn a good income, but also to act like a traditional Asian woman. Distress can arise when she is expected to fulfil dual roles without dual benefits to her:

    > An asylum-seeker came and we married here. It was not a good match. I did not know he was already married in Pakistan . . . I was educated here. But after marriage, I was expected to behave in the same manner as a wife from Pakistan or India. There are many cases of attempted suicide [relating to situations like this], where women harm themselves. If they got support, things would be better.

4. She is not appreciated and is not valued by the family.

The husband was considered key in setting the standard for his wife's treatment in the family. It was assumed that if the husband gave her his respect and support, good treatment by her in-laws and children would follow. If he mistreated or demeaned her, so would all others.

## Perceived role of depression

Depression was infrequently mentioned as a proximal cause of suicide attempts, and only as an outcome of social problems. The emphasis of women in the focus groups was much more on the importance of social stressors and social support in suicidality in Asian women. Mental distress was always implied as a consequence of the social problems. Depressed mood, when it was occasionally mentioned, was always a result of a social problem, with the clear expectation that if the social problem were solved, suicidality would also be resolved.

## Solution and prevention of suicidality – support for Asian women

> There are many cases of attempted suicide, women harming themselves. If they got support, things would be better.

No focus group participant mentioned the medical or psychiatric treatment of depression as a solution or prevention for suicide attempts in Asian women. Rather, in keeping with their knowledge of suicidality as a consequence of social and familial problems, they emphasised the need for support for Asian women who feel isolated and trapped. Support seemed to be thought of as providing Asian women with outlets for talking about their situations and distress, and perhaps the possibility of examining options with someone who provides moral support and validation of the woman.

## Differences between different subgroups of Asian women in the focus groups

### *Age*

Young and older participants overall agreed on the variety of contributors to suicide attempts, but their emphasis was somewhat different. Young Asian women, the group at highest risk for suicide attempts, often mentioned conflict with parents as a factor. Intergenerational conflict was frequently due to culturally based differences in expectations between generations. Disagreements often centred on choice of marriage partner, the degree of independence of children from parents in decision making, and cultural aspects of life style. Forced marriage by a father in face of a daughter's preferred, mixed-race relationship was mentioned as a direct cause of suicide attempts in young women. In addition to mentioning risk factors shared with young, white, British women, e.g. love relationship problems and career pressure, they also noted the stress of living between two religions or cultures as a factor.

Some older women complained about problems with daughter-in-laws and young women, which often related to intergenerational cultural differences and dissatisfaction with how younger women fulfilled family roles and duties, e.g. frustration with a younger female relative who 'won't cook'. Two interrelated factors were considered by focus groups to place older women at risk of attempted suicide. One factor related to the general theme of Asian women being bearers of blame. For older women, this was considered to occur when older children do not turn out well and the mother bears the blame for this within the family and community. The second factor relates to a general theme that a risk factor for an Asian woman is when she receives little respect from her husband, with children learning by example not to respect her either. Focus groups described older women considering suicide as a cumulative effect of being unappreciated and attributed low family worth by husbands and children.

### *Religion*

Focus group participants did not describe any relationship between suicide and religion. There were no differences between Muslim, Sikh, and Hindu women in what they considered to be causes of suicide attempts or in the frequency with which these causes were mentioned. However, there were differences in how women related to their religions in considering issues that arose in focus group discussions.

In contrast to Hindu women, Muslim and Sikh women almost always referred to religion in the course of their focus group discussions. This could have been due to some selection bias because all the Sikh women were recruited from gurudwaras, where they congregate to reflect upon the religious teachings of the guru. However, even in comparison to Hindu women recruited from Hindu temples, there were still relatively more allusions to religion. Muslim and Sikh participants seemed to make more conscious and direct connections to their religion when considering matters at hand. For example, when talking about counsellors, they often said that counsellors should be sensitive towards religion, not passing judgement on religion, e.g. 'Asian, even white counsellors are needed, but they should be sensitive to religion.' Sikh participants recruited from gurudwaras sometimes suggested religion as a solution to coping with stressors which could lead to suicide:

You should take the name of God.

You should devote more time to religious thought.

Whenever you have distress, you should come to the gurudwara.

There is no use going to the counsellor. You should go to the gurudwara.

In regard to study recruitment, the researcher found that Muslim women responded most quickly to focus group recruitment and were particularly eager to participate in both the focus groups and in the pre-pilot testing of the educational pamphlet. She found it more difficult to recruit Hindu and Sikh women. The project link worker was not Muslim herself, so recruiter–recruit matching would not explain this finding. Any number of other explanations are possible: an especially high level of concern or awareness of the problem of depression and suicide for Asian women; eagerness for a forum for expressing their opinions; a strong desire to comment on the situations faced by Asian women; or sample bias. Except for the possible explanation of sample bias, the high level of interest of these Muslim women in participating in this study bodes well for future studies examining Muslim Asian women's concerns.

## PHASE 2: DEVELOPMENT OF THE EDUCATIONAL PAMPHLET

1. The pamphlet was developed based on three sources of information:
   - the study focus groups with Asian women living in the community on causes of attempted suicide
   - ethnography and participant observation in the London Asian community over previous years
   - findings from a previous study of British Asian women who had attempted suicide (Bhugra et al., 1999a).
2. The pamphlet was pre-pilot-tested by the researcher with focus group members to get preliminary feedback. Research team members also provided feedback. A series of revisions were made of pamphlet prior to its final pilot form.
3. A directory of sources of help in the Ealing area was compiled for incorporation into the pamphlet.
4. Contents of the educational pamphlet: it began with an introduction to the problem of suicide attempts in Asian women and its relevance to all Asian families. It was addressed to Asian women who might be at risk and also to Asian families in general. Information was provided on:

- recognising suicide risk factors
- how to prevent suicidality in family members and the importance of family support
- recognising depression
- effective treatments for depression
- how to cope with feeling overwhelmed
- where to go and whom to talk to about feeling depressed or suicidal
- local sources of help.

The section on suicide risk factors included the main familial and sociocultural risk factors that had been described in the Asian women focus groups. A copy of the pilot test educational pamphlet is included in AppendixII; translations are available.

5. The educational material was designed as a pamphlet which fits onto a two-sided piece of A4 paper which can be easily and cheaply photocopied and disseminated. Single copies can therefore be distributed, to a wide variety of surgeries, charities, and individuals at low cost. The recipients can then reproduce the number of pamphlets they need at low cost to themselves.
6. Due to limited funds, the pamphlet for this study was produced in English and three other Indian languages – Hindi, Urdu, and Gujarati. Copies of these were sent to community mental health centres and selected GP surgeries in Southall.

## PHASE 3: PILOT TEST INTERVENTION WITH EDUCATIONAL PAMPHLET

### Goals

- To test the effect of the pamphlet on attitudes toward help seeking for depression and suicidality.
- To test the effect of the pamphlet on increasing awareness of risk factors and resources for depression and suicide in Asian women.
- To get systematic feedback on whether the pamphlet was considered acceptable and useful for Asian communities.
- To field test the feasibility of using the pamphlet in the UK Asian community.
- To familiarise key staff at participating GP surgeries, Asian community organisations and at the local Accident and Emergency (A&E) department with the pamphlet and its directory of local services.

## Methods for pilot testing the educational pamphlet

### *Subject recruitment*

- Asian community organisations and GP surgeries with large South Asian patient populations in the London area were contacted by the researcher and asked to allow recruitment of subjects from their sites. The goals and nature of the study were explained.
- A convenience sample was drawn from South Asians aged 15 to 75 years attending participating GP surgeries or on registers with participating Asian community organisations. Recruitment from GP surgeries took place in waiting rooms for general patient surgeries, mother and well baby clinics, and antenatal clinics.
- The pamphlet and study questionnaires used in pilot testing were in English. This decision was made for two reasons. First, we placed a priority on pilot testing the pamphlet in the group of Asians known to be at highest risk for suicide and attempted suicide – younger Asian women. Younger UK Asians are most likely to be comfortable with written English rather than with written South Asian languages. Second, an adequate sample size was needed to obtain meaningful pilot test results, which could not be obtained with multiple, small samples divided by different languages. A result of this decision was that subject recruitment was limited to Asians who were literate in English.
- GP surgeries and some of the community organisations preferred to have their own staff distribute the study questionnaire packets to possible participants rather than allowing the link worker to distribute them.
- In the case of GP surgeries, it was usually a nurse who distributed the questionnaire packet. For most of the community organisations, the researcher was able to recruit subjects and distribute the questionnaire packets directly.
- For this study, recruitment by participating site staff rather than our link worker had the disadvantages of no assurance of equality in distribution of the pamphlet or in recruitment of subjects, and inadequate data from which to determine accurate refusal rates or characteristics of refusals. However, accepting this requirement of some participant sites respected their right to control access to their clients, to protect the confidentiality of their clients, and to retain autonomy, and was considered to allow adequate conditions under which to pilot test the pamphlet within the aims of this study.
- At GP surgery sites, surgery staff gave potential participants a stamped, self-addressed envelope with each questionnaire packet so that they could return the form directly to the study after completion.

At community organisations, the link worker was given access to contact information for individuals on organisation registers. The link worker then contacted individuals at listed households by phone to explain the study. Those who agreed were sent a questionnaire packet by post along with a stamped, self-addressed envelope for the completed questionnaires to be returned to the study.

- Based on contact information given in returned questionnaire packets, the link worker sent follow-up questionnaires 4 to 6 weeks later by post. A stamped, self-addressed envelope was included for returning the follow-up questionnaire to the study.
- Those subjects who did not return the follow-up questionnaire by post were contacted by phone by the link worker, reminded, and offered the option of completing the follow-up by phone.

### *The study questionnaire packet and follow-up questionnaire*

Questionnaires and the pilot pamphlet were in English and answered by self-report. Data collection using the study questionnaire packet was done over a 6-week period. The questionnaire packet generally took 30 to 40 minutes to complete and consisted of four parts:

1. A written *consent form* describing the study and its aims which participants signed to document their consent. The consent form made it clear that their choice of whether to participate would be confidential and would affect their care in no way.
2. A *baseline questionnaire* which was answered prior to reading the educational pamphlet. It began with questions about contact information, demographic characteristics, and identity. It then continued with questions which were later duplicated in the post-pamphlet questionnaire and the follow-up questionnaire: likeliness to get involved if someone were depressed or suicidal; recognition of depression and suicidality in others; knowing of ways to help others with depression or suicidality; relative suicide rates of white and Asian British women; what can help a person with depression; causes of suicide attempts in Asian women; and if the subject were to have depression or suicidal thoughts herself the likelihood that she would tell listed potential confidants.

   Except in the case of a few open-ended questions, respondents selected their answers from a limited list of possibilities. The questionnaire was modified and derived in large part from the 'Depression Knowledge Questionnaire' (Bhugra et al., 1997b) which was pilot tested in London Asians and itself derived from the longer MORI questionnaire on depression (Maddox, Levi, & Thompson, 1994; Priest, Vize, Roberts, & Tylee, 1996).

3. The educational *pilot pamphlet* (included in the Appendix II).
4. The *post-pamphlet questionnaire* which was answered immediately after reading the pamphlet. It repeated baseline questions on self-report attitudes and had three added questions on whether she or he liked the pamphlet, whether it was useful for the community, and an open-ended question asking for suggestions to improve the pamphlet.

The *follow-up questionnaire* was administered four to six weeks after the participant had completed the initial questionnaire packet. It repeated questions asked in the baseline and post-questionnaires in order to test retention of pamphlet information and the pamphlet's longer term impact on attitudes.

### *Analysis*

For questions regarding attitude, opinion, or anticipated behaviour, answer choices were on a scale of 1 to 4. Depending on the question, choices were either 'Strongly agree', 'Agree', 'Disagree', and 'Strongly Disagree' or 'Very Likely', 'Likely', 'Unlikely', and 'Very Unlikely'.

For the purpose of analysing results with clearer clinical relevance, the four possible responses were recategorised as either positive or negative: 'Likely' vs. 'Unlikely' and 'Agree' vs. 'Disagree'. In cases where age was recategorised into 'age categories', these categories were '20 years or less', '21–30', '31–40', '41–50', '51–60' and 'over 60'.

Intercooled Stata 5.0 software was used for statistical analysis. Two-tailed significance tests were used. The $\chi^2$ test was used for independent, categorical variables. McNemar's $\chi^2$ test was used for matched, paired, categorical variables, e.g. when comparing how a subject answered a question before and then after reading the pamphlet. The Student's *t* test was used for continuous, dichotomous variables that met requirements for parametric tests. For continuous, dichotomous variables with nonparametric distributions, the Mann–Whitney U test (Wilcoxon rank sum test) was used. Analysis of multiple, continuous variables used one-way ANOVA when requirements for parametric tests were met. The Kruskal-Wallis test was used to analyse medians of multiple, continuous variables with nonparametric distributions. All confidence intervals for results are for 95%. Backwards, stepwise logistic regression was used to determine whether factors were independently associated with the outcome of interest.

## Results of educational pamphlet intervention

### *Participation*

Nine GP surgeries and 24 community organisations agreed to participate in the study as sites for subject recruitment. A total of 350 study questionnaire packets were distributed by the researcher to participating sites at GP surgeries and through community organisations in the London area. Of these, 300 were given to potential participants in the study and 50 were returned unused. Of this total of 300 packets received by potential study subjects, 182 questionnaire packets were returned completed. Although this gives an estimated minimum refusal rate of 39%, some potential participants declined to accept the questionnaire packet in the first place and these individuals were not recorded. Of the 182 packets, 85 (47%) were completed through GP surgeries and 97 (53%) through community organisations. Reasons for not accepting study questionnaire packets or not returning questionnaire packets included: not reading English; losing the form; unfamiliarity with reasons and methods of research studies; fear of getting into a problem by getting involved; desire not to reveal contact information for the follow-up; feeling the topic was not relevant because of no problems with depression or suicidality; lack of time due to work and family; fear that information would reach social services or governmental agencies.

Only two questionnaire packets had been completed by men and so were dropped from the analysis. This resulted in a final convenience sample of 180 South Asian women participating in the study. The extremely low number of Asian men participating in the study was due to a combination of factors. Far fewer Asian men attended the daytime hours of participating GP surgeries due to their work schedules. At GP surgeries and over the phone when recruitment was done from community organisation listings, the vast majority of Asian men who were contacted declined participation in the study.

This seemed to be because men considered the topic of health in Asian women as lacking relevance to themselves, and perhaps also that men have no role in Asian women's health matters. In addition to this segregation of interests, an element of segregation of the sexes in communication had an effect. Asian men tended to direct the female researcher to their female household members rather than talk to her themselves. It may be that a male researcher is needed in order to engage Asian men in discussing their role in the health of families and women. There may have been another factor in that participating site staff might not have offered as many men the opportunity to participate because of their own sense that the topic of Asian women's depression and suicidality did not pertain to Asian men.

### *Demographic characteristics*

Demographic characteristics of the participants are shown in Table 13.1. The mean age was 35 years old, with an age range of 15 to 75 years. Ethnicity and immigration history showed statistically significant associations with median age. Women who were Bangladeshi and Pakistani were younger. Younger age, which is a risk factor for suicide attempts Bhugra et al., 1999a,

Table 13.1
Demographic characteristics (total $n = 180$)

| | *N (%)* | *Mean age* (SD)* | *p value for age difference between subcategories** |
|---|---|---|---|
| *Age* | | 35 (13.2) (range 15 to 75) | |
| *Years lived in UK* | | | 0.0001† |
| ≤ 5 | 32 (18%) | 27 (7.5) | |
| 6–15 | 26 (14%) | 34 (8.2) | |
| >15 | 74 (41%) | 45 (11.5) | |
| whole life | 48 (27%) | 26 (9.6) | |
| *Highest education* | | | 0.21‡ |
| Primary school | 2 (1%) | 58 (24.7) | |
| Junior school | 11 (6%) | 36 (11.6) | |
| Secondary school | 42 (23%) | 36 (11.9) | |
| Vocational school | 15 (8%) | 31 (15.1) | |
| University | 97 (54%) | 35 (13.3) | |
| Other | 13 (7%) | 35 (12.1) | |
| *Self-designated ethnicity* | | | 0.002† |
| Asian | 39 (22%) | 36 (13.6) | |
| Indian | 94 (52%) | 37 (13.2) | |
| Pakistani | 20 (11%) | 29 (9.0) | |
| Bangladeshi | 5 (3%) | 22 (3.0) | |
| British–Asian | 15 (8%) | 32 (15.6) | |
| British | 0 | | |
| Other | 7 (4%) | 43 (9.1) | |
| *Nationality* | | | 0.79‡ |
| British | 108 (60%) | 36 (14.1) | |
| Indian | 59 (33%) | 35 (12.2) | |
| Pakistani | 6 (3%) | 30 (9.5) | |
| Other | 7 (4%) | 34 (8.1) | |
| *Religion* | | | 0.21‡ |
| Hindu | 99 (55%) | 36 (13.0) | |
| Muslim | 47 (26%) | 33 (13.9) | |
| Christian | 6 (3%) | 30 (10.0) | |
| Other | 26 (14%) | 37 (12.7) | |
| None | 2 (1%) | 49 (8.5) | |

* For the 171 subjects who answered the age item.
† Using the Kruskal-Wallis test.
‡ Using one-way ANOVA.

1999b; Neeleman, Jones, Van, & Murray, 1996) and completed suicide (Neeleman, Mak, & Wessely, 1997) in Asian women, was also found in the newly immigrated and native-born groups in this sample. Long-term immigrants were older.

When the ethnicity category of 'Other' was excluded, ethnicity was associated with immigration status, 'Indian' forming the largest ethnic group in all immigrant categories (Pearson $\chi^2$ (12) = 29.53; $p$ = .003). When calculated for the four immigration categories, there were no statistically significant differences regarding education categories. However, when education was recategorised as 'less than secondary school' vs. 'secondary school or more', a statistically significant association between immigration and education developed (Pearson $\chi^2(3) = 7.97$; $p = .047$). Of new immigrants, 100% had at least a secondary school education vs. 96% of '6–15 years' and of 'whole life', and 86% of 'over 15 years'. The finding of more new immigrants having higher education in this study is not surprising because the English language questionnaire created a selection bias for more highly educated new immigrants. This indicates that translation of the pamphlet into South Asian languages is necessary to make it useful for new immigrants and long-term Asian residents who have less education and low English literacy. Such translations have now been done.

Regarding occupation, the largest groups were 'housewife' (24%), 'clerical' (23%), 'student' (15%), and 'professional' (12%). Additional categories were 'retired', 'unemployed', 'manager', 'own business', 'teacher', 'labourer', and 'creative arts', which ranged from 0.6% to 8% of women.

### *Demographic differences between GP surgery and community organisation subsamples*

Women from GP surgeries were younger (mean age of 33 years vs. 37 years; *t* test: two-tailed *p* of the difference = 0.047; CI 0.06 to 7.9). They also had lower education levels than those from community organisations. More women from GP surgeries had their highest education level at secondary school level (35% vs. 13%; Pearson $\chi^2(1) = 11.6$; $p = .001$) and fewer had a university degree (35% vs. 70%; Pearson $\chi^2(1) = 22.26$; $p < .001$). Occupation differed in that the community sample had more teachers (8% vs. 0%; Pearson $\chi^2(1) = 7.16$; $p = .007$). GP surgeries had fewer with self-identified ethnicity of 'Indian' (39% vs. 64%, Pearson $\chi^2(1) = 11.53$; $p = .001$) and more self-identified as 'Pakistani' (18% vs. 5%; Pearson $\chi^2(1) = 7.56$; $p = .006$). Nationality in the GP sample was less often 'Indian' (22% vs. 42%; Pearson $\chi^2(1) = 8.6$; $p = .003$) and more often 'Pakistani' (7% vs. 0%; Pearson $\chi^2(1) = 7.25$; $p = .007$). Immigration status differed in that the GP sample had fewer who had lived in the UK '5 years or less' (11% vs. 24%; Pearson $\chi^2(1) = 5.07$; $p = .024$) and more who have lived in Britain their whole life (35% vs. 20%; Pearson

$\chi^2(1) = 5.39$; $p = .02$). The GP sample had fewer Hindus (42% vs. 66%, Pearson $\chi^2(1) = 10.25$; $p = .001$) and more Muslims (41% vs. 13%, Pearson $\chi^2(1) = 17.61$; $p = <.001$).

### *Follow-up*

Of the 180 women who completed the initial questionnaire packet, 160 completed the follow-up questionnaire 4 to 6 weeks later and 20 (11%) refused or were lost to follow-up. Of follow-ups, 98 (61%) were returned by post and 62 (39%) were completed over the phone. Administration of the follow-up questionnaire by phone allowed the link worker to gather additional comments about issues raised by questions, which are included in reports of findings below.

Women who did and who did not follow up were compared. Univariate analysis indicated that of the group lost to follow-up more were Bangladeshis (10% vs. 1.9%; Pearson $\chi^2(1) = 4.35$; $p <.05$) and more had lived in Britain their whole life (45% vs. 24%; Pearson $\chi^2(1) = 3.87$; $p <.05$). There were no statistically significant differences in any other demographic factors, in willingness to get involved if someone else were depressed or suicidal, in beliefs about useful interventions for depression, in willingness to tell others if depressed or suicidal themselves, or in their attitude toward liking the pamphlet and believing it useful for the community. Chi-squared testing indicated no differences in willingness to tell potential confidants if they were depressed or suicidal, either at baseline or immediately after reading the pamphlet.

When multivariate analysis was done using backward, stepwise logistic regression to examine for independent effects of demographic characteristics and sample site (GP surgery vs. community organisation) there were no differences between the two groups and the effects of ethnicity and immigration history were lost. Of the women who did not follow up, 100% reported that they 'like this pamphlet' and think that 'this pamphlet is useful for increasing awareness in the community', with no difference on these two questions compared with women who did follow-up.

## Causes of suicide attempts in Asian women: Baseline opinions in the pilot survey

Table 13.2 describes the proportions of women who 'strongly agreed', 'agreed', 'disagreed', or 'strongly disagreed', with each possible cause of suicide attempts in Asian women. The top three factors that women agreed are causes of suicide attempts by Asian women were 'Violence by the husband' (92%), 'Being trapped in an unhappy family situation' (90%), and 'Depression' (90%). Of the 92% of women who agreed that 'Violence by

Table 13.2
Asian women's baseline opinions about causes of suicide attempts
(Possible causes are listed in the same order as in the questionnaire. Numbers are the percentage of women who chose that answer. $n = 180$)

| *In your opinion, are these causes of suicide attempts in Asian women?* | *Strongly agree* | *Agree* | *Disagree* | *Strongly disagree* | *Cumulative agreement* |
|---|---|---|---|---|---|
| Marital problems | 34 | 53 | 10 | 3 | 87 |
| Violence by the husband | 40 | 52 | 6 | 2 | 92 |
| Family conflict or pressure | 33 | 54 | 11 | 2 | 87 |
| Trapped in an unhappy family situation | 37 | 53 | 8 | 2 | 90 |
| In-law problems | 31 | 50 | 16 | 3 | 81 |
| Depression | 37 | 53 | 7 | 3 | 90 |
| Fear of shame, rejection, or loss of reputation in society | 28 | 54 | 14 | 3 | 82 |
| Break-ups or losses in relationships | 23 | 55 | 19 | 3 | 78 |
| Abuse by other family members | 29 | 51 | 15 | 4 | 80 |
| Problems with the children | 10 | 41 | 36 | 13 | 51 |

the husband' is a factor, 40% chose 'Strongly Agree'. This was the largest proportion at baseline to 'Strongly Agree' with any item being a factor in suicide attempts by Asian women.

The list of potential causes of suicide attempts that we offered in the questionnaire was largely based on our findings from the Asian women focus groups. The high proportions of women in the pilot survey who agreed with the listed potential factors suggest that the findings from the study's focus groups did represent opinions of the wider Asian women community. A notable exception is that 90% of women agreed that 'depression' is a factor in Asian women suicide attempts when offered the item in the questionnaire. But depression was rarely mentioned as a factor in suicide attempts within the focus groups, where women focused instead on describing social factors.

### *Demographic factors and beliefs about causes of suicide*

Backward, stepwise logistic regression was done to examine for independent effects of demographic factors on baseline opinions about causes of suicide attempts. Demographic factors checked were age, occupation, education (recategorised as less than secondary school vs. secondary school or more), ethnicity, nationality, years lived in UK, religion, and sample site (GP surgery vs. community organisation). Results of Pearson $\chi^2$ tabulation and testing are reported in some cases to aid in the interpretation of belief patterns associated with demographic factors. Demographic factors had no effect on agreement with 'violence by husband', 'depression', or 'problems with the children' as causes of suicide attempts.

A statistically significant finding using backwards, stepwise logistic regression was that 'Years lived in the UK' was associated with agreement with 'Family conflict or pressure' ($p = .03$) and 'Abuse by other (nonspouse) family members' ($p = .03$) as perceived causes of suicide attempts by Asian women.

New immigrants tended to have the lowest agreement with family causes, and those living in the UK '6–15 years' or their 'whole life' tended to agree most with family factors causing suicide attempts. The proportions who agreed with 'Family conflict or pressure' in the four categories of 'Years lived in the UK' were 75% of '5 years or less' ($n = 32$), 96% of '6–15 years' ($n = 26$), 86% of 'over 15 years' ($n = 74$), and 94% of 'whole life' ($n = 48$) (Pearson $\chi^2(3) = 8.28$; $p = .041$). Proportions who agreed with 'Abuse by family members' as a cause in the four categories of 'Years lived in the UK' were 66% of '5 years or less', 88% of '6–15 years', 78% of 'over 15 years', and 90% of 'whole life' (Pearson $\chi^2(3) = 8.31$; $p = .04$).

Younger age was associated with higher agreement with 'Trapped in an unhappy family situation' as a cause of suicide attempts ($p = .014$). When age categories were examined, agreement ranged from 100% in those aged 20 or younger, 93–94% in aged 20–40, 84% in age 41–50, and 71–75% in those age 51 and higher.

Higher education was associated with greater agreement with 'Marital problems' as a perceived cause of suicide attempts in Asian women ($p = .019$). A total of 62% with less than a secondary school education vs. 89% of those with secondary school or more agreed with this cause (Pearson $\chi^2(1) = 7.66$; $p = .006$). Higher education was also associated with greater agreement with 'in-law problems' ($p = .02$). A total of 54% with less than a secondary school education vs. 83% of those with secondary school or more agreed with this cause (Pearson $\chi^2(1) = 6.80$; $p = .009$). The fact that higher education was correlated with greater agreement that marital and in-law conflict cause suicide attempts might be related to the situation described in focus groups of husbands and in-laws wanting Asian wives to be educated yet to remain within traditional roles.

Women sampled from GP surgeries were more likely than those from community organisations to agree that 'Fear of shame, rejection, or loss of reputation in society' is a cause of suicide attempts (89% vs. 76%, respectively; Pearson $\chi^2(1) = 5.07$; $p = .024$).

Agreement with 'Break-ups or losses in relationships' as a perceived cause of suicide attempts was associated with 'Years lived in the UK' ($p = .001$) and nationality ($p = .007$). New immigrants agreed least often with this cause (66%), and those living in the UK their 'whole life' agreed most (90%). By nationality, British nationals had the lowest agreement (75%) and Pakistani nationals the highest (100%).

The finding of this study that young Asian women who are lifelong UK residents strongly believe that suicide attempts are caused by 'Family conflict or pressure' and 'Abuse by family members' correlates with Bhugra et al.'s (1999a) suggestion, based on interviews with Asian suicide attempters, that family conflict contributes to suicide attempts, particularly in young Asian women who experience cultural conflict and identity flux between traditional Asian and western cultures. Being 'Trapped in an unhappy family situation' was also considered a very important factor by younger Asian subjects, further reinforcing the importance of family context for suicide attempts in young Asian women.

## Effect of pamphlet on knowledge and willingness to intervene in depression and suicidality

Table 13.3 shows subjects' baseline, post-pamphlet and follow-up responses regarding: willingness to get involved in others' depression or suicidality; self-assessed ability to recognise depression or suicidality; knowledge of resources for help; and knowledge about relative suicide attempt rates for white and Asian women.

### *Willingness to get involved if someone else seemed depressed or suicidal*

At baseline, 20% of women would not get involved. Reading the pamphlet was associated with a transitory, immediate decrease to 12% in the proportion of women who would not get involved. However, at follow-up 4 to 6 weeks later the proportion of women willing to get involved was indistinguishable from baseline, indicating that the pamphlet had no long-lasting effect in this area. Comments made to the researcher during phone follow-ups indicated that women would only get involved with very close friends or close family members who might be depressed. They would not get involved with distant relatives or acquaintances.

Backward, stepwise logistic regression indicated that there was no independent effect of age, years in the UK, ethnicity, nationality, religion, or education on willingness to get involved if someone else is depressed or suicidal. Sample site was independently associated with likelihood to get involved in that women from GP surgeries were twice as likely not to get involved than women from the community sample (67% vs. 33%; Pearson $\chi^2(1) = 7.65$; $p = .006$).

### *Recognition of depression and suicidality and knowing ways to help*

Both immediately after reading the pamphlet and 4 to 6 weeks later, there was an increase in the proportion of women who self-assessed that they could recognise depression or suicidal thoughts in others (9% increase at follow-up

Table 13.3
Comparison of respondent views before reading pamphlet, immediately after, and at follow-up 4–6 weeks later

| | *Baseline vs. immediately after pamphlet* | | | | | *Baseline vs. at 4–6 weeks follow-up* | | | |
|---|---|---|---|---|---|---|---|---|---|
| | *n* | *Baseline* | *After* | *Difference* (95% CI)* | *p value†* | *n* | *Follow-up* | *Difference* (95% CI)* | *p value†* |
| If you thought someone you knew might be depressed or suicidal, you would not get involved. | 180 | 20 | 32 | 12 (4 to 21) | <.01 | 160 | 18 | –2 (–10 to 7) | .62 |
| You would be able to recognise if someone you knew had depression or suicidal thoughts. | 180 | 77 | 90 | 13 (6 to 20) | <.001 | 160 | 84 | 9 (0 to 17) | <.05 |
| If someone you knew were depressed or suicidal, you know of ways to help him or her. | 179 | 72 | 93 | 22 (14 to 29) | <.001 | 159 | 91 | 19 (11 to 28) | <.001 |
| In Britain, a white woman is more likely to attempt suicide that an Asian woman. | 172 | 31 | 24 | –6 (–14 to 1) | .08 | 153 | 16 | –14 (–23 to –5) | <.01 |

* Proportions and their differences are rounded. Differences for 'Baseline vs. follow-up' are based only on subjects who completed both baseline and follow-up questions.
† P values are analysed using McNemar's test for paired, categorical data.

from baseline; CI 0–17; $p < .05$). There was also a substantial improvement the proportion that believed they knew of ways to help (19% increase at follow-up from baseline; CI 11–28; $p < .001$).

In the analysis of demographic variables associated with these two topics, univariate, chi-squared analysis initially suggested that immigration background was associated with 'knowing ways to help', with the highest proportion knowing of ways to help in new immigrants who had lived in the UK five years or less (94% of $n = 32$). However, backward stepwise logistic regression showed that this effect was actually due to an association between higher education ($p = .011$), with immigration a confounder in that new immigrants had higher levels of education (Pearson $\chi^2(3) = 7.97$; $p = .047$). There was no difference between GP and community samples regarding baseline opinions on self-assessed ability to recognise if someone has depression or suicidal thoughts or knowing ways to help.

### *Beliefs about relative rates of attempted suicide*

At baseline, 31% of Asian women agreed with the statement 'In Britain, a white woman is more likely to attempt suicide than an Asian woman'. When they read the pamphlet, it included the information 'In Britain, Asian women attempt suicide much more than any other group'. At follow-up 4 to 6 weeks later, the proportion that agreed incorrectly with the survey question had decreased by 14% (CI of difference –23 to –5, $p < .01$).

Backward stepwise logistic regression showed that the incorrect belief that white women are more likely to attempt suicide was associated with more recent immigration and lower education, and with no independent effects from other demographic variables or sample site. The more recent the immigration, the higher the proportion who agreed incorrectly with the statement: 50% of those living in the UK '5 years or less' ($n = 30$); 33% of '6–15 years' ($n = 24$); 30% of 'over 15 years' ($n = 73$); and of 17% 'whole life' ($n = 46$) (Pearson $\chi^2(3) = 9.18$; $p = .027$).

## What can help depression? Baseline opinions and effect of pamphlet

Table 13.4 describes the results of the effect of the pamphlet on baseline opinions of Asian women of factors that can help a person with depression. These findings have been reported in part in the paper 'Help-seeking Attitudes toward Depression and Suicidality in UK South Asian Women: Effects of an Educational Pamphlet' (Bhugra & Hicks, forthcoming).

At baseline, the largest proportion of Asian women agreed that counselling can help a person with depression (91%), followed by family involvement (86%), decreasing problems causing stress (85%), antidepressants (51%), and

**Table 13.4**

**What can help depression? Baseline opinions and effect of pamphlet**

(Proportions of women who agree that the factor is helpful for depression before reading the pamphlet, immediately after, and at follow-up 4–6 weeks later. Factors are listed in the same order as in the questionnaire)

| | *Baseline vs. immediately after pamphlet (n = 180)* | | | | *Baseline vs. at 4–6 weeks follow-up (n = 160)* | | |
|---|---|---|---|---|---|---|---|
| *In your opinion, can these factors help a person with depression?* | *Baseline* | *After* | *Difference* (95% CI)* | *p value†* | *Follow-up* | *Difference* (95% CI)* | *p value†* |
| Family involvement | 86 | 96 | 10 (4 to 16) | <.001 | 93 | 8 (0 to 15) | <.05 |
| Having the person deal with it alone | 23 | 22 | –1 (–8 to 6) | .72 | 16 | –8 (–16 to 0) | <.05 |
| Counselling‡ | 91 | 96 | 4 (0 to 9) | <.05 | 96 | 4 (–1 to 9) | .08 |
| Antidepressant tablets | 51 | 67 | 17 (9 to 24) | <.001 | 66 | 15 (6 to 24) | <.001 |
| Decreasing the problems causing stress‡ | 85 | 92 | 6 (1 to 12) | <.05 | 90 | 4 (–3 to 12) | .24 |

* Proportions and their differences are rounded. Differences for 'Baseline vs. follow-up' are based only on subjects who completed both baseline and follow-up questions.
† *p* values are analysed using McNemar's test for paired, categorical data.
‡ *n* for this item is one less: $n = 179$ for Baseline vs. immediately after; and $n = 159$ for Follow-up.

dealing with it alone (23%). After reading the pamphlet which suggested that all the first four methods listed above are effective solutions for depression, belief in the efficacy of 'counselling', 'family involvement', and 'decreasing problems' remained high. During follow-up interviews done over the phone, subjects often pointed out to the researcher that 'family involvement' would be helpful only in situations where family members were not the source of the problem. Subjects noted that if the woman's depression or suicidality were due to her husband or in-laws, the most frequently mentioned culprits, their involvement would only make her condition worse.

Baseline agreement with the utility of antidepressants was relatively low at 51%. After reading the pamphlet, the proportion of women agreeing with the use of 'antidepressant tablets' increased by 17% (CI of difference 9 to 24; $p < .001$), an increase which was sustained at follow-up 4 to 6 weeks later (15% higher than baseline; CI of difference 6 to 24; $p < .001$). Comments were often made to the link worker during follow-up phone interviews at this point, mostly to the effect that antidepressants cannot solve the woman's problem, but can help somewhat. It was also felt that antidepressants can help for only a short period and that ultimately benevolent involvement by trustworthy family members was the solution.

### *Demographic factors and beliefs about what can help depression*

Backward stepwise logistic regression indicated that there were no independent effects from age, nationality, ethnicity, religion, years lived in the UK, education, occupation, or sample site on whether 'Family involvement', 'Dealing with it alone', 'Counselling' or 'Decreasing the problems causing stress' can be helpful for depression. There was no statistically significant difference in beliefs between the women who did and did not participate in the follow-up 4 to 6 weeks later.

Regarding baseline belief in the efficacy of antidepressants, backward, stepwise logistic regression indicated no independent effects from age, nationality, ethnicity, religion, or sample site. There were independent effects from immigration ($p = .002$), education ($p = .024$), and occupation ($p = .02$). Having less belief in the efficacy of antidepressants was associated with higher education, fewer years lived in the UK, and certain occupations such as being unemployed, the owner of a business, or in the creative arts. In these occupational groups 20 to 25% believed antidepressants were helpful, as opposed to 73% of professionals.

Baseline agreement with antidepressants was lowest in newest immigrants and highest in those who had lived in the UK 'over 15 years' (60%). Only 25% of women who lived in the UK for '5 years or less' ($n = 32$) thought that antidepressants were helpful (Pearson $\chi^2(3) = 14.08$; $p = .003$). For these new immigrants, reading the pamphlet increased agreement with antidepressants by 28% (95% CI of difference = 7 to 49; McNemar's $\chi^2(1) = 7.36$; $p < .01$). Due to lower numbers at follow-up, statistical significance faded but still showed a strong trend in the same direction ($n = 29$; increase of 21%; 95% CI of difference = –3 to 44; McNemar's $\chi^2(1) = 3.60$; $p = .058$).

With regard to the effect of education, 77% of the 13 women with less than a secondary school education vs. 49% of the 167 women with a secondary school education or more believed at baseline that antidepressants were helpful (Pearson $\chi^2(1) = 3.89$; $p = .048$). The proportion of the more educated women who agreed with antidepressants increased by 16% immediately after the pamphlet (95% CI of difference = 8 to 24; McNemar's $\chi^2(1) = 16.20$; $p = .0001$). This was retained at follow-up (95% CI of difference = 7 to 25; McNemar's $\chi^2(1) = 12.52$; $p < .001$).

## Help seeking for depression and suicidality: Effects of pamphlet

The pilot pamphlet was found to have a strong and positive impact on help-seeking attitudes for depression and suicidality in the study sample. These findings have been reported (Bhugra & Hicks, 2004).

Table 13.5 describes the effect of the pamphlet on help-seeking attitudes. At baseline, immediately after reading the pamphlet and at the 4- to 6-week follow-up, subjects were presented with a list of potential confidants and asked about the likelihood that they would tell them 'if you had depression or suicidal thoughts yourself'. Respondents could choose multiple potential confidants except in the case that they chose 'no one'.

At baseline, prior to intervention with the educational pamphlet, the highest proportion of Asian women were 'likely' to tell a 'friend' (84%), 'spouse' (74%), 'GP' (67%), or 'counsellor' (64%), if they had depression or suicidal thoughts. In descending order of frequency, the proportions 'likely' to tell other potential confidants at baseline were: 'relative' (58%); 'psychiatrist' (56%); 'Helpline, e.g. Samaritans' (49%); 'nurse or health visitor' (49%); 'social worker' (48%); 'religious leader' (21%); 'no one' (21%). Immediately after reading the pamphlet there were statistically significant increases in the proportions willing to tell all types of confidant except 'helpline', 'relative', or 'religious leader'. The proportion likely to tell 'no one' decreased from 21% to 12% (CI of difference –16 to –2; $p$ of difference = <.01).

The improvement in help-seeking attitudes after reading the pamphlet remained present at follow-up 4 to 6 weeks later. Only 8% would still tell 'no one' if they had depression or suicidal thoughts (decrease of 13%; 95% CI of difference –21 to –6; $p$ = <.001). At follow-up, increases remained statistically significant in the proportions of women 'likely' to tell a 'GP'

Table 13.5

**Effect of pamphlet on Asian women's help-seeking attitudes for depression and suicidality**

(Proportions 'likely' to tell the potential confidant 'if you had depression or suicidal thoughts yourself' before reading the pamphlet, immediately after, and at follow-up 4–6 weeks later. Baseline proportions reflect attitudes present before any intervention)

| | *Baseline vs. immediately after pamphlet (n = 180)* | | | | *Baseline vs. at 4–6 weeks follow-up (n = 160)* | | |
|---|---|---|---|---|---|---|---|
| *Potential confidant* | *Baseline* | *After* | *Difference* (95% CI)* | *p value†* | *Follow-up* | *Difference* (95% CI)* | *p value†* |
| GP | 67 | 82 | 15 (9 to 21) | <.001 | 79 | 14 (5 to 22) | <.001 |
| Counsellor | 64 | 83 | 19 (12 to 26) | <.001 | 78 | 13 (4 to 22) | <.01 |
| Psychiatrist‡ | 56 | 73 | 17 (10 to 24) | <.001 | 72 | 16 (6 to 25) | <.001 |
| Nurse or health visitor‡ | 49 | 64 | 15 (7 to 23) | <.001 | 55 | 7 (−2 to 16) | .10 |
| Social worker‡ | 48 | 60 | 12 (4 to 19) | .001 | 51 | 3 (−6 to 12) | .47 |
| Helpline, e.g. Samaritans‡ | 49 | 50 | 2 (−5 to 9) | .61 | 54 | 5 (−4 to 14) | .25 |
| Friend | 84 | 90 | 6 (0 to 12) | <.05 | 94 | 10 (4 to 16) | <.01 |
| Spouse | 74 | 82 | 8 (2 to 13) | <.01 | 86 | 12 (5 to 19) | <.001 |
| Relative | 58 | 63 | 5 (−2 to 12) | .13 | 68 | 11 (1 to 20) | <.05 |
| Religious leader‡ | 21 | 22 | 1 (−5 to 7) | .68 | 21 | 2 (−7 to 10) | .63 |
| No one‡ | 21 | 12 | −9 (−16 to −2) | <.01 | 8 | −13 (−21 to −6) | <.001 |

* Proportions and their differences are rounded. Differences for 'Baseline vs. follow-up' are based only on subjects who completed both baseline and follow-up questions.
† p values are analysed using McNemar's test for paired, categorical data.
‡ $n$ for this item is one less: $n = 179$ for Baseline vs. immediately after; and $n = 159$ for Follow-up.

(increase of 14%; CI 5 to 22; $p < .001$), 'counsellor' (increase of 13%; CI 4 to 22; $p < .01$), 'psychiatrist' (increase of 16%; CI 6 to 25; $p < .001$), 'friend' (increase of 10%; CI 4 to 16; $p < .01$), 'spouse' (increase of 12%; CI 5 to 19; $p < .001$) and 'relative' (increase of 11%; CI 1 to 20; $p < .05$).

During follow-up phone interviews, subjects expanded on the difficulties of confiding in friends and family members. Women felt they would have to be quite selective not to confide in relatives who might exploit the situation. It was generally felt that relatives from the in-law's side were 'no good' as confidants, that relatives in general were likely to have 'a jealous feeling' and would tell others in society about the woman's problem. Women commented that only a sister or mother could be helpful to a depressed or suicidal woman. In comparing women who did ($n = 160$) and who did not ($n = 20$) participate in the follow-up questionnaire, there were no differences in willingness to tell potential confidants if they were depressed or suicidal, either at baseline or immediately after reading the pamphlet.

## Factors associated with baseline help-seeking attitudes

### *Confiding in a GP*

Backward stepwise logistic regression indicated that age ($p < .001$) and sample site (GP vs. community) ($p < .001$) were independent factors associated with whether a woman would tell a GP of depression or suicidality at baseline. The likelihood of telling a GP increased with age and with being sampled from a GP surgery. Of women in the age category of 20 or under ($n = 13$), 46% would tell their GP. The percentage steadily increased with age to reach over 80% in all categories age 41or older (Pearson $\chi^2(5) = 12.48$; $p = .03$). Although univariate testing had initially suggested a statistically significant association between years lived in the UK and baseline likelihood of telling a GP, this effect was lost when multivariate logistic regression controlled for the factors of age and sample site. The illusory effect of immigration was because newer immigrants were younger. Other factors with no effect were education, ethnicity, nationality, occupation, and religion.

### *Confiding in other health professionals*

Baseline likelihood of telling other professional confidants was checked with backward stepwise logistic regression to examine for independent effects of the demographic factors of age, religion, years lived in UK, education (defined as less than secondary school vs. secondary school or higher), ethnicity, nationality, occupation, and sample site. None of these factors were shown to have independent effects on whether an Asian woman would tell a counsellor, psychiatrist, or helpline of depressed or suicidal feelings.

Univariate testing suggested an association between ethnicity and the likelihood of telling a psychiatrist, with Bangladeshis having the lowest likelihood (20% of N = 5), British Asians having a likelihood of 73% ($n$ = 15), and 'Other' the highest likelihood of 100% ($n$ = 7). Statistical significance of the effect of ethnicity was lost when other demographic factors were incorporated using stepwise logistic regression ($p$ = .14), although an effect could become statistically significant in a larger sample.

Baseline willingness to confide in 'a nurse or health visitor' was associated with religion ($p$ = .03) and education ($p$ = .04) using backward stepwise logistic regression. Women with less than a secondary school education were more likely to confide in a nurse than women who attained secondary school or higher (77% vs. 47%; Pearson $\chi^2(1) = 4.32$; $p = .04$). Of Muslim women, 64% ($n$ = 47) vs. 39% of Hindu women ($n$ = 98) would tell a nurse or health visitor (Pearson $\chi^2(1) = 8.01$; $p = .005$).

Education was independently associated with the likelihood of telling a social worker, using stepwise logistic regression ($p$ = .034). Women with less than a secondary school education were more likely to tell a social worker than women with secondary school or higher (77% vs. 46%; Pearson $\chi^2(1) = 4.68$; $p = .03$).

### *Confiding in family and community members*

Demographic factors and sample site had no association with whether an Asian woman would tell a spouse, friend, relative, or 'no one' of depressed or suicidal feelings. In all ethnic and religious categories of Asian women, religious leaders were among those least likely to be confided in about depressed or suicidal thoughts. Stepwise logistic regression suggested that age ($p$ = .02) and education ($p$ = .01) were independently associated with the likelihood of confiding in a religious leader. Greater likelihood of telling a religious leader was associated with higher age and lower education.

## Primary care and community populations of Asian women – effects of educational pamphlet

Analysis was done on the effect of the pamphlet on women sampled from GP surgeries and on women sampled from community organisations. This was done to examine the potential usefulness of the educational pamphlet for primary care intervention in clinical Asian populations and for public health education in Asian community populations. Compared to women from community organisations, women from GP surgeries were younger (mean age of 33 years vs. 37 years; test: two-tailed $p$ of the difference = .047; CI 0.06 to 7.9) and had lower levels of education. GP surgeries also had fewer new immigrants and more lifelong residents, fewer ethnic Indians, more Pakistanis, fewer Hindus, and more Muslims.

The only statistically significant difference between the GP surgery and community organisation samples in their baseline willingness to tell different types of potential confidants was that women from GP surgeries were more likely to tell a GP of depressive or suicidal thoughts (82% vs. 55%; $\chi^2 = 15.12$; $p \leq 0.001$). The high baseline level of willingness to disclose symptoms to GPs in the surgery sample was not a transient effect of filling out the questionnaire within the immediate environment of the surgery, as was shown by the persistence of this high level (84%) in the follow-up done from home 4 to 6 weeks later. Tables 13.6 and 13.7 show the immediate and residual effects of reading the pamphlet on baseline help-seeking attitudes in GP surgery and community organisation samples of Asian women.

### *Effect of pamphlet on Asian women from GP surgeries*

At baseline, women sampled from GP surgeries were most likely to tell a friend (88%) or their GP (82%) if they had depression or suicidal thoughts. There were sustained increases in the proportions of women likely to confide in a counsellor, psychiatrist, and spouse 4 to 6 weeks after reading the pamphlet, with the greatest increase of 19% for psychiatrists. The baseline proportion of 22% of women likely to tell 'no one' of their depression or suicidality decreased substantially after reading the pamphlet and remained low at 6% 4 to 6 weeks later.

### *Effect of pamphlet on Asian women from the community*

At baseline, only 55% of Asian women sampled through community organisations would tell their GP if they had depression or suicidal thoughts. Immediately after reading the pamphlet, 22% more women reported that they would confide in their GP, an increase that was sustained 4 to 6 weeks later. At follow-up, increases were sustained in the proportions of women likely to confide in psychiatrists, nurses or health visitors, and friends. At baseline, 21% of Asian women in the community were likely to tell 'no one' if they were depressed or suicidal, with a trend to decrease immediately after reading the pamphlet to 16%, and to 10% at 4 to 6 weeks, although not reaching statistical significance in this sample size.

**Table 13.6**

**Effect of pamphlet on help-seeking attitudes of women from GP surgeries**

(Proportions 'likely' to tell the potential confidant 'if you had depression or suicidal thoughts yourself' before reading the pamphlet, immediately after, and at follow-up 4–6 weeks later)

| | *Baseline vs. immediately after pamphlet* | | | | *Baseline vs. 4–6 weeks follow-up* | | |
|---|---|---|---|---|---|---|---|
| *GP surgery group* | *Total n = 83* | | | | *Follow-up n = 70* | | |
| *Potential confidant* | *Baseline* | *After* | *Difference* (95% CI)* | *p value†* | *Follow-up* | *Difference* (95% CI)* | *p value†* |
| GP | 82 | 89 | 7 (0 to 14) | <.05 | 84 | 3 (−9 to 15) | .59 |
| Counsellor | 66 | 87 | 20 (9 to 32) | <.001 | 83 | 17 (2 to 32) | <.05 |
| Psychiatrist‡ | 59 | 79 | 21 (10 to 31) | <.001 | 77 | 19 (5 to 33) | <.01 |
| Nurse or health visitor‡ | 55 | 71 | 16 (3 to 29) | <.01 | 52 | −1 (−15 to 12) | .82 |
| Social worker‡ | 48 | 63 | 16 (4 to 28) | <.01 | 51 | 4 (−11 to 19) | .53 |
| Helpline, e.g. Samaritans‡ | 49 | 51 | 2 (−9 to 14) | .64 | 55 | 6 (−9 to 20) | .39 |
| Friend | 88 | 94 | 6 (−3 to 15) | .13 | 93 | 6 (−4 to 15) | .16 |
| Spouse | 71 | 81 | 10 (1 to 19) | <.05 | 86 | 17 (5 to 29) | <.01 |
| Relative | 60 | 69 | 8 (−3 to 20) | .13 | 71 | 11 (−3 to 26) | .09 |
| Religious leader‡ | 24 | 27 | 2 (−6 to 11) | .53 | 23 | 0 (−15 to 15) | 1.00 |
| No one‡ | 22 | 7 | −15 (−25 to −4) | <.01 | 6 | −19 (−30 to −7) | <.001 |

* Proportions and their differences are rounded. Differences for 'Baseline vs. follow-up' are based only on subjects who completed both baseline and follow-up questions.

† p values are analysed using McNemar's test for paired, categorical data.

‡ *n* for this item in the GP sample is one less: $n = 82$ for Baseline vs. immediately after; and $n = 69$ for Follow-up.

**Table 13.7**

**Effect of pamphlet on help-seeking attitudes of women from community organisations**

(Proportions 'likely' to tell the potential confidant 'if you had depression or suicidal thoughts yourself' before reading the pamphlet, immediately after, and at follow-up 4–6 weeks later)

| | *Baseline vs. immediately after pamphlet* | | | | *Baseline vs. 4–6 weeks follow-up* | | |
|---|---|---|---|---|---|---|---|
| *Community organisation group* | *Total n = 97* | | | | *Follow-up n = 90* | | |
| *Potential confidant* | *Baseline* | *After* | *Difference* (95% CI)* | *p value†* | *Follow-up* | *Difference* (95% CI)* | *p value†* |
| GP | 55 | 76 | 22 (12 to 31) | <.001 | 76 | 22 (11 to 34) | <.001 |
| Counsellor | 63 | 80 | 18 (8 to 27) | <.001 | 73 | 10 (–2 to 22) | .08 |
| Psychiatrist | 55 | 68 | 13 (3 to 24) | <.01 | 69 | 13 (0 to 27) | <.05 |
| Nurse or health visitor | 44 | 58 | 13 (3 to 24) | <.01 | 58 | 13 (1 to 26) | <.05 |
| Social worker | 48 | 57 | 8 (–1 to 18) | .06 | 51 | 2 (–10 to 14) | .69 |
| Helpline, e.g. Samaritans | 48 | 49 | 1 (–8 to 10) | .81 | 53 | 4 (–9 to 17) | .45 |
| Friend | 81 | 87 | 5 (–4 to 14) | .20 | 94 | 13 (4 to 23) | <.01 |
| Spouse | 77 | 84 | 6 (–1 to 13) | .06 | 86 | 8 (–2 to 17) | .07 |
| Relative | 56 | 58 | 2 (–7 to 11) | .62 | 64 | 10 (–3 to 23) | .09 |
| Religious leader | 18 | 18 | 0 (–9 to 9) | 1.00 | 20 | 3 (–7 to 14) | .49 |
| No one | 21 | 16 | –4 (–14 to 5) | .32 | 10 | –9 (–19 to 1) | .06 |

* Proportions and their differences are rounded. Differences for 'Baseline vs. follow-up' are based only on subjects who completed both baseline and follow-up questions.

† *p* values are analysed using McNemar's test for paired, categorical data.

## Community education and feedback during study

While working with GPs, nurses, surgery staff, volunteer organisation staff, community leaders, and community members to recruit participants for focus groups and to pilot test the pamphlet intervention, the researcher familiarised these individuals with the pamphlet. During this process, she carried out informal teaching regarding the pamphlet's contents, including its directory of local resources for Asian women and families. As well as getting feedback on the acceptability and usefulness of the pamphlet, this functioned as a collegial training and dissemination of information to increase suicide risk awareness, recognition of risk factors, and knowledge on sources of help. In addition, both the researcher and Dr Bhugra met with the Ealing Hospital deliberate self-harm nurse to review the contents and use of the educational pamphlet.

The pamphlet was well received by professionals and paraprofessionals in the GP surgeries and community organisations, with feedback that it filled an important gap in Asian public health. Many facilities decided to make the pamphlet generally available to their clients. Translation and formatting of the pamphlet into multiple Asian languages was possible only for three South Asian languages within the financial constraints of this grant and was not fully justifiable until results of this pilot testing were known to establish the efficacy and acceptability of the pamphlet.

## Study limitations

Because the pamphlet was pilot tested only in English, this probably selected for more educated or acculturated women in the immigrant population, thus under-representing immigrant Asian women with less education and poorer English language skills. This may affect the generalisability of the findings. In addition, the sample size of this pilot study was relatively small and subject selection was non-random.

## Suggestions from study participants for improving pamphlet

As part of the pilot testing of the pamphlet, the 180 participants were asked the open-ended question 'Do you have any suggestions for improving the pamphlet?'. Most women left this question blank. Of those who responded, the majority commented positively and felt the pamphlet was satisfactory as it was written. The most frequent criticism or suggestion from women was that the pamphlet should be made available in multiple South Asian language translations. Some suggested wide distribution of the pamphlet at GP offices, to students, to men, at grocery shop check-outs, and 'to all Asian family households'.

### Modification of the pilot tested pamphlet based on study findings

Qualitative feedback during the process of pilot testing suggested that Asian men had no interest in reading the pamphlet because of the emphasis on 'Asian women' in the heading, considering this to be a signal that the subject matter would be outside their own interests. There was some suggestion that the pamphlet would likely be distributed only to Asian women by staff and paraprofessionals for the same reason.

Because community education on attitudes of all family members is important in identifying and preventing the risk of suicide in Asian women, we have subsequently modified the heading of the pamphlet from 'For All Asian Women & Asian Families' to 'For All Asian Families'. This modified version contains all the same information (see Appendix II).

## CONCLUSIONS

- Based on 10 focus groups with 43 Asian women, community opinions on main causes and contributors to suicide attempts in Asian women were gathered. These contributed to development of a pamphlet for depression and suicidality in Asian women, which was pilot tested in a convenience sample of 180 Asian women from GP surgeries and community organisations.
- Causes of suicide attempts: focus groups considered the primary causes of suicide attempts in Asian women to be isolation after immigration to the UK, in-law problems, marital problems, and dowry conflict. Analytic themes that emerged from discussions of suicide were 'being trapped', 'suicide is a distress in quietness', and 'no way out'. During pilot testing of the educational pamphlet, a survey of baseline opinions was done. The 180 women surveyed considered the top three causes of suicide attempts by Asian women to be 'Violence by the husband' (92%), 'Being trapped in an unhappy family situation' (90%), and 'Depression' (90%).
- Reading the pilot pamphlet resulted in marked improvement in help-seeking attitudes. In the baseline survey of help-seeking attitudes, over a fifth (21%) of Asian women were likely to tell 'no one' if they felt depressed or had suicidal thoughts. Reading the pamphlet was associated with an immediate reduction of this proportion to 12%, with a retained positive effect remaining at follow-up 4 to 6 weeks later in that only 8% would still tell 'no one' if they had depression or suicidal thoughts (decrease of 13%; CI –21 to –6; $p < 0.001$).
- Some 4 to 6 weeks after reading the pamphlet, Asian women showed sustained improvement in their willingness to report depression and

suicidality to a GP (increase of 14%; CI 5 to 22; $p < .001$), counsellor (increase of 13%; CI 4 to 22; $p < .01$), psychiatrist (increase of 16%; CI 6 to 25; $p < .001$), friend (increase of 10%; CI 4 to 16; $p < .01$), spouse (increase of 12%; CI 5 to 19; $p < .001$), and relative (increase of 11%; CI 1 to 20; $p < .05$). At baseline, 55% of Asian women sampled from nonclinical community sites were likely to tell their GP of depression or suicidality. This proportion increased by 22% after reading the pamphlet and was sustained at follow-up 4 to 6 weeks later (CI 11 to 34; $p < .001$).

- Potential role of the pamphlet in suicide prevention and Asian public health: quantitative and qualitative feedback on the pamphlet from study subjects, professionals, and Asian community members was strongly in favour of the appropriateness, acceptability, and feasibility of the pamphlet for use in the Asian community. It was felt to fill a gap in the health-care needs of Asian women.
- These findings suggest that the pamphlet could contribute to a reduction in suicide attempts by increasing access to social support, decreasing isolation, increasing communication with professionals for diagnosis and treatment of depression, and increasing access to professional support in addressing the social problems that contribute to suicide attempts. The findings of the study support the efficacy and feasibility of the pamphlet for use in both public health and primary care.
- Focus group participants reported that 'support' is the main way to prevent and address suicide attempts in Asian women, which they attributed primarily to social causes. Baseline reports on help seeking, gathered during pilot testing of the pamphlet, indicated that after telling a friend or spouse, depressed or suicidal women would be most likely to tell a GP or counsellor of such feelings. For women who are suicidal due to social isolation or marital mistreatment, GPs and counsellors might be the only source of help they would choose to access. These findings underline the importance of GPs as a resource for Asian women with depression and suicidality.
- Because of the limits on GP resources, it is essential that they have available a directory of local Asian charity organisations for counselling patients, and that such charities are adequately funded to provide support for women in their community. The pamphlet pilot tested in this study meets an important need by being a resource that GPs can give to patients which lists sources of counselling and advice. In addition, we have demonstrated that it significantly improves the willingness of women to seek help from both professional and social resources if they are depressed or suicidal.

## RECOMMENDATIONS

1. In judging whether the pamphlet should be translated into the major Asian languages of Britain's Asian population and made generally available, one chooses between three alternatives:
   - no translation or distribution of the pamphlet
   - translation and pilot testing of the pamphlet in Asian languages to establish their efficacy in these forms
   - proceeding to translate and distribute the pamphlet based on this pilot test.

   We recommend the last alternative, based on the strength of the study findings of positive impact on help-seeking attitudes, our estimate that the findings are highly likely to be replicated in pilot tests with non-English-speaking Asian women, and the strongly positive feedback from professionals and Asian women about the pamphlet which was accompanied by their urging that it be made available to address the current unmet needs of Asian women.
2. Translation and formatting of the modified pamphlet entitled 'For All Asian Families' into the major Asian languages used in the British population so that it can be used by the many Asian women and family members who do not read English. This study has carried this out for three South Asian languages.
3. Distribution of one copy of the modified pamphlet in each of its translated versions to all GP surgeries, temples, gurudwaras, and Asian voluntary organisations in the Ealing area, so that they can make their own photocopies. It should be suggested to recipient organisations that the pamphlet be made generally available in waiting areas, in order to maximise its usefulness as an educational and preventative tool.
4. Consider making the pamphlet available to other Health Trusts with large Asian populations so that they can use it as it is or modify it by substituting a directory of their local resources.

CHAPTER FOURTEEN

# Conclusions and the way forward

## CONCEPTUAL MODEL OF AETIOLOGICAL FACTORS

It is clear that the rates of attempted suicide among Asian adolescents are no different from their white counterparts (Goddard et al., 1996) but these rates increase dramatically once female adolescents reach the age of eighteen or nineteen. It is likely that this period is the most likely to be stressful because the individual might have either left home or be getting ready to do so, and will be individuating. Dusevic et al. (2002), working in Australia, developed a framework for suicide prevention across cultures. In it, they highlight the role of key stakeholders in trying to understand the role of immigration and acculturation. In setting up their priorities they aimed to survey key stakeholders by asking them about perceptions of immigrant suicides, experiences with immigrant suicide behaviour, service initiatives including suicide, policy, education packages, and their views on immigrant suicides and prevention. They found that a majority of respondents did agree that suicide was indeed a problem for migrant populations in Australia and that 70% of these populations had little or no awareness of initiatives to reduce rates of suicide, even though some of the key stakeholders themselves were working in the healthcare delivery field. Although the response rates were low it is clear that issues in Australia are not dissimilar to those in the UK.

The concept of self-identity and self-esteem is crucial in the development of the individual. Such factors can work as intermediate components when the individual is growing up, when identity formation and individuation become vital. One factor that might explain the higher-than-expected rates in young females is the fact that younger females might have left home and be studying independently at college or university.

The dynamics of deliberate self-harm consist of discharge of aggressive tendencies towards oneself or others. It is likely that the emotional crises that trigger suicide are usually those that provoke insecurity, weaken the person's self-image or threaten loneliness and reduced function in life (Figure 14.1).

Aggression against oneself or others, appeal, and ambivalence all contribute to suicidal gestures and to completed suicide. When studying suicide among black people in America, Hendin (1964b) felt that there was a narrow border between homicide and suicide. Inner feelings of rage, guilt, and punishment might be projected onto external factors and individuals by adolescents for whom rage and self-hatred are part of their cultural and racial experience. The individual's rejection of culture and family could contribute to a sense of rage, which might become internalised and lead to self-harm. Having observed that being black in America was a stressor, Hendin (1964b)

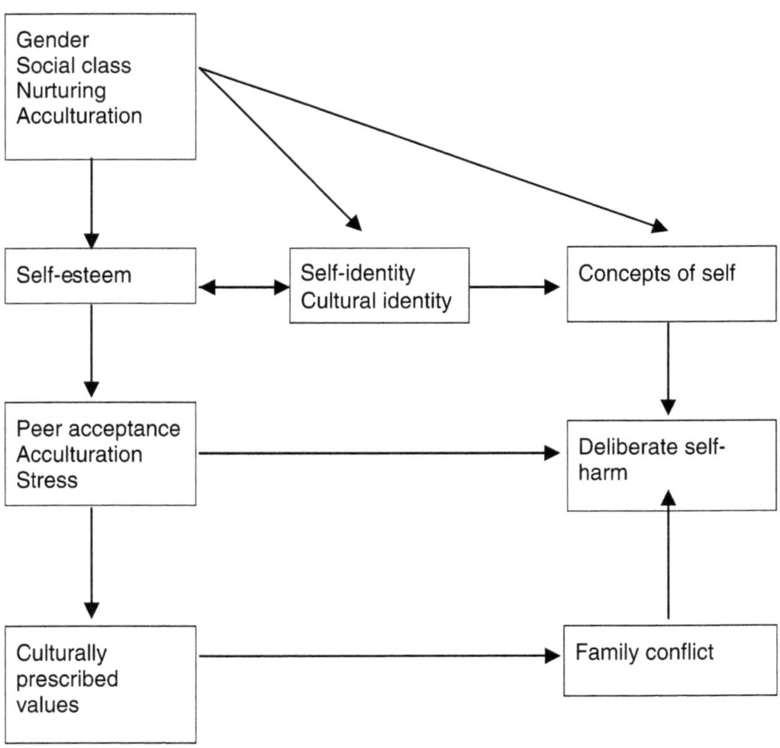


**Figure 14.1** Interrelation of factors in deliberate self-harm

noted that black people's concept of race related to self-hatred, and that violence contributed to anger and destruction.

The differences between adolescents at school and adolescents at college are noticeable. Delinquency and provocative and defiant behaviour towards parents are common in younger adolescents, although they might appear sociable to deal with their individuation, friendship, and social acceptance. However, Hendin (1982) argues that their social contracts might remain shallow and that they might be uneasy at the possibility of intimacy. Their rebellious behaviour could mask the fact that they are depressed and fear separation from their families, despite their underlying unhappiness with them.

The different rates of deliberate self-harm between Asian adolescents and Asian females can be attributed to common factors such as culture conflict, sexual or physical abuse, and stress in the family or at school. The rates in older Asian females are related to factors like being in an arranged marriage, having liberal attitudes, and having fewer religious beliefs. Thus any preventive strategy must take varying factors into account for different groups. Figure 14.2 shows the interaction of the factors that play a role in the process of deliberate self-harm. An awareness of these factors can highlight where preventive strategies need to be implemented.

Although deliberate self-harm can often be seen as a cry for help, Pritchard (1995) argues that this undermines the meaning of the behaviour. The repetition of such behaviour, seen in nearly one-quarter of our sample of young females (Bhugra et al., 1999b), has major implications for service development. Like in previous studies, this study found that females attempt suicide more often than males. There can be more than one possible explanation for this discrepancy. Gender role and gender role expectations are certainly important factors in explaining some of the high rates that are observed. The key characteristics of adolescents is that they respond to the immediate present with great intensity of delight or despair (Pritchard, 1995).

In their focus group consultations, Dusevic et al. (2002) found that the key stakeholders were clear about both vulnerability and protective factors for migrant groups. Among the protective factors they included family cohesiveness, support, religious beliefs, low alcohol use, employment, acceptance of hardship, and self-esteem. The risk factors included stigma in seeking help from outside the family, cultural and linguistic gaps, isolation, problem drinking, individualism, and marginalisation.

For migrant young people, the risk factors identified included cultural and language gaps, academic pressures, school bullying, drug abuse, and abuse. For older people, isolation and family problems were seen as the most common causes. Thus, social isolation and marginalisation and social support become important factors in a fight to reduce rates of attempted and completed suicide. Resilience can work at individual, school, and community levels and should be encouraged at all these levels.

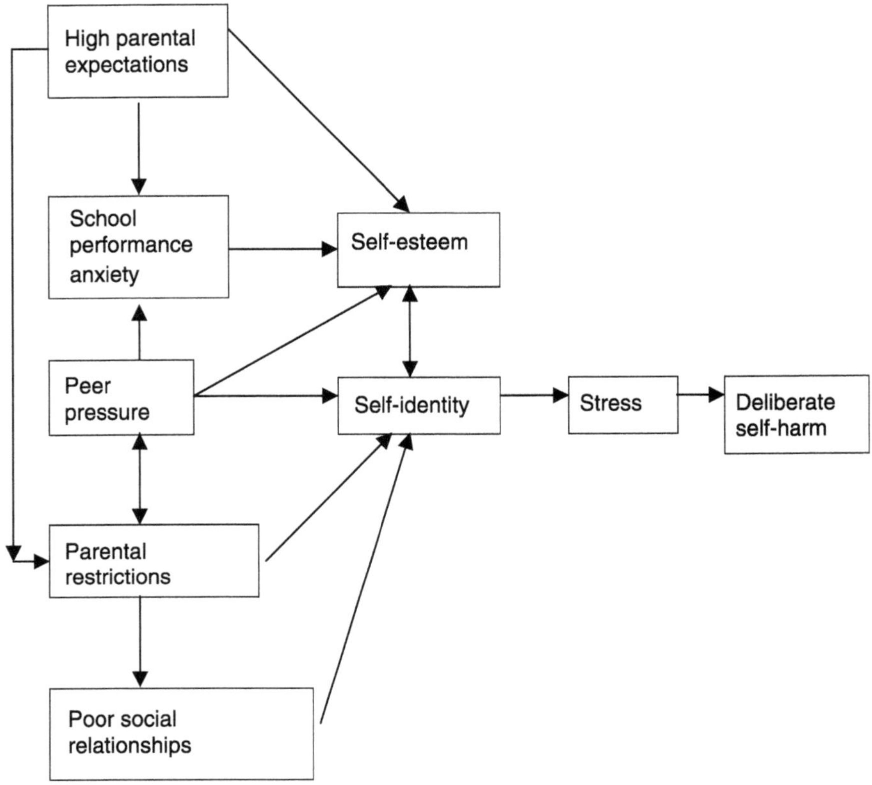


**Figure 14.2** Interrelation of school and parental pressures

## A NEW HYPOTHESIS

Ethnic groups might set themselves apart using superiority or inferiority on the basis of real or alleged physical characteristics, as well as the cultural physical criteria that set the group apart. Racial identity refers to a sense of group or collective identity based on one's perception that the individual shares a common racial heritage with a particular racial group. The racial group is one in which the person is seen as inside or outside a particular biological group. This differentiation is helpful but can also be criticised for helping to create stereotypes and overgeneralisations, thereby further compounding the complexity of the problem. The concepts of 'ethnic', 'racial', and 'cultural identities' are not often easily distinguishable. Acculturation and cultural identity have to be studied at both individual and group levels. In these series of studies we looked at individual identities but future studies need to evaluate group identities.

## Beliefs, explanatory models and cultural identity

Individuals' cultural beliefs go with them everywhere and influence not only their idioms of distress but how these idioms are then used to express symptoms and employ help-seeking patterns. For example, we found that among Punjabi women who had been in the UK for a number of years, some still believed that depression was not a medical condition (Bhugra et al., 1997b). The respondents not only recognised the symptoms of depression but were also able to identify various aetiological and perpetuating factors. However, their method of help seeking was related to their explanatory models and determined where and how they sought help. Their argument was that not only would going to a GP stigmatise them and their families, depression was a part of life's ups and downs and there was nothing that doctors could do.

A person's identity can thus defined as the totality of one's self, which is very strongly influenced by culture. Two points need to be emphasised here. First, racial, ethnic, and cultural identities form part of one's identity, and second, the development of identity and resulting changes due to acculturation will change the construction of identity. Gender, familial, and socioeconomic identities are also part of the identity. There is no doubt that these are linked with the concept of the self.

## National character

On a national/cultural level, national character might have a role to play – a factor that has been unduly ignored over the last decade or two. Inkeles (1997) sees nationalcharacter as a particular way of looking at the coherence of culturally defined values or behaviour patterns – referring to personality patterns that are common or standardised in a given society. It has been seen as a model personality structure – a great variety of individual personality structures.

National character needs to be studied on the basis of collective policies and products, rituals, child-rearing practices, institutional structures, folk lore, media, and mass communication – psychological analysis of which can contribute significantly to the overall psychological characterisation of society (Inkeles, 1997) National character might or might not be a direct influence on an individual. Social changes lead to changes in identity and possibly further diversification of personality types. The nature of the national character and the relationship with acculturation is worth studying. However, a further important point is that of Hofstede's descriptions of cultures (Hofstede, 1980, 1984)as individualistic and collectivist. Individualism refers to societies and cultures in which the ties between individuals are loose and individuals are expected to look after themselves and their immediate family, whereas collectivism refers to societies and cultures in which people from birth onwards are integrated into strong cohesive in-groups, which protect them throughout their lifetime in exchange for unquestioning loyalty. Hofstede (1984) suggests that individualistic societies emphasise 'I' consciousness – autonomy, emotional independence, individual initiative, right to privacy, pleasure seeking, financial security, need for specific friendship, and universalism. Collective societies stress 'we' consciousness – collective identity, emotional dependence, group solidarity, sharing, duties and obligations, need for stable and predetermined friendship, group decision making, and particularism. These two types of society or culture, are paralleled at the individual psychological level by idiocentrism and allocentrism, respectively (Triandis et al., 1985). Triandis et al. (1985) propose that two dimensions – family integrity and interdependence with sociability – are crucial for collectivism. They suggest that for individualism the dimensions are separation from in-groups and self-reliance with hedonism. For individualism, the key principles are regulation, rules, and laws; characteristics are individuation, self-fulfilment, uniqueness, autonomy, freedom of choice, and assertiveness. The three key principles for collectivism are roles, duties, and obligations; characteristics include self-cultivation, interdependence, nurturance, succorance, common fate and compliance (see Kim et al., 1994).

Individualistic societies support the basic tenets of liberalism whereas those of collectivist societies support traditionalism. The former assumes that individuals are rational and able to use reason to make personal choices and therefore they should be given individual rights to choose freely and to define their own goals. At interpersonal level they are seen as discreet, autonomous, self-sufficient, and respectful to the rights of others. From a societal point of view they are abstract and universal, and their status and role are defined by their achievement (e.g. occupational, economic, and educational status). Their interaction with others are based on equality, equity, non-interference, and detachability. Collectivist societies, therefore, prioritise common good and social harmony over individual interests. Individuals are bound by relationships that emphasise common fate. Individuals are encouraged to put the interests of other people and of the group before their own. Concession and compromise are essential ingredients in promoting role-based and virtue-based conceptions of justice, institutions are seen as an extension of the family, and paternalism and legal moralism reigns supreme.

Individuals in certain settings can behave in a collective fashion even if they are in individualistic societies, but the crux is that they are more often than not likely to behave like the society by which they were influenced.

Individualism has been shown to be related to high levels of gross national product (GNP; Hofstede 1980) but extreme individualism can lead to forms of social pathology such as high crime, suicide, divorce, child abuse, emotional stress, and physical and mental illness.

Allocentric persons tend to have happy marriages and are more likely to receive the social support that acts as a buffer against life-change stresses. Allocentric individuals define self in terms of in-group relationships and know more about others than themselves. In-group goals have primacy over personal goals and cognitions are context dependent. The attitudes of allocentric individuals reflect interdependence and their values are those of security, obedience, duty, in-group harmony, hierarchy, and personalised relationships. A major calamity for members of this group is ostracisation by others. Their social behaviours can make such individuals difficult to know but once relationships are established they become intimate.

Idiocentric individuals see individuals as basic unit of social perception. Self is defined as a separate identity and these individuals know more about their own self than about others. Self is less similar to friends than friends to self. They experience much cognitive dissonance and personal goals have primacy over in-group goals. Cognitions are context independent and they favour beliefs that reflect independence and emotional detachment from in-groups.

Thus it is likely that allocentric individuals from a collectivist society will face new types of stress if they migrate to an individualistic society and their social links are with idiocentric individuals. It has been argued that Idiocentric persons in collectivist cultures yield to group norms less than allocentric persons in individualistic cultures. Similarly, idiocentric individuals from a collectivist society who migrate to an individualistic society and meet idiocentric individuals will have different experiences (Figure 14.3). This interaction must be studied at both individual and cultural group levels. Theoretically, it would enable us to understand processes of and responses to migration, especially if national character is included in the equation. The

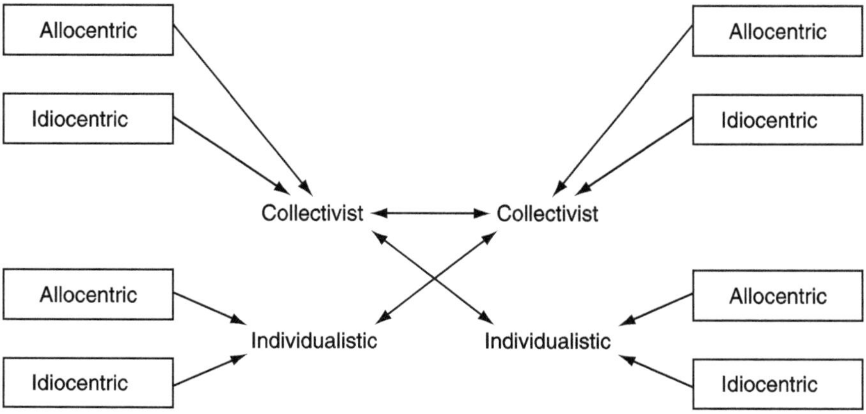


**Figure 14.3** Possible interactions at different levels

complex interaction, therefore, will provide a valuable insight into how different migrant groups and individuals respond to migratory stress, how their stress leads to mental illness, and how their identities are formed/changed to deal with it. In addition, such insights will help determine social support and sources of social network. The relationship between these individuals and their cultural group is of paramount interest.

## Ethnic diversity versus ethnic identity

The feelings of alienation and attempts to belong to one group can act as chronic, continuing difficulties, making vulnerable individuals more prone to psychosis (Figure 14.4).

Figure 14.4 illustrates how different components of the model can be measured and studied. There is no doubt that individualistic/collectivist or allocentric/Idiocentric constructs, although identified and portrayed as bipolar, are not necessarily so. My view is that cultures that are basically sociocentric but are then transplanted onto an individualistic culture will face problems, especially if individuals are egocentric. Hence Asian women who are individuating are more likely to be faced with this conflict, which places them in in a vulnerable position where self-harm becomes the only open option for expressing their distress. These ideas need to be studied further in ecological studies. The sociocentric self will therefore differ from the egocentric self in terms of responses to stress, as well as help seeking. Sociocentric individuals are likely to come from societies that are based on kinship and their social and individual identity is likely to be based on relationships with others. On the other hand, egocentric individuals and individualistic societies might well encourage individuals to have a more independent existence and more one-to-one relationships than family or kinship loyalties. Thus another layer of societal functioning is created.

Thus, when the clinicians talk of deliberate self-harm it is essential that they understand the concept of self in that particular individual and in the community or the group the individual comes from. This can be illustrated by the example of individuals deliberating harming the 'other' within their selves, so the act of deliberate self-harm might be targeted at their parents or extended family. After migration, the process of acculturation might well influence some layers illustrated in the Hsu (1985) model, but not other layers. Dusevic et al. (2002) argue that the degree of divergence between traditional and host cultural values and world view (i.e. the degree of cultural distance) will influence the amount and degree of stress and could lead to culture shock. This, in turn, might lead to acts of self-harm to find some relief and time out from the stressors. Suffice it to say here that there are four levels: (i) assimilation (complete adoption of the culture of the new society); (ii) integration (blending of elements of traditional culture with elements of the

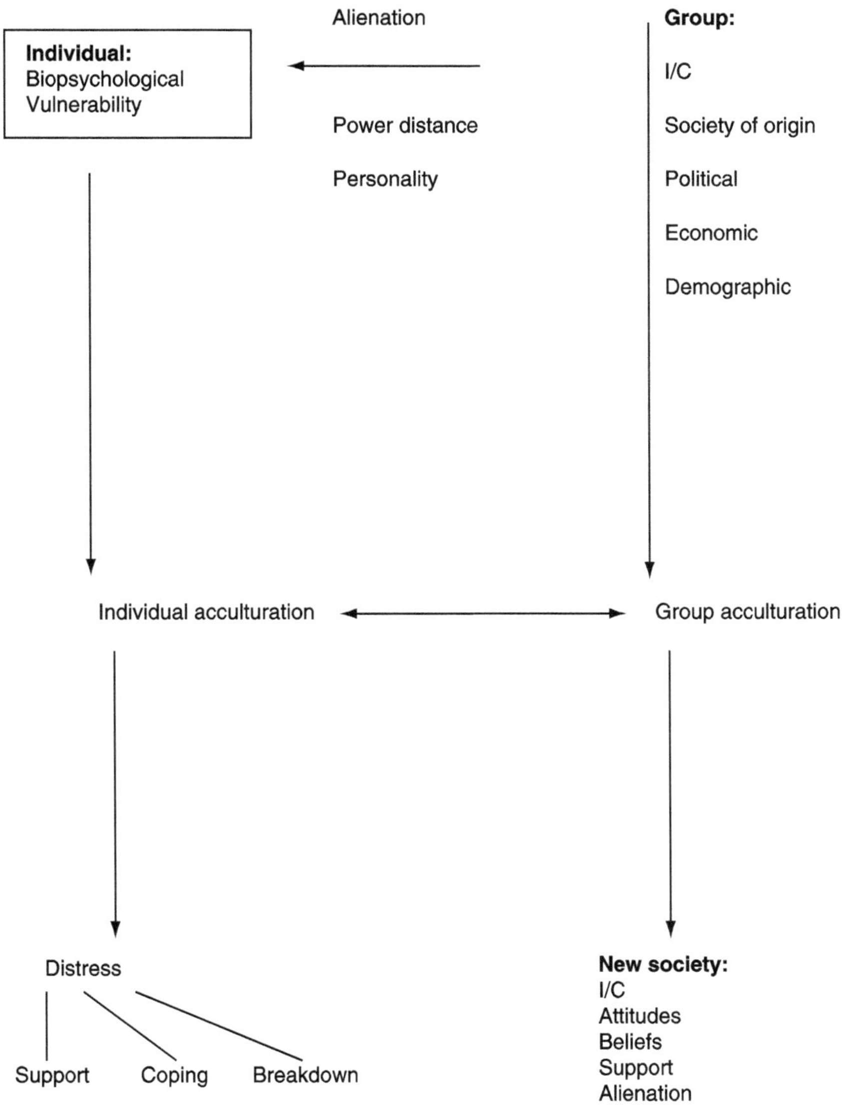


**Figure 14.4** Model of vulnerability

new society); (iii) separation (exclusive commitment to the culture of origin); and (iv) marginalisation (neither affiliation to the original culture nor to the new one).

Acculturation will be influenced by a number of factors, including cultural and geographical distance, ease of migration, languages spoken and commonality of language with the new culture, age, reasons for migration, educational and economic status, etc. An additional factor is the difference between achievement and expectation, and how first-generation of migrants respond to the process of migration and to the concepts of self inherited by their children, who might feel torn from the parental culture of origin but not assimilated/accepted by the new culture in which they were born.

## CONCLUSIONS

The independence and interdependence of migrants can be related to the societies or cultures they originate from. The type of society, national character, and individual and group acculturation all provide a link to the way an individual deals with stress, creates social networks or buffers, and survives. The theoretical implications for studying identity, beliefs and distress are many. Independence and formal education (both of which can be contributing factors) are culture-specific goals of development and are internalised in such a way that they travel with individuals into new societal contexts. The majority, dominant view consists of both assimilation and accommodation. Cultural adaptation must therefore be studied at both individual and group levels. The heterogeneity of the individuals and the societies they came from are useful indicators in trying to understand the impact of migration and development and changes in cultural identity. Cultural identity is fluid and is likely to be influenced by number of factors, which clinicians must bear in mind.

APPENDIX I

# The Asian Cultural Identity Schedule (ACIS)

## INTRODUCTION

This schedule was developed at the Institute of Psychiatry by Professor Bhugra. A generic version suitable for African/Caribbean and Asian populations was adapted specifically for each of these groups, making the questions more directly relevant. This is an 80-item questionnaire with closed questions, but also with opportunities for more verbatim responses and expansion of themes where appropriate and where the specific interview situation and population requires.

There is an introductory section seeking demographic information including self-identity and identity of the household members. There is a second section on religion and a third on language, followed by sections on marriage/family including some life style variables such as cooking preferences, shopping behaviours, child rearing preferences.

The schedule is at an early stage of development and all users are requested to register its use with Professor Dinesh Bhugra. It is recommended that reliability (test/re-test and inter-rater) are performed each time it is used and that each of the items and overall ratings are validated on each sample population using consensus groups from the relevant cultural and ethic background. This might be done on five or ten subjects with a view to classifying into those who fall into strongly identified with own culture group and strongly identified with host culture group. The theoretical background to the schedule is covered in a published article (Bhugra et al., 1999c). An early validation paper showed that discordance of identity across the main domains measured in this schedule was associated with deliberate self-harm in Asian women and also in children and adolescents. More specifically, adolescents who attempt deliberate self-harm showed as untraditional in their aspirations as compared to their parents and control group adolescents. The parents of control group adolescents were more traditional, reflecting the protective effect of traditionalism. Women who attempted deliberate self-harm showed less traditional attitudes to social conduct and aspirations than control women (Bhugra et al., 1999c).

We propose that the existing schedule is carefully scrutinised for face and content validity to the population of interest and that the terms are changed only where necessary following piloting. We recommend that William Berry's model of acculturation is taken account of in the scoring for the schedule (1980). This involves identifying those that are biculturally identified with both host and own culture; those that are identified with neither; and those that are strongly identified with one or other, but not both or neither. This produces four groups each with different vulnerabilities to the development of distress.

## CULTURE AND IDENTITY SCHEDULE

### INTRODUCTION

Interviewers should introduce themselves and describe the purpose of the interview. It should be emphasised that the respondent is not on trial and the purpose of the interview is not to assess the mental state of the respondent.

The objective is to gain insight into the extent to which Asians identify with the British cultural environment or retain, (re)create or adapt their own cultural signifiers. Interviews should aim to get some idea about the experiences and the attitudes of people of Asian origin or descent living in the cultural context of the United Kingdom and the level of comfort they feel in that culture.

The responses remain completely confidential and the respondents cannot be identified by their responses.

### Legend

### Instructions to interviewer/prompt questions

| **Centre/Project** | **Subject/Patient No:** | **Resp ID No:** | **Ethnic ID No.** | **Schedule/Card** |
|---|---|---|---|---|
| ☐☐ | ☐☐☐ | ☐ | ☐☐ | ☐☐ |
| **1 2** | **3 4 5** | **6** | **7 8** | **9 10** |

To begin with, I would like to get some background information:

1. How old are you now? ☐☐ **11–12**
2. (2a) Where were you born? **[13–15]**

   (2b) ***[If born abroad]*** How old were you when you came to this country?

   99 = Not applicable ☐☐ **16–17**

   ***CARD 1***

3. ***[If born here]***How old were your parents when they came to this country? ☐☐ **18–19**

   Probe of (3a) Father, (3b) Mother ☐☐ **20–21**

   99 = If either born here
4. If not born here, where are your parents from? **[22–25]**
5. Do you think of yourself as primary: ☐☐ **26–27**

1 = British

2 = Asian British

3 = Indian

4 = Pakistani

5 = Bangladeshi

6 = Sri Lankan

7 = Asian

8 = Other

6. What do you understand by the term black or black British **[31–35]**

7. Do the members of your household or your relatives think of themselves as primarily: ☐☐ **36–37**

1 = British

2 = Asian British

3 = Indian

4 = Pakistani

5 = Bangladeshi

6 = Sri Lankan

7 = Asian

8 = Other

8. Who does?

***CARD 1***

## RELIGION

9. What religion are you? ☐☐ **38–39**

   1. Catholic
   2. Church of England
   3. Methodist
   4. Muslim
   5. Hindu
   6. Sikh

7. Pentecostal
8. Rastafarian
9. Other (please specify) ______________________________
10. None

10. Have you changed your religion ☐ **40**

1 = Yes

2 = No

11. If yes, from what to what and why? **[41–45]**

12. Do you go to religious assembly?

***[This would include religious assembly at subject's or someone else's home]*** ☐ **46**

1 = Yes

0 = No

9 = Not applicable

***[If No, Cut off to Q16 – If Yes, Proceed]***

13. Over the last year how often have you attended? ☐ **47**

1 = Less than once a month

2 = At least once a month

3 = At least once a week

4 = Daily

9 = Not applicable

***CARD 1***

14. The last time you went to a religious assembly, the people attending were:

4 = Mostly Asian ☐ **48**

3 = Mostly white

2 = Equal Asian and white

1 = Other

15. The leader of the religious assembly you attend most is:

2 = Asian ☐ **49**

1 = White

8 = Other

9 = Not known/applicable

## LANGUAGE

16. Do you speak Hindi/Punjabi/Urdu or any other Asian language? ☐ **50**

1 = Never/rarely

2 = Sometimes

3 = Frequently

17. Where do you speak it? ☐ **51**

1 = Home

2 = Socialising

3 = Work

4 = All three
***[Score the highest number you are able to]***

18. Do you have difficulty understanding what white English people say? ☐ **52**

1 = Never/Rarely

2 = Sometimes

3 = Frequently

**[If score 2 or 3]**

19. Why is that? **[53–55]**

20. Do white English people have difficulty in understanding what you say? ☐ **56**

1 = Never/Rarely

2 = Sometimes

3 = Frequently

21. Why is that? **[57–60]**

22. Do you have difficulty understanding what Asian people say in your own language? ☐ **61**

1 = Never/Rarely

2 = Sometimes

3 = Frequently

23. Do Asian people have difficulty in understanding what you say when you speak in your own language?

1 = Never/Rarely ☐ **62**

2 = Sometimes

3 = Frequently

## MARRIAGE/FAMILY

24. Are you married/*or in a relationship?*

4 = Yes, married ☐ **63**

3 = Yes, in a relationship (e.g. cohabiting; visiting etc.)

2 = Not in a relationship/Not married

1 = Other
***[If married, Proceed] If not, go to Q29]***

25. How old were you when you got married? ☐☐ **64–65**

***26–28 not appropriate here (they are for African–Caribbeans)***

26. ☐ **66**

27. ☐ **67**

28. ☐ **68**

**[For All Respondents]**
29. What do you think is the best age to get married?

**[If the answer is never code 99]**

For men ☐☐ **69–70**

30. For a woman ☐☐ **71–72**

31. What is your view about arranged marriages? **[73–75]**

32. How would you describe arranged marriage? **[76–80]**

***CARD 2***

33. Do you think an arranged marriage is a good idea? ☐ **1**

2 = Yes

1 = No

34. Would you prefer your daughter/sister to have an arranged marriage?

2 = Yes ☐ **2**

1 = No

35. Would you prefer your son/brother to have an arranged marriage?

2 = Yes ☐ **3**

1 = No

36. Is it OK to live with a partner before you are married?

1 = Yes ☐ **4**

2 = No

37. Is it OK to have children with a partner before you are married?

1 = Yes ☐ **5**

2 = No

38. Have you ever had a (sexual/romantic) relationship (not friendship) with a white person?

1 = Yes ☐ **6**

2 = No

9 = Not applicable

39. Would you approve of your children or siblings ***[whichever appropriate]*** having a relationship with a white person?

1 = Yes ☐ **7**

2 = No

40. Would you (have you ever) consider(ed) marrying a white person?

1 = Yes ☐ **8**

2 = Don't know/depends

3 = No

41. Should children be mostly the responsibility of:

3 = Their father ☐ **9**

2 = Their mother

1 = Equally

9 = Don't know

42. If something happened to the parents [or if parents not available] who should look after the children? ***[Try to get a firm answer one way or the other]***

3 = Their father's family ☐ **10**

2 = Their mother's family

1 = Equally

9 = Don't know

***For those married [or in relationship] proceed:***

***[For those living with family, cut off to Q47]***
***[For those living alone, cut to Q51]***

43. In your home, who usually makes decisions about domestic matters, e.g. cooking/shopping, household chores?

1 = Self ☐ **11**

2 = Partner

3 = Equally

44. Decisions about family matters e.g. children ***[where applicable]. [Probe: children's schooling, visiting family, discipline].***

1 = Self ☐ **12**

2 = Partner

3 = Equally

45. Decisions about holidays?

1 = Self ☐ **13**

2 = Partner

3 = Equally

46. Decisions about large purchases [over £200?]

1 = Self ☐ **14**

2 = Partner

3 = Equally

***[For those living with parents/or extended family]***

***For the following questions, substitute father and mother with father-in-law and mother-in-law where appropriate]***

47. In your home who usually makes decisions about domestic matters? ***[e.g. cooking, shopping, domestic chores]***

    1 = Father and mother equally ☐ **15**

    2 = Self

    3 = Mother

    4 = Father

    5 = Other specify ......................................................

    9 = Don't know

48. Decisions about family matters?

    ***[Probe children's schooling, visiting family, discipline]***

    1 = Father and mother equally ☐ **16**

    2 = Self

    3 = Mother

    4 = Father

    5 = Other specify ......................................................

    9 = Don't know

***CARD 2***

49. Decisions about holidays?

    1 = Father and mother equally ☐ **17**

    2 = Self

    3 = Mother

    4 = Father

    5 = Other specify ......................................................

    9 = Don't know

50. Decisions about large purchases ***[e.g. more than £200]***

    1 = Father and mother equally ☐ **18**

    2 = Self

    3 = Mother

4 = Father

5 = Other specify ......................................................

9 = Don't know

***[For all respondents:]***

51. In a relationship/marriage who ought to make decisions about domestic matters? ***[cooking, shopping, domestic chores]***

1 = Equally ☐ **19**

2 = Partner

3 = Self

4 = Don't know

52. Decisions about family matters?

***[Probe children's schooling, visiting family, discipline]***

1 = Equally ☐ **20**

2 = Partner

3 = Self

4 = Don't know

53. Decisions about holidays?

1 = Equally ☐ **21**

2 = Partner

3 = Self

4 = Don't know

54. Large purchases (e.g. more than £200)

1 = Equally ☐ **22**

2 = Partner

3 = Self

4 = Don't know

55. Do you think that it is OK for a couple without children for the man to work and the woman to stay at home?

1 = No ☐ **23**

2 = Don't know/depends upon income/if that is the woman's decision

3 = Yes

57. For the woman to work and the man to stay at home?

1 = No ☐ **25**

2 = Don't know/depends upon income

3 = Yes

58. For a couple with children, do you think it is OK for the man and the woman to stay at home?

1 = No ☐ **26**

2 = Don't know/depends upon income

3 = Yes

59. For both the man and the woman to work?

1 = No ☐ **27**

2 = Don't know/depends upon income

3 = Yes

60. For the woman to work and the man to stay at home?

1 = No ☐ **28**

2 = Don't know/depends upon income

3 = Yes

***[The aim in the following question is to gain access to extreme positions]***

61. Would you say that children from Asian families living in Britain (in general) tend to:

***[Probe for various contexts such as at school, at home and towards authority]***

1 = Behave better than white children ☐ **29**

2 = No difference/depends upon the family

3 = Behave worse than white children

9 = No opinion

62. Explain why you feel this way:

    ***[e.g. Children born in the Indian sub-continent are more respectful whilst those born in the UK are more influenced by their peers etc.]*** ☐ **[30–33]**

63. Have you ever thought that schools which specifically emphasise ethnicity or culture in their curriculum are necessary for children of ethnic minorities?

    2 = Yes ☐ **34**

    1 = No

    9 = No opinion

64. Explain why? **[35–37]**

65. Would you like to see any elements of your culture ***[probe for language, music, religion, history etc.]*** included in the regular school curriculum?

    1 = No ☐ **38**

    2 = Yes

66. Why? **[39–40]**

67. Would you say that white parents generally tend to treat their children:

    1 = Too leniently ☐ **41**

    2 = About right

    3 = Too strictly

    9 = No opinion

68. Explain in what respect? **[42–45]**

69. Do Asian parents generally tend to treat their children:

    1 = Too strictly ☐ **46**

    2 = About right

    3 = Too leniently

    9 = No opinion

70. Explain in what respect? **[47–50]**

71. Do you have relatives in this country?

    2 = Yes ☐ **51**

1 = No

0 = Not asked
***[If Yes to above]***

72. Do you keep in contact with them?

1 = Never/Rarely ☐ **52**

2 = Sometimes

3 = Frequently

9 = Not applicable

73. ***[If the subject has children]*** Do any of your relatives help you with childcare?

2 = Yes ☐ **53**

1 = No

9 = Not applicable

74. ***[If Yes],*** who? **[54–55]**

***[For all respondents:]***

75. Do you help any of your relatives with childcare?

2 = Yes ☐ **56**

1 = No

9 = Not applicable

76. ***[If Yes],*** who? **[57–60]**

77. If you had any children, do you think your relatives would help you with childcare?

2 = Yes ☐ **61**

1 = No

9 = Not applicable

78. ***[If Yes],*** who? **[62–65]**

79. Do you have any relatives abroad?

2 = Yes ☐ **66**

1 = No
***[If No, go to Q83]***

80. Do you keep in contact with relatives abroad?

*[If Yes, ascertain the frequency]*

0 = No ☐ **67**

1 = Rarely (at least once a year)

2 = Sometimes (at least once a month)

3 = Frequently (at least once a week)

81. *[If Yes,]* how?

1 = Letter ☐ **68**

2 = Phone

3 = Both

4 = Other specify ................................................

82. Do you send money to relatives abroad?

1 = No ☐ **69**

2 = Yes

9 = Not applicable

## EMPLOYMENT AND HOUSING *CARD 2*

83. Are you employed at present?

1 = Yes ☐ **70**

2 = No

84. The people you work with (or worked with) are:

4 = Mostly Asian ☐ **71**

3 = Equally Asian and white

2 = Mostly white

1 = Other

85. If you had a choice would you work with people who are:

4 = Mostly Asian ☐ **72**

3 = Equally Asian and white

2 = Mostly white

1 = Not bothered

86. Do you find that working with Asian people is:

1 = Less pleasant than working with white people ☐ **73**

2 = No different

3 = More pleasant than working with white people

87. Why do you say that? **[74–75]**

88. Do you think that generally:

1 = Asian people work harder that white people ☐ **76**

2 = No different in the way in which people work

3 = white people work harder than Asian people
***[If the response is "that depends upon the kind of work", score 2]***

89. Do you live close to people of the same ethnic group as yourself?

2 = Yes ☐ **77**

1 = No

90. Would/does it matter to you if you lived/that you live in a neighborhood where there were few Asians?

2 = Yes ☐ **78**

1 = No

9 = Don't know

91. If No, why? **[79–80]**

## LEISURE

***CARD 3***

92. Do you have friends outside the family:

1 = Yes ☐ **1**

2 = No

93. ***[If Yes]***, are they:

4 = Mostly Asian ☐ **2**

3 = Equally Asian and white

2 = Mostly white

1 = Others

94. Do you spend most of your leisure time:

1 = By yourself ☐ **3**

2 = With your friends

3 = With your family

4 = Other

9 = Don't have spare time

95. Do you read Hindi/Punjabi/Urdu newspapers or magazines e.g. *Des Pardes, India Today*, Asian-based newspapers, etc.

0 = No ☐ **4**

1 = Never/Rarely

2 = Sometimes

3 = Frequently

96. ***[If No, or never/rarely]***, why is that? **[5–10]**
***[Probe, are they difficult to get hold of? You don't like them?]***

97. Do you read or buy books which feature Indian personalities or are written by Indian authors?

0 = No ☐ **11**

1 = Never/Rarely

2 = Sometimes

3 = Frequently

98. ***[If No or never/rarely],*** why is that? **[12–15]**
***[Probe, are they difficult to get hold of, you don't like them?]***

99. Do you make a special effort to watch programmes or films concerning Asian people on television/at the cinema?

2 = Yes ☐ **16**

1 = No

100. ***[If No],*** why not **[17–20]**

101. Are you satisfied with the portrayal of Asian people in these programmes?

2 = Yes ☐ **21**

1 = No

102. ***[If No],*** why not? **[22–25]**

103. Would you like to see greater participation/representation of Asian people on the TV or the cinema?

2 = Yes ☐ **26**

1 = No

104. ***[If No],*** why not **[27–30]**

105. Do you watch Hindi films on video or at the cinema?

2 = Yes ☐ **31**

1 = No

8 = No interested

106. ***[If Yes,]*** how often

1 = Average once a year ☐ **32**

2 = Between once a year and once a month

3 = At least once a month

4 = At least once a week

5 = More than once a week

107. Are you a member of any kind of club or organisation?

1 = Yes ☐ **33**

2 = No

108. [***If Yes],*** please describe what it is: **[34–35]**
[***If No, skip to Q110]***

109. ***[If Yes],*** does it have:

1 = Mostly white members ☐ **36**

2 = Equally white and Asian members

3 = Mostly Asian members

4 = Only Asian members

110. What kind of music do you listen to?

1 = Rarely listen to music ☐ **37**

2 = Non-Asian music

3 = Mixture of Asian and other music

4 = Only Asian music

111. Do you go to the Indian subcontinent?

1 = No ☐ **38**

2 = Yes

9 = Not applicable

112. [*If Yes,*] How often in the last 5 years? ☐ **39**

113. *[If not]* why not? **[40–45]**

114. If you had enough money, would you go to India?

1 = Yes ☐ **46**

2 = No

115. *[If Yes,]* how often in the next 5 years?

0 = Never ☐ **47**

1 = Once

2 = Twice

3 = 3 times

4 = More than 4 times

116. *[If No,]* why not **[48–50]**

## FOOD AND SHOPPING

117. Do you eat Indian food at home?

1 = Never/Rarely ☐ **51**

2 = Sometimes

3 = Frequently

118. *[If score 2 or 3]* How often has that been in the last one year?

1 = Average once a year ☐ **52**

2 = Between once a year and once a month

3 = At least once a month

4 = At least once a week

5 = More than once a week

119. Do you cook Indian food at home? 

1 = Never/Rarely ☐ **53**

2 = Sometimes

3 = Frequently

120. ***[If score 1]*** Why not? **[54–55]**

121. ***[If score 2 or 3]*** How often?

1 = Average once a year ☐ **56**

2 = Between once a year and once a month

3 = At least once a month

4 = At least once a week

5 = More than once a week

122. Do you shop in stores which specialise in Asian goods?

1 = No ☐ **57**

2 = Yes

123. ***[If score 2]*** How often?

1 = Average once a year ☐ **58**

2 = Between once a year and once a month

3 = At least once a month

4 = At least once a week

5 = More than once a week

124. What kind of food would you prefer to eat when you are out at a restaurant?

1 = Never go to a restaurant ☐ **59**

2 = English/take away food

3 = Asian food

4 = Other

125. Why would that be? **[60–65]**

## ASPIRATIONS

126. Are there people who you admire greatly in public life?

1 = Yes ☐ **66**

0 = No

127. Are they:

1 = Mostly white ☐ **67**

2 = Equally Asian and white

3 = Mostly Asian

8 = Other

9 = Not known

128. Are these people identified with

1 = Yes

2 = No

a) Religion ☐ **68**

b) Sport ☐ **69**

c) Music/Media ☐ **70**

d) Politics ☐ **71**

e) Community ☐ **72**

f) Other ☐ **73**

## SELF ATTITUDES

129. Do you use skin lightening products?

1 = Yes ☐ **74**

2 = No

9 = Not asked

130. [If Yes] Why is that? **[75–77]**

131. Why do you think that Asian people use skin lightening products? **[78–80]**

***(Questions 132–143 not applicable here; these are for other groups)***

135. When you retire, do you expect to move to the Indian sub-continent?

0 = No ☐ **11**

1 = Unsure

2 = Yes

136. ***[If not]*** Why not? **[12–15]**

137. Do you own property in the Indian subcontinent?

1 = No ☐ **16**

2 = Yes

138. **[If No],** If you could afford it would you wish to own property there?

1 = No ☐ **17**

2 = Yes

139. Why? **[18–20]**

140. If you had given your word that you would do something you really didn't want to, would you:

1 = Avoid doing it if possible ☐ **21**

2 = Do it only if it was convenient

3 = Try your best to do it

4 = Make sure you did it, no matter what

141. Do you think that people of Asian origin or descent have difficulty/problems with fitting into British culture and the British way of life? **[22–25]**

Thank you for your help.

APPENDIX II

# Educational pamphlet

## What Asian Women Can Do:

- Identify the family members or friends you can talk to. Start now to build a bond of trust.
- Don't feel shy or hesitant to get help. People often don't help unless you ask because they don't know and may be reluctant to interfere. Take the first step.
- Tell your GP if you are depressed or suicidal. He or she will offer confidential help, as will the other professionals listed on this pamphlet.
- Make it through that moment of desperation when you're thinking of suicide. Whatever it takes, just make it through that moment. No matter how bad the situation seems, other options will become clear with time. Call someone to talk.
- Remember - You are not alone. No matter how terrible or unusual your situation, other women have experienced the same thing. If they found the strength to hope, to have courage, and to ask for help, so can you.
- Are you imagining suicide to be a solution? Suicide won't solve the problem. There are better options for coping. Look to your strengths. Ask for advice.
- Do you put your own needs last? Feel self-blame, lack of confidence, guilty or ashamed? You deserve respect from yourself and others. Affirm your positive points. Take good care of yourself. Break the habit of automatic self-blame.
- Ask yourself, "What are my aims in life?" Focusing on your goals and priorities will give you strength. Give yourself time and encouragement to learn new skills. Develop financial independence.

## Where you can get Advice and Help

- Tell your GP or Nurse. They can help.
- For general advice and counseling:

**Asian Family Counseling Service**
0208 997-5749 (Hindi, Punjabi, Gujrati, Urdu)
**Relate** (individuals, couples, families)
0208 427-8694 (Hindi, Bengali, Gujrati, Urdu)
**Nafsiyat Intercultural Therapy Centre**
0207 263-4130
**TASHA** (Hindi, Punjabi, English)
0208 569-9933
**Ealing Psychotherapy Department** (English)
0208 967-5235
**Sangam Advice Centre** (on welfare rights)
0208 952-7062

- Support especially for Women:

**Asian Women's Resource Centre**
0208 961-6549/5701 (Hindi, Punjabi, Gujrati)
**Harrow Women's Association** (for Asian women)
0208 381-1622
**Women's Support Group** (domestic violence)
0208 572-8656 (Hindi, Punjabi and others)
**Muslim Women's Helpline**
0208 904-8193
**Women's Therapy Centre**
0207 263-6200 (Punjabi, English)
**Rape Crisis Centre**
0207 837-1600 (also past experiences of abuse)
**Sahara**, Box 324, Reading, Berks, RG1 6AW
(housing for Asian women subjected to abuse)

- For alcohol or drug problems:

**Ealing Drugs Advisory Service**
0208 579-5585 (Hindi, Punjabi, Gujrati, Urdu)
**Southall Alcohol Advisory Service**
0208 574-5244 (Hindi, Punj., Beng., Urdu, Engl.)

- If feeling overwhelmed or suicidal:

**Samaritans** (24 hours)
0208 427-7777
0345 909090 (at local rates)
**Call your GP or hospital Accident & Emergency.**

* **For All** *

# Asian Families

* *********** *

## Creating Harmony Preventing Despair

In Britain, Asian women attempt suicide much more than any other group. Young Asian women are especially at risk. Deliberate self-harm or attempted suicide is a silent but serious cry for help.

**Prevention is the Solution.**

Suicide is an irreversible tragedy, so prevention is key. You can recognize when someone you know is feeling overwhelmed or suicidal. Here are the many ways this problem can be detected and prevented.

**It can happen to any person in any family.**

Funded by the Department of Health

## How Can You Identify the Problem in Your Family?

In almost every case of suicide, there are hints that the act is about to occur.
Be sensitive to that hint and act to prevent it.
Don't ignore it.

## Recognize High-Risk Situations:

The more of these common situations you have, the higher the risk of a suicide attempt:

- The woman has developed **depression, hopelessness** or **feels desperate**.
- There is **poor communication**, e.g. between parents and children or husband and wife.
- The woman receives **little support, praise or affection** from husband or family.
- The woman has a **break-up** or **conflict** with husband, boyfriend, parents or best friend.
- The woman fears **shame, failure** or **loss of reputation**.
- There has been **emotional, physical or sexual abuse** by family. There is **domestic violence**.
- She is **overburdened with responsibilities**, without getting any reward or return.
- She feels **trapped, rejected** or **pressured** by others - feels 'All doors are closed'.
- She feels there is **no one she can tell**.

## What Asian Families Can Do:

- Family can identify and give emotional support to the distressed person and help her to face the situation with courage.
- How does your family communicate? Asian family members in Britain may face different issues, have different values, and disagree. Listening, patience, respect and flexibility from all sides are needed to solve problems. Explain the reasons for your opinions.
- Does your family express affection, offer praise, and allow women and younger members to express their true opinions? Doing this won't spoil them. It strengthens family bonds. It creates confidence, good self-image and improves function at work, school and home. True family stability doesn't rely on the silence of women and children.
- Do you blame women for problems? Using the woman as a scapegoat causes severe stress. Rejection and blame increase her risk of suicide. So even if you are very angry, try to understand the whole situation. Your consideration and tolerance are very important to her.
- To live a life of dignity, a woman needs respect from others and all her family. Don't expect sacrifice only from the women all the time. Their needs should also be addressed.
- Has there been violence or sexual abuse? Stopping the abuse is essential. Families should offer support to the woman. Join her in letting the person know that she is not helpless, not alone, and violence won't be tolerated. In addition to the woman's suffering, children do worse at school and have more psychological problems if there is violence in the family.
- Does your family have different standards for men and women? Having stricter standards for the women than the men causes high stress and burden. It contributes to feelings of shame, self-blame and guilt, which are factors in suicide.
- Is reputation more important than the woman? Comparing your family to a community ideal is not realistic. No family is perfect. It's more important that a woman be healthy and content with her life.
- Must girls and women be protected? Overprotection prevents her developing good judgment, responsibility, and maturity so that she can cope with life's problems. Also, overcontrol can lead to rebellion.
- You can be alert for signs of depression. Ask what's wrong and listen. Support her in asking for help from a professional. Counseling is confidential.

*****************************

## Signs of Depression or Stress

* Feels sad, anxious, depressed or empty
* Low enjoyment. Low interest.
* Feels guilt, self-blame or worthlessness
* Poor sleep, or sleeps too much
* Poor appetite. Loses weight
* Low energy. Poor concentration.
* Has many physical pains and problems.
* Acts slowed down, erratic or frantic
* Cries easily. Hopeless. Thinks a lot of death.
* Thoughts or Threats of self-harm or suicide

## Effective Solutions for Depression:

- Family offers support and understanding.
- Counseling
- Antidepressant medications are very helpful.
- Decreasing problems that cause the stress.

*****************************

APPENDIX IIIA

# DSH Assessment by Clinicians (DACS)

## (Adolescent version)

**Demographic details**

Name: ______________________________

Date of birth: ______________ Sex (M/F): ______________

Address: ______________________________

______________________________

Name and address of GP: ______________________________

______________________________

Ethnicity: ______________________

**Catchment Consultant**

Ethnic status (please ☑)

| | | | |
|---|---|---|---|
| ☐ White | ☐ Bangladeshi | ☐ Black British | ☐ Chinese |
| ☐ Black Caribbean | ☐ Pakistani | ☐ African | ☐ Indian |

☐ Other (please specify): ____________________

**Self-ascribed ethnic status:** ____________________

Place of birth: ____________________

Parental place of birth: ____________________

Employed: ☐ Yes ☐ No

Current employment, if any: ______________________________

Past employment, if any: ______________________________

**Marital status of parents:** ☐ Single ☐ Married ☐ Cohabiting

☐ Separated ☐ Divorced ☐ Widowed

**Biological Parents:** ☐ Living together ☐ As married ☐ Living separately
☐ Child with M/F
Degree of contact with parent not living with: ________

**Ethnic status of:** Biological father: ____________
Biological mother: ___________
Biological father's partner: ____
Biological mother's partner: ___

**School year:** Exams: ____________________
Bullying: ☐ Yes ☐ No ☐ Don't know
Give details:
_______________________________________________
Any change of school: ☐ Yes ☐ No
☐ Don't know
Attendance record: ☐ Absences ☐ Truancy
☐ Illness
Exclusion:

**Legal status of child:** ______________________________________________

**Current status:** ____________________________________________________

**Previous history:** __________________________________________________

Episodes in care: ________________________________
Ever on Child Protection Register (CPR)?
☐ Yes ☐ No

**Name and address of school:** ________________________________________

_______________________________________________________________________

**Animosity between natural parents, if any (please detail):** __________________

_______________________________________________________________________

_______________________________________________________________________

**Siblings**

| Name | Age | Sex | School, if applicable | Problems | Living at home? Y/N | Relationship quality |
|---|---|---|---|---|---|---|
| 1. | | | | | | |
| 2. | | | | | | |
| 3. | | | | | | |
| 4. | | | | | | |
| 5. | | | | | | |
| 6. | | | | | | |

**Any siblings on CPR/in care?** ☐ Yes ☐ No

*If yes*, specify who: ______________________________

How long for? ______________________________

Why? ______________________________

**Details of deliberate self-harm (DSH):**

Date of assessment: ______________ Date of admission: ______________

Date of DSH: ______________________ Time: ______________________

**Method:** ☐ Overdose ☐ Violent acute cutting ☐ Other (please specify)

**Overdose:**

Tablet type: ________ Strength: ________ Number taken: ________

Time taken: _______ Blood level: _______ Source of tablets: _______

Discomfort (e.g. vomiting): ☐ Yes ☐ No

**Violent acute cutting:**

Please state number, length, site and depth of cuts. ***If other***, please describe here as well:

______________________________________________________________________

______________________________________________________________________

______________________________________________________________________

How did they get to medical services? ____________(e.g. self, friend, family)

Duration between presentation and DSH? ______________________________

Where did they get the idea from? ________(e.g. past history, family history, friends, peers, TV, magazine, newspapers)

**Alcohol:**

Amount: ______________________________________

Type: ____________ Time taken: ___________

Length of time planning: _____ Impulsive: ☐ Yes ☐ No

**How was the patient feeling at the time?** ______________________________

____________________________________________________________________

Directed at anyone? ☐Yes ☐ No

***If yes***, who? ___________________________________________________

**Why DSH** (in own words): ___________________________________________

____________________________________________________________________

____________________________________________________________________

Did the patient think it would kill him/her? ☐ Yes ☐ No

***If no***, what did the patient think would happen? _________________________

____________________________________________________________________

Had the patient left a suicide note? ☐ Yes ☐ No

***If yes***, what were the contents of the note? (Enclose copy if possible) _______

____________________________________________________________________

What efforts were made to avoid detection? _____________________________

How was the patient discovered? ______________________________________

Any regrets at still being alive? ☐ Yes ☐ No

What did the patient think the consequences would be of:

(i) non-discovery? ______________________________________________

(ii) discovery? _________________________________________________

Worries about information to boy-friend, girl-friend, family, peers, schools, etc:

______________________________________________

______________________________________________

**Precipitating factors**

Immediately? ☐ Yes ☐ No *If yes*, note: ____________

Last 3 months ☐ Yes ☐ No *If yes*, note: ____________

Last 6 months ☐ Yes ☐ No *If yes*, note: ____________

**What were the reactions of relatives at whom in DSH aimed?**

______________________________________________

Any past history of DSH? ☐ Yes ☐ No

*If yes*, write number of overdoses injuries: ____________

**Does the patient fulfil criteria for any of the following?** ☐ Yes ☐ No

*If yes*, (ICD coding)

☐ Depression

☐ Alcohol dependence

☐ Drug dependence

☐ Psychotic illness

☐ Personality disorder

☐ Eating disorder

☐ Abuse – sexual/physical

☐ Any other diagnosis,

*please specify*: ____________

____________

**Reasons for making the above diagnosis**

1. ____________________
2. ____________________
3. ____________________
4. ____________________
5. ____________________

**Is the patient still at risk of self-harm?** ☐ Yes ☐ No

***If yes,***

In the next few days? ☐ Yes ☐ No

In the long term? ☐ Yes ☐ No

***If yes***, please state why: ______________________________

______________________________

______________________________

**Date of admission** (if applicable): ______________

What would have needed to have been different/or to change for the patient not to have self-harmed? ______________________________

When did the patient first think about DSH? ______________

Had the patient told anyone about the thoughts? ☐ Yes ☐ No ***If yes***, who? ______________________________

Under what circumstances would the patient repeat DSH? ______________

______________________________

If the patient did repeat, what would he/she do differently next time? ______

______________________________

Speciality admitted under (please circle all groups if transferred between specialities):

[MED] [PSYCH] [SURGERY] [ORTHO] [PED]

**Discharge to where?** ☐ Home/LA ☐ Psych Hosp

**Name of assessor:** ______________________________

Grade: [SHO] [REG] [SR] [Staff Grade] [Clin Assis] [CON]

APPENDIX IIIB

# DSH Assessment by Clinicians (DACS)

## (Adult version)

**Demographic details**

Name: ____________________

Date of birth: ____________ Sex (M/F): ____________

Address: ____________________

____________________

Name and address of GP: ____________________

____________________

Ethnicity: ____________

**Catchment Consultant**

Ethnic status (please ☑)

| | | | |
|---|---|---|---|
| ☐ White | ☐ Bangladeshi | ☐ Black British | ☐ Chinese |
| ☐ Black Caribbean | ☐ Pakistani | ☐ African | ☐ Indian |

☐ Other (please specify): ____________

**Self-ascribed ethnic status:** ____________

Place of birth: ____________

Parental place of birth: ____________

Employed: ☐ Yes ☐ No

Current employment, if any: ____________________

Past employment, if any: ____________________

**Marital status of parents:** ☐ Single ☐ Married ☐ Cohabiting ☐ Separated ☐ Divorced ☐ Widowed

**Previous History:** ______________________________

**Animosity between natural parents, if any (please detail):** ______________

______________________________________________

**Siblings**

| Name | Age | Sex | School, if applicable | Problems | Living at home? Y/N | Relationship quality |
|---|---|---|---|---|---|---|
| 1. | | | | | | |
| 2. | | | | | | |
| 3. | | | | | | |
| 4. | | | | | | |
| 5. | | | | | | |
| 6. | | | | | | |

**Details of deliberate self-harm (DSH):**

Date of assessment: __________ Date of admission: __________

Date of DSH: ______________ Time: ______________

**Method:** ☐ Overdose ☐ Violent acute cutting ☐ Other (please specify) _

**Overdose:**
Tablet type: _______ Strength: _______ Number taken: _______

Time taken: ______ Blood level: ______ Source of tablets: ______

Discomfort (e.g. vomiting): ☐ Yes ☐ No

**Violent acute cutting:**

Please state number, length, site and depth of cuts. ***If other***, please describe here as well:

______________________________________________

______________________________________________

______________________________________________

How did they get to medical services? __________(e.g. self, friend, family)

Duration between presentation and DSH? ____________________________

Where did they get the idea from? ________(e.g. past history, family history, friends, peers, TV, magazine, newspapers)

**Alcohol:**

Amount: ______________________________

Type: ___________ Time taken: ___________

Length of time planning: ______ Impulsive: ☐ Yes ☐ No

**How was the patient feeling at the time?** ____________________________

________________________________________________________________

Directed at anyone? ☐Yes ☐ No

***If yes***, who? ______________________________________________

**Why DSH** (in own words): ____________________________________

________________________________________________________________

________________________________________________________________

Did the patient think it would kill him/her? ☐ Yes ☐ No

***If no***, what did the patient think would happen? ____________________

________________________________________________________________

Had the patient left a suicide note? ☐ Yes ☐ No

***If yes***, what were the contents of the note? (Enclose copy if possible) _______

________________________________________________________________

What efforts were made to avoid detection? ______________________

How was the patient discovered? ________________________________

Any regrets at still being alive? ☐ Yes ☐ No

What did the patient think the consequences would be of:

(i) non-discovery? ______________________________________

(ii) discovery? _________________________________________

Worries about information to boy-friend, girl-friend, family, peers, schools, etc: ________________________________________________________

________________________________________________________________

**Precipitating factors**

Immediately? ☐ Yes ☐ No *If yes*, note: ____________________

Last 3 months ☐ Yes ☐ No *If yes*, note: ____________________

Last 6 months ☐ Yes ☐ No *If yes*, note: ____________________

**What were the reactions of relatives at whom in DSH aimed?**

______________________________________________________________

Any past history of DSH? ☐ Yes ☐ No

*If yes*, write number of overdoses injuries: ____________________________

**Does the patient fulfil criteria for any of the following?** ☐ Yes ☐ No

*If yes*, (ICD coding)

☐ Depression ☐ Eating disorder

☐ Alcohol dependence ☐ Abuse – sexual/physical

☐ Drug dependence ☐ Any other diagnosis,

☐ Psychotic illness *please specify*: ____________

☐ Personality disorder ______________

**Reasons for making the above diagnosis**

1. ________________________________________
2. ________________________________________
3. ________________________________________
4. ________________________________________
5. ________________________________________

**Is the patient still at risk of self-harm?** ☐ Yes ☐ No

***If yes,***

In the next few days? ☐ Yes ☐ No

In the long term? ☐ Yes ☐ No

*If yes*, please state why: ____________________________________________

______________________________________________________________

______________________________________________________________

**Date of admission** (if applicable): ________________

What would have needed to have been different/or to change for the patient not to have self-harmed? ______________________________________________

When did the patient first think about DSH? ____________________________

Had the patient told anyone about the thoughts? ☐ Yes ☐ No *If yes*, who? ______________________________________________

Under what circumstances would the patient repeat DSH? ______________

______________________________________________

If the patient did repeat, what would he/she do differently next time? ______

______________________________________________

Speciality admitted under (please circle all groups if transferred between specialities):

[MED] [PSYCH] [SURGERY] [ORTHO] [PED]

**Discharge to where?** ☐ Home/LA ☐ Psych Hosp

**Name of assessor:** ____________________________

Grade: [SHO] [REG] [SR] [Staff Grade] [Clin Assis] [CON]

# References


Acosta-Rua, M. V. (1991). Child and adolescent suicide. *Journal of the Florida Medical Association, 78*, 295–298.

Adityanjee (1986). Suicide attempts and suicide in India. *International Journal of Social Psychiatry, 28*, 1–7.

Ahmed, S. H. (1983). Pakistan. In L. A. Headley (Ed.), *Suicide in Asia and the Far East*. Berkeley, CA: University of California Press.

Ahmed, S. H., & Zuberi, H. (1981). Changing pattern of suicide and parasuicide in Karachi. *Journal of the Pakistan Medical Association, 31*, 76–78.

Ali, A. (1979). Girmit: The indenture experience. *Fiji Bulletin 5*. Suva: The Fiji Museum.

Al-Issa, I. (2000). Culture and mental illness in Algeria. In I. Ai-Issa (Ed.), *Al-Junun: Mental illness in the Islamic world*. New York: International Universities Press.

Allen, D. (1997). Social constructions of self. In W. W. Allen (Ed.), *Culture and self*. Boulder, CO: Westview, pp. 3–26.

Andrews, C., & Pearson, W. (1916). *Indentured labour in Fiji*. Allahad: League for Abolition of Indentured Labour.

Arap Mengech, H. N., & Dhadphale, M. (1984). Attempted suicide (parasuicide) in Nairobi, Kenya. *Acta Psychiatrica Scandinavica, 69*, 416–419.

Arffa, S. (1983). Cognition and suicide: A methodological review. *Suicide and Life-Threatening Behaviour, 13*, 109–121.

Asad, T. (1997). Remarks on the anthropology of the body. In S. Oakley (Ed.), *Religion and the body*. Cambridge: Cambridge University Press, pp. 42–52.

Ashraf, M. (1964). The problem of suicide in Karachi. *Pakistan Armed Forces Medical Journal, 14*, 156–167.

Bagley, C. (1995). *Child sexual abuse and mental health in adolescents and adults*. Aldershot: Avebury.

Bagley, C. (1997). The taxonomy of completed suicide in adolescents and the role of schools in suicide prevention. In C. Bagley & R. Ramsey (Eds), *Suicidal behaviour in adolescents and adults*. Aldershot: Ashgate.

Bagley, C., & Greer, S. (1971). Clinical and social predictors of repeated attempted suicide. *British Journal of Psychiatry, 119*, 515–521.

Bagley, C., & McDonald, M. (1984). Adult mental health sequels of child sexual abuse, physical abuse and neglect in maternally separated children. *Canadian Journal of Community Mental Health, 6*, 5–26.

Bagley, C., & Ramsey, R. (1986). Sexual abuse in childhood. *Journal of Social Work and Human Sexuality, 4*, 33–47.

Bagley, C., & Ramsey, R. (1997). *Suicidal behaviour in adolescents and adults*. Aldershot: Ashgate.

Bagley, C., & Tremblay, P. (1996). On the prevalence of homosexuality and bisexuality in a random community survey of 750 men aged 18–27. *Journal of Homosexuality, 36(2)*, 1–18.

Bagley, C., & Young, L. (1987). Juvenile prostitutes and child sexual abuse: A controlled study. *Canadian Journal of Community Mental Health, 6*, 5–26.

Baller, R. D., & Richardson, K. (2000). Social integration, imitation and the geographic patterning of suicide. *American Sociological Review, 67*, 873–888.

Barnett, P., & Gotlib, I. (1988). *Personality and depression: new scales and a model of relationships*. Paper presented at the Canadian Psychological Association Meeting, Montréal.

Basu, A. (1997). Reducing concern with self: Parfit and the ancient Buddhist schools. In D. Allen (Ed.), *Culture and self*. Boulder, CO: Westview Press, pp. 97–110.

Batchelor, I. R. (1954). Repeated suicidal attempts. *British Journal of Medical Psychology, 27*, 158–163.

Batchelor, I., & Napier, M. (1954). The sequelae and short-term prognosis of attempted suicide. *Journal of Neurology and Psychiatry, 17*, 261–266.

Bayet, A. (1922). *Le suicide et la morale*. Alcan, Paris: Libraire Felix.

Beck, A., Lester, D., & Kovacs, M. (1973). Attempted suicides by males and females. *Psychological Reports, 33*, 865–866.

Beck, A., Resnik, H., & Lettieri, D. (Eds.) (1974). *The Prediction of Suicide*. Bowie, MD: Charles Press.

Beck, U. (1992). *Risk society*. London: Sage.

Bell, A., & Weinberg, M. (1978). *Homosexuality: A study of diversity among men and women*. New York: Simon & Schuster.

Benedict, R. (1934). *Patterns of culture*. London: Routledge.

Bergman, B., & Brismar, B. (1991a). Suicide attempts by battered wives. *Acta Psychiatrica Scandinavica, 83*, 380–384.

Bergman, B., & Brismar, B. (1991b). A 5-year follow-up study of 117 battered women. *American Journal of Public Health, 81*, 1486–1489.

Berman, A. L., & Schwartz, R. H. (1990). Suicide attempts among adolescent drug users. *American Journal of Diseases of Children, 144*, 310–314.

Berrios, G., & Mohanna, M. (1990). Durkheim and French psychiatric views on suicide during the 19th century. *British Journal of Psychiatry, 156*, 1–9.

Berry, J. (1980). Acculturation has varieties of adaptation. In A. M. Padilla (Ed.), *Acculturation*. Boulder, CO: Interview Press.

Berry, J. (1990). Psychology of acculturation. In R. W. Brislin (Ed.), *Applied cross-culture psychology*. Newbury Park, CA, Sage, pp. 232–253.

Bettridge, B., & Favreau, D. (1995). The dependency needs and perceived availability and adequacy of relationships in female adolescent suicide attempters. *Psychology of Women Quality, 19*, 517–531.

Bhatia, S. C., Khan, M. H., Mediratta, R. P., & Sharma, A. (1987). High-risk suicide factors across cultures. *International Journal of Social Psychiatry, 33*, 226–236.

Bhugra, D. (1991). Politically motivated suicides. *British Journal of Psychiatry, 159*, 594–595.

Bhugra, D., Baldwin, D., Desai, M. (1997a). Focus groups: Implications for primary and cross-cultural psychiatry. *Primary Care Psychiatry, 3*, 45–50.

Bhugra, D., Baldwin, D., & Desai, M. (1997b). A pilot study of the impact of fact sheets and guided discussion on knowledge and attitudes regarding depression in an ethnic minority sample. *Primary Care Psychiatry, 3*, 135–40.

Bhugra, D., Baldwin, D., Desai M., & Jacob K. S. (1999a). Attempted suicide in west London II. Intergenerational comparisons. *Psychological Medicine, 29*, 1131–139.

Bhugra, D., Bhui K., Desai M., Singh J., Baldwin D., Mallett, R., & Leff, J. (1999c). Cultural identity and its measurements: A questionnaire for Asians. *International Review of Psychiatry, 11*, 213, 244–249.

Bhugra, D., Bhui, K., Desai, M., Singh, J., & Baldwin, D. (1999d). The Asian Cultural Identity Schedule (ACIS): an investigation of culture and self harm. *International Journal of Methods in Psychiatric Research, 8*, 212–218.

Bhugra, D., Desai, M., & Baldwin, D. S. (1999a). Attempted suicide in west London, I. Rates across ethnic communities. *Psychological Medicine, 29*, 1125–1130.

Bhugra, D., & Hicks, M. H. (2004). *Help-seeking attitudes toward depression and suicidality in UK South Asian women: Effects of an educational pamphlet*. Psychiatric Services.

Bhugra, D., Thompson, N., Singh, Z., & Fellow-Smith, E. (2003). Inception rates of deliberate self-harm among adolescents in West London. *International Journal of Social Psychiatry, 49*, 247–250.

Biswas, S. (1990) Ethnic differences in self-poisoning: A comparative study between Asians and white adolescent groups, *Journal of Adolescence, 13*, 189–193.

Bjarnason, T. & Thorlindsson, T. (1994). Manifest predictors of past suicide attempts in a population of Icelandic adolescents. *Suicide and Life Threatening Behaviour, 24*, 350–358.

Blos, P. (1962). *On adolescence*. New York: Free Press.

Boldt, M. (1982). Normative evaluations of suicides and deaths: A cross-generational study. *Omega, 13*, 145–157.

Bonner, R., & Rich, A. (1987). Toward a predictive model of suicidal ideation and behaviour. *Suicide and Life-Threatening Behaviour, 17*, 50–63.

Brent, D. (1995). Risk factors for adolescent suicide and suicidal behaviour: Mental and substance abuse disorders, family environment factors and life stress. *Suicide and Life Threatening Behaviour, 25* (suppl), 52–63.

Brent, D. A., Kolko, D., Wartella, M., Boylan, M., Moritz, G., Baugher, M., & Zelenak, J. P. (1993). Adolescent psychiatric patients risk of suicidal attempts at 6 months follow-up. *Journal of the American Academy of Child and Adolescent Psychiatry, 32*, 95–105.

Brent, D. A., Perper, J., Moritz, G., Allman, C., Friend, A., Schweers, J., Roth, C., Balach, L., & Harrington, K. (1992). Psychiatric effects of exposure to suicide among the friends and acquaintances of adolescent suicide victims. *Journal of the American Academy of Child and Adolescent Psychiatry, 31*, 629–640.

Brent, D., Perper, J., Goldstein, C., Kolko, D., Allan, M., Allman, C., & Zelenak, J. (1988). Risk factors for adolescent suicide. *Archives of General Psychiatry, 45*, 581–588.

Briere, J., & Runtz, W. (1986). Suicidal thoughts and behaviours in former sexual abuse victims. *Canadian Journal of Behavioural Science, 18*, 413–423.

Briere, K., & Zaidi, L. (1989). Sexual abuse histories and sequelae in female psychiatric emergency room patients. *American Journal of Psychiatry, 146*, 1602–1606.

Brockington, J. L. (1996). *The sacred thread*. Edinburgh: Edinburgh University Press.

Bronstein P. (1988). Father–child interaction. In P. Bronstein, & C. P. Cowan (Eds.), *Fatherhood today: Men's changing role in the family*. New York: Wiley, pp. 107–124.

Brown, K. M. (1994). Comment: Good mothers and bad mothers in the rituals of Sati. In M. J. S. Hawley (Ed.), *Sati: The blessing and curse*. New York: Oxford University Press, pp. 91–100.

Brown, M., King, E., & Barraclough, B. (1995). Nine suicide pacts: a clinical study of consecutive series 1974–1993. *British Journal of Psychiatry, 167*, 448–451.

Buglass, D., & Horton J. (1974). A scale for predicting subsequent suicidal behaviour. *British Journal of Psychiatry, 124*, 575–578.

Bukstein, O. G., Brent, D. A., Perper, J. A., Moritz, G., Baugher, M., Schweers, J., Roth, C., & Balach, L. (1993). Risk factors for completed suicide among adolescents with a lifetime history of substance abuse: A case-control study. *Acta Psychiatrica Scandinavica, 88*, 403–408.

Burke, A. (1974). Sociocultural aspects of attempted suicide among women in Trinidad and Tobago. *British Journal of Psychiatry, 125*, 374–377.

Burke, A. (1976a). Attempted suicide among Asian immigrants in Birmingham. *British Journal of Psychiatry, 128*, 528–532.

Burke, A. (1976b). Sociocultural determinants of attempted suicide among West Indians in Birmingham. *British Journal of Psychiatry, 129*, 261–266.

Canetto, S. (1992). Gender and suicide in the elderly. *Suicide & Life-Threatening Behaviour, 22*, 80–97.

Canetto, S., & Feldman, L. (1993). Overt and covert dependence in suicidal women and their male partners. *Omega, 27*, 177–194.

Canetto, S., & Lester, D. (1995). The epidemiology of women's suicidal behaviour. In S. S. Canetto & D. Lester (Eds.), *Women and suicidal behaviour*. New York: Springer, pp. 61–70.

Cantor P. (1972). The adolescent attempters: Sex, sibling position and family constellation. *Suicide and Life-Threatening Behaviour, 21*, 252–261.

Cappelli, M., Chilow, M. K., Goodman, J. T., Davidson, S. I., Feder, S. H., Baron-Manion, I., McGrath, P. (1995). Identifying depressed and suicidal adolescents in teen health clinic. *Journal of Adolescent Health, 16*, 64–70.

*Caraka Samhita*, (1949). Jamnagar: Shree Gulab Kunverba Ayurvedic Society (six volumes).

Carpenter, L., & Brockington, I. (1980). A study of mental illness in Asians, West Indians and Africans living in Manchester. *British Journal of Psychiatry, 137*, 201–205.

Caruso, M., & Moussaoui, D. (1992). Tentative de suicide, pratique religieuse et insertion sociale. *Review Maghrebine de Psychiatrie, 2*, 29–32.

Chambers, D., & Harvey, J. (1989). Inner urban and national suicide rates: A simple comparative study. *Medicine Science and Law, 29* (3), 183–185.

Cheetham, R. W., Edwards, S. R., Naidoo, L. R., Griffiths, J. A., & Singh, V. G. (1983). Deculturation as a precipitant of parasuicide in an Asian group. *South African Medical Journal, 63*, 942–945.

Cheung, P. (1995). Acculturation and psychiatric morbidity among Cambodian refugees in New Zealand. *International Journal of Social Psychiatry, 41*, 108–119.

Chiu, L. P. W (1989). Attempted suicide in Hong Kong. *Acta Psychiatrica Scandinavica, 79*, 425–430.

Clarke, C. F. (1988). Deliberate self-poisoning in adolescents. *Archives of Disease in Childhood, 63*, 1479–1483.

Clifton, K., & Lee, D. (1995). *Gender socialisation and women's suicidal behaviour*. New York: Springer, pp. 35–40.

Cochrane, R. (1977). Mental illness in immigrants in England and Wales: An analysis of mental hospital admissions. *Social Psychiatry, 12*, 25–35.

Cochrane, R. (1999). Ethnicity, drinking patterns and alcohol problems. In D. Bhugra & V Bahl (Eds.), *Ethnicity: An agenda for mental health* (pp. 70–84), London: Gaskell.

Cochrane, R., & Robertson, A. (1973). The Life Events Inventory: A measure of the relative severity of psychological stressors. *Journal of Psychosomatic Research, 17*, 133–139.

Cochrane, R., & Stopes-Roe, M. (1981). Psychological symptom levels in Indian immigrants in London – a comparison with native English. *Psychological Medicine, 11*, 319–327.

Cohen-Sandler, R., Berman, A., & King, R. (1982). A follow-up study of hospitalised suicidal children. *Journal of the American Academy of Child and Adolescent Psychiatry, 21*, 398–403.

Cole, W. O. & Sambhi, P. S. (1989). *The Sikhs: Their religious beliefs and practices*. Calcutta: Rupa.

Conrad, N. (1991). Where do they turn? Social support systems of suicidal high school adolescents. *Journal of Psychosocial Nursing & Mental Health Services, 29*, 15–19.

Coomaraswamy, A. K. (1957). *The dance of Shiva*. New York: Noonday Press.

Cotgrove, A., Zirinsky, L., Black, D., & Weston, D. (1995). Secondary prevention of attempted suicide in adolescents. *Journal of Adolescence, 18*, 569–577.

Courtright, P. B. (1994). The iconographies of Sati. In J. S. Hawley (Ed.), *Sati: The blessing and the curse*. New York: Oxford University Press, pp. 149–158.

Crome, P. (1993). The toxicity of drugs used for suicide. *Acta Psychiatrica Scandinavica*, suppl. *371*, 33–37.

Crooke, W. (1896). *The popular religion and folklore in Northern India*. New Delhi: Munshiran Manoharlal, reprinted 1978.

Crumley, F. E. (1979). Adolescents suicide attempts. *Journal of the American Medical Association, 241*, 2404–2407.

Culberg, J., Wasserman, D., & Stefansson, C.-G. (1988). Who commits suicide after a suicide attempt? *Acta Psychiatrica Scandinavica, 77*, 598–603.

Cutler, S., & Nolen-Hoeksemma, S. (1991). Accounting for sex differences in depression through female victimization: Childhood sexual abuse. *Sex Roles, 24*, 425–438.

Dahlgren, K. G. (1977). Attempted suicide – 35 years afterward. *Suicide & Life-Threatening Behaviour, 7*, 75–79.

Daly, M., Conway, C. & Kellerher, M. (1986). Social determinants of self-poisoning. *British Journal of Psychiatry, 148*, 406–413.

Daradekh, T. K. (1989). Suicide in Jordan 1980–1985. *Acta Psychiatrica Scandinavica, 79*, 241–244.

Davies, J. (1904). Suicide with some illustrative cases. *Journal of the American Medical Association, 43*, 121–123.

Dean, G., Walsh, D., Downing, H., & Shelley, E. (1981). First admissions of native born and immigrants to psychiatric hospitals in south east England in 1976. *British Journal of Psychiatry, 139*, 506–512.

De Man, A., & Leduc, C. P. (1995). Suicidal ideation in high school students: Depression and other correlates. *Journal of Clinical Psychology, 51*, 173–181.

De Wilde, E., Kienhörst, I., Diekstra, R., & Wolters, W. (1992). The relationship between adolescent suicidal behaviour and life events in childhood and adolescence. *American Journal of Psychiatry, 149*, 45–51.

De Wilde, E., Kienhörst, I., Diekstra, R., & Wolters, W. (1993). The specificity of psychological characteristics of adolescent suicide attempts. *American Journal of the Academy of Child & Adolescent Psychiatry, 32*, 51–59.

De Young, M. (1982). Self-injurious behaviours in incest victims. *Child Welfare, 61*, 577–584.

DHHS (1999). *Mental health: A report of the Surgeon General*. Rockville, MD: US Department of Health and Human Services.

DHHS (2001). *Mental health: Culture, race and ethnicity*, Rockville, MD: US.

Diekstra, R. F. (1992). Epidemiology of suicide: Aspects of definition, classification and prevention policies. In P. Creper, G. Ferrari, S. Platt, & M. Bellini (Eds.), *Suicidal behaviour in Europe*. Rome: John Libey CIC, 15–45.

Diekstra, R. F., & Gulbinat, W. (1993). The epidemiology of suicidal behaviour: A review of three continents. *World Health Statistics Quarterly, 46*, 52–68.

Diekstra, R. F., & Garnefski, N. (1995). On the nature, magnitude and causality of

suicidal behaviours: An international perspective. *Suicide & Life Threatening Behaviour 25*, 36–57.
Dissanayake, S., & De Silva, P. (1983). Sri Lanka. In L. A. Headley (Ed.), *Suicide in Asia and the Far East*. Berkeley, CA: University of California Press.
Doniger, W., & Smith, B. (1991). *The Laws of Manu*. New Delhi: Penguin.
Dubois, A. J. A. (1906). *Hindu manners, customs and ceremonies*. Trans by H. K. Beauchamp. Delhi: Oxford University Press (reprint 1989).
Dumont, L. (1970). *Homo hierarchicus: The caste system and its implications*. London: Weidenfeld and Nicholson.
Durkheim, E. (1879/1951). *Suicide: A sociological study*. Trans. by J. Spaulding & G. Simpson. London: Routledge and Kegan Paul. (Original work published 1879).
Dusevic, N., Baume, P., Malak, A-E. (2002). *Cross-cultural suicide prevention*. NSW, Australia: Transcultural Mental Health Centre.
Eisenthal, E., Farberow, N., & Shneidman, E. (1966). Follow-up of neuropsychiatric patients in suicide observation status. *Public Health Reports* (Wash), *81*, 977–990.
Embree, A. T. (1994). Comment: Widows as cultural symbols. In J. S. Hawley (Ed.), *Sati: The blessing and the curse*. New York: Oxford University Press, 149–158.
Erikson, E. (1968). *Identity: Youth and crisis*. New York: Norton.
Esmail, A. (1996). Islamic communities and mental health. In D. Bhugra (Ed.) *Psychiatry and religion: Context, consensus and controversies*. London: Routledge.
Ettlinger, R. (1975). Evaluation of suicide prevention after attempted suicide. *Acta Psychiatrica Scandinavica*, suppl 1. *250*.
Ettlinger, R. W. (1984). Suicides in a group of patients who had previously attempted suicide. *Acta Psychiatrica Scandinavica, 40*, 363–378.
Farberow, N. (1975a). *Suicide in different cultures*. Baltimore, MD: University Park Press.
Farberow, N. (1975b). Cultural history of suicide. In N. Farberow (Ed.), *Suicide in different Cultures*. Baltimore, MD: University Park Press, 1–15.
Fennigs, S. & Carlson, G. A. (1995). Advances in the study of mood disorders in childhood and adolescence, *Current Opinion in Paediatrics, 7*, 401–404.
Fergusson, D. M., & Lynskey, M. T. (1995). Childhood circumstances adolescent adjustment and suicide attempts in New Zealand birth cohort. *Journal of the American Academy of Child and Adolescent Psychiatry, 34*, 612–622.
Figueira, D. M. (1994). Die Flambierte Frau: Sati in European culture. In J. S. Hawley (Ed.), *Sati: The blessing and the curse*. New York: Oxford University Press, pp. 55–71.
Finkelhor, D. (1984). *Child sexual abuse: New theory and research*. New York: Free Press.
Fridell, S. R., Zucker, K., Bradley, S., & Maing, D. (1996). Physical attractiveness of girls with gender identity disorders. *Archives Sexual Behaviour, 25*, 17–31.
Ganesvaran, T., & Raja Rajaswaran, R. (1988). Fatal deliberate self harm in a Sri Lankan hospital. *British Journal of Psychiatry, 152*, 420–423.
Ganesvaran, T., Subramaniam, S., & Mahadevan, K. (1984). Suicide in northern town of Sri Lanka. *Acta Psychiatrica Scandinavica, 69*, 420–425.
Ganzler, S. (1967). Some interpersonal and social dimensions of suicide behaviour. *Dissertation Abstracts, 28*, 1192 B–1193 B.
Garfinkel, B., Froese, A., & Hood, J. (1982). Suicide attempts in children and adolescent deliberate self-harm. *Journal of Adolescence, 19*, 513–527.
Garrison, C., Addy, C., Jackson, K., McKeown, R., & Waller, J. (1991). A longitudinal study of suicidal ideation in young adolescents. *Journal of the American Academy of Child and Adolescence Psychiatry, 30*, 597–606.
Garzotto, N., Siani, R. T., Tansella, C., & Tansella, M. (1976) Cross-validation of a predictive scale of subsequent suicidal behaviour in an Italian sample. *British Journal of Psychiatry, 128*, 137–140.

Gasquet, I. & Choquet, M. (1993). Factors determining hospital and post hospital care of adolescents admitted to general hospital after suicide attempts: an epidemiological perspective. *Psychologie Medicale, 25*, 400–404.

Gautam, S., Nijhawan, M., & Kamal, P. (1987). Standardisation of Hindi version of Goldberg's General Health Questionnaire. *Indian Journal of Psychiatry, 29*, 65–66.

Ghubash, R. (1993). *Sociocultural change and psychiatric disorder*. University of London, PhD thesis.

Giddens, A. (1978). *Durkheim*. London: Fontana.

Giddens, A. (1992). *The transformation of intimacy, sexuality, love and eroticism in modern societies*. Cambridge: Polity Press.

Glenn, J. & Urbach, H. (1981). Adaptive and non adaptive action in adolescence. In S. Orgel and B.D. Fine (Eds.), *Clinical psychoanalysis*. New York: Jason Aronson, pp. 259–292.

Glover, G. R., Marks F., & Nowers, M. (1989). Parasuicide in young Asian women. *British Journal of Psychiatry, 154*, 271–272.

Goddard, N., Subotsky, F., & Fombonne, E. (1996). Ethnicity and adolescent deliberate self-harm. *Journal of Adolescence, 19*, 513–527.

Goldberg, D. P. (1972). *The detection of psychiatric illness by questionnaire.* Oxford: Oxford University Press.

Goldberg, D., & Hodes, M. (1992). The poison of racism and the self-poisoning of adolescents. *Journal of Family Therapy, 14*, 51–67.

Goldney, R., Harris, L., Badri, A., Michael, S., & Fisher, L. (1998). Suicidal ideation in Sudanese women. *Crisis, 19*, 154–158.

Goldney, R., Winefield, A., Tiggeman, M., & Winefield, H. (1991). Suicidal ideation: Its enduring nature and associated morbidity. *Acta Psychiatrica Scandinavica, 83*, 115–120.

Goldston, D. B., Daniel, S. S., Reboussin, D. M., Kelley, A. E., & Frazier, P. H. (1998). Psychiatric diagnosis of previous suicide attempters, first time attempters on an adolescent inpatient psychiatry unit. *Journal of American Academy of Child and Adolescent Psychiatry, 37*, 924–932.

Goldston, D. B., Daniel, S. S., Reboussin, D. M., Kelley, A., Ievers, C., & Brunstetter, R. (1996). Frist time suicide attempters, repeat attempters and previous attempters on an adolescent inpatient psychiatry unit. *Journal of American Academy of Child and Adolescent Psychiatry, 35*, 631–639.

Gordon, M. M. (1964). *Assimilation in American life*. New York: Oxford University Press.

Granboulan, V., Rabain, D. & Basquin, M. (1995). The outcome of adolescent suicide attempts. *Acta Psychiatrica Scandinavica, 91*, 265–270.

Graves, T. (1967). Psychological acculturations in a tri-ethnic community. *South Western Journal of Anthropology, 23*, 337–350.

Greer, S., & Bagley, C. (1971). Effect of psychiatric intervention in attempted suicide. *British Medical Journal, 1*, 310–312.

Gupta, S., & Singh, H. (1981). Psychiatric illness in suicide attempters. *Indian Journal of Psychiatry, 23*, 6974.

Gururaj, G., & Isaac, M. (2001). *Epidemiology of suicides in Bangalore*. Bangalore: NIMHANS (pub. no. 43).

Haider, I. (1968). Suicidal attempts in children and adolescents. *British Journal of Psychiatry, 114*, 1113–1134.

Hallstrom, T. (1977). Life – weariness, suicidal thoughts and suicidal attempts among women in Gothenburg. *Acta Psychiatrica Scandinavica, 79*, 481–489.

Handy, S., Chithiramohan, R., Ballard, C., & Silveira, W. R. (1991). Ethnic differences in adolescents self-poisoning: A comparison of Asian and caucasian groups. *Journal of Adolescence, 14*, 157–162.

Hanson, W., & Wang, A. (1984). Suicide attempts in a Danish region. *Social Psychiatry & Psychiatric Epidemiology, 19*, 197–201.
Harischandra D. V. J. (1998). *Psychiatric aspects of Jataka stories*. Galle, Sri Lanka: Upuli.
Harlan, L. (1994). Perfection and devotion: Sati traditions in Rajasthan. In J. S. Hawley (Ed.), *Sati: The blessing and the curse*. New York: Oxford University Press, pp. 79–90.
Harrington, R., & Dyer, E. (1993). Suicide and attempted suicide in adolescence. *Current Opinions in Psychiatry, 6*, 467–469.
Harvey, P. (2000). *An introduction to Buddhist ethics*. Cambridge: Cambridge University Press.
Hassan, R. (1970). *Some sociological aspects of suicide in Singapore*. W.F.M.H. workshop in sea. Singapore: Roche Far East Research Foundation, pp. 60–73.
Hawley, J. S. (1994). Introduction. In J. S. Hawley (Ed.), *Sati: The blessing and the curse*. New York: Oxford University Press, pp. 3–26.
Hawton, K. (1986). Suicide and attempted suicide among children and adolescents. *Developmental clinical psychology and psychiatry*. London: Sage
Hawton, K. Cole, D., O'Grady, J., & Osborn, M. (1982a). Motivational aspects of deliberate self-poisoning in adolescents. *British Journal of Psychiatry, 141*, 286–291.
Hawton, K., & Fagg, J. (1988). Suicide and other causes of death following attempted suicide. *British Journal Psychiatry, 152*, 359–366.
Hawton, K. & Fagg, J. (1992). Deliberate self-poisoning and self-injury in adolescents. A study of characteristics and trends in Oxford 1976–1989. *British Journal of Psychiatry, 161*, 816–823.
Hawton, K., Fagg, J., Simkin, S., Harriss, L., & Malmberg, A. (1998). Methods used for suicide by farmers in England and Wales. *British Journal of Psychiatry, 173*, 320–324.
Hawton, K., O'Grady, J., Osborn, M., & Cole, D. (1982b). Adolescents who take overdoses. *British Journal of Psychiatry, 140*, 118–123.
Haynes, R. (1966). *Attempted suicide in Trinidad and Tobago*. Trinidad: Institute of Social and Economic Research.
Haynes, R. (1984). Suicide in Fiji – a preliminary study. *British Journal of Psychiatry, 145*, 433–438.
Haynes, R. (1987). Suicide and social response in Fiji. *British Journal of Psychiatry, 151*, 21–26.
Headley, L. (Ed.) (1983). *Suicide in Asia and the Near East*. Berkeley, CA: University of California Press.
Hendin, H. (1964a). *Suicide and Scandinavia*. New York: Free Press.
Hendin, H. (1964b). *Black suicide*. New York: Free Press.
Hendin, H. (1982). *Suicide in America*. New York: Free Press.
Hicks, M., & Bhugra, D. (2003). Perceived causes of suicide attempts by UK South African women. *American Journal of Orthopsychiatry, 73*, 455–462.
Hoberman, H., & Garfinkel, B. (1988). Completed suicide in children and adolescents. *Journal of the American Academy of Child & Adolescent Psychiatry, 27*, 689–695.
Hodges, W. (1793). *Travels in India during the years 1780, 1781, 1782 and 1783*. London: J. Edwards.
Hodgman, C. H. & McAnarney, E. R. (1992). Adolescent depression and suicide: Rising problems. *Hospital Practice, 27*, 4.
Hofstede, G. (1980). *Cultures consequences*. Beverly Hills: CA: Sage.
Hofstede, G. (1984). *Cultures consequences: Abridged*. Beverly Hills, CA: Sage.
Hollinger, P. & Offer, D. (1982). Prediction of adolescent suicide: A population model. *American Journal of Psychiatry, 139*, 302–307.
Hovens, J. G., Cantwell, D., & Kiriakos, R. (1994). Psychiatric co morbidity in hospitalised adolescent substance abusers. *Journal of the American Academy of Child and Adolescent Psychiatry, 33*, 476–483.
Hsu, F. L. K. (1985). The self in cross-cultural perspective. In A. Mersealla & F. L. K. Hsu (Eds.), *The self in a cross-cultural perspective*. New York: Tavistock, pp. 24–55.

Hutchinson, G., Daisley, H., Simmonds, V., & Gordon, A. (1991). Suicide by poisoning. *West Indies Medical Journal, 40*, 69–73.

Hutchinson, G., Daisley, H., Simeon, D., Simmonds, V., Shetty, M., & Lynn, D. (1999). High rates of paraquat induced suicide in Southern Trinidad. *Suicide and Life-Threatening Behaviour, 29*, 186–191.

Iga, M., & Tatai, K. (1975). Characteristics of suicides and attitudes towards suicides in Japan. In N. L Farberow (Ed.), *Suicide in different cultures*. Baltimore, MD: University Park Press.

Inkeles, A. (1997). National character. New Brunswick: Transaction Publishers.

Jacob, K. S., Bhugra, D., & Mann, A. (1997). The validation of the 12 item GHQ among ethnic Indian women living in the United Kingdom. *Psychological Medicine, 27*, 1215–1217.

Jamil, H. (1990). Acute poisoning: A review of 1900 cases. *Journal of the Pakistan Medical Association, 40*, 131–133.

Jamil, H., Khan A., Akhtar. S., & Sultana, N. (1977). Patients with acute poisoning. *Journal of the Pakistan Medical Association, 27*, 91–93.

Johnsson-Fridell, E., Ojehagen, A., & Traskman-Bendz, L. (1996). A 5-year follow-up study of suicide attempts. *Acta Psychiatrica Scandinavica, 93*, 151–157.

Kalish, R., Reynolds, D., & Farberow, N. (1974). Community attitudes toward suicide. *Commmunity Mental Health Journal, 10*, 301–307.

Kalupahana, D. J. (1987). *The principles of Buddhist psychology. SUNY Series in Buddhist Psychology.* NY: SUNY Press.

Kane, P. V. (1973). *History of Dharmasastra*. Poona: Bhandarkar Oriental Research Institute.

Kaplan, A. & Klein, R. (1989). Women and suicide. In D. Jacobs and H. N. Brown (Eds.). *Suicide: understanding and responding*. Madison, CT: International Universities Press, pp. 257–282.

Karim, J., & Price, J. (1973). Suicide in Fiji. *Fiji Medical Journal, 1*, 49–53.

Kasturiaratchi, N., De Silva, H., & Ellawala, N. (1996). *A study of suicide in Sri Lanka. Report Faculty of Medicine*. Peradeniya: University Of Peradeniya.

Kelleher, M. J., Daly, M., Keohane, B., Daly, C., Daly, F., Crowley, M., & Kelleher, M. J. A. (1994). Deprivation and long-term outcome of deliberate self poisoning. In M. J. Kelleher (Ed.) *Divergent perspectives in suicidal behaviour* (pp. 71–78). Cork: UCC 5th European symposium on suicide.

Kennedy, R. H. (1843). The suttee: The narrative of an eye witness. *Bentley's Miscellany, 13* (75), 241–256.

Kerfoot, M. (1988). Deliberate self-poisoning in childhood and early adolescence. *Journal of Child Psychology & Psychiatry, 29*, 335–343.

Khan, M. M., & Reza, H. (1998). Gender differences in nonfatal suicidal behaviour in Pakistan: Significance of sociocultural factors. *Suicide and Life-Threatening Behaviour, 28*, 62–68.

Kienhörst, I. C., De Wilde, E., Diekstra, R., & Wolters, W. (1992). Differences between adolescent suicide attempters and depressed adolescents. *Acta Psychiatrica Scandinavica, 85*, 222–225.

Kim, U., Triandis, H., Kitayama, C., Chin, S-C., & Yoon, G. (1994). Introduction. In U. Kim, et al. (Eds.), *Individualism and collectivism: Theory, method and applications.* Thousand Oaks, CA: Sage, 1–18.

King, C. A., Naylor, M. W., and Segal, H. G., Evans, T., & Shain, B. N. (1993). Global self worth, specific perceptions of competence and depression in adolescents. *Journal of the American Academy of Child and Adolescent Psychiatry, 32*, 745–752.

Kingsbury, S. (1994). The psychological and social characteristics of Asian adolescent overdose. *Journal of Adolescence, 17*, 131–135.

Kjelsberg, E., Winther, M. & Dahl, A. A. (1995). Overdose deaths in young substance abusers. Accidents or hidden suicides. *Acta Psychiatrica Scandinavica, 91*, 236–242.

Kokkevi, A. & Stefanis, C. (1995). Drug abuse and psychiatric co-morbidity. *Comprehensive Psychiatry, 36*, 329–337.

Kontaxakis, V., Markdis, M., Vaslamatzis, G., Ionnaides, H., & Stefanis, C. (1988). Attempted suicide by jumping: Clinical and social features. *Acta Psychiatrica Scandinavica, 77*, 435–437.
Kosky, R., Silburn, S., & Zubrick, S. (1990). Symptomatic depression and suicidal ideation: A comparative study with 628 children. *Journal of Nervous and Mental Disorders, 174*, 523–528.
Kovacs, M., & Goldston, D. (1991). Cognitive and social cognitive development of depressed children and adolescents. *Journal of Neurochemistry, 30*, 388–392.
Kovacs, M., Goldston, D., & Gatsons, C. (1993). Suicidal behaviour and childhood onset depressive disorders: A longitudinal investigation. *Journal of the American Academy of Child & Adolescent Psychiatry, 32*, 820.
Kreitman, N. (1978). *Parasuicide*. London: Wiley.
Kreitman, N., Carstairs, M., & Duffy, J. (1991). Associations of age and social class with suicide among men in Great Britain. *Journal of Epidemiology & Community Health, 45*, 195–202.
Kumar, R. S. (1990). Like wild fire. *Times Of India Sunday Review 21*, 2 October.
Kumar, S. P. N. (1998). Age and gender related analysis of psychosocial factors in attempted suicide. *Indian Journal of Psychology., 40*, 338–345.
Kushner, H. I. (1995). Women and suicidal behaviour: Epidemiology, gender and lethality in historical perspective. In S. S. Canetto & D. Lester (Eds.), *Women and suicidal behaviour*. New York: Springer, pp. 11–34.
Ladely, S. J., & Puskar, K. R. (1994). Adolescent suicide: Behaviours, risk factors and psychiatric nursing interventions. *Issues in Mental Health Nursing, 15*, 497–504.
Lal, N., & Sethi, B. B. (1976). Demograhic and socioeconomic variables in attempted suicide by poisoning. *Indian Journal of Psychiatry, 17*, 100–107.
Lamb, J., & Parker, K. (1991). School based adolescent mental health project survey of depression, suicidal ideation and anger. *Journal of Child & Adolescence Psychiatric Nursing, 4*, 101–104.
Lamminpaa, A. (1995). Alcohol intoxication in childhood and adolescence. *Alcohol and Alcoholism, 30*, 5–12.
Larsson, B., Melin, L., Breitholtz, E., & Andersson, G. (1991). Short term stability of depressive symptoms and suicide attempts in Swedish adolescents. *Acta Psychiatrica Scandinavica, 83*, 385–390.
Leslie, J. (1989). *The perfect wife*. Delhi: Oxford University Press.
Lester, D. (1984). Suicide. In C. P. Widom (Ed.), *Sex roles and psychopathology*. New York: Plenum Press, pp. 145–456.
Levav, I., & Aisenberg, E. (1989). Suicide in Israel: Cross-national comparison. *Acta Psychiatrica Scandinavica, 79*, 468–473.
Lewis, R. J. (1994). Comment: Sati and the nineteenth century British self. In J. S. Hawley (Ed.), *Sati: The blessing and the curse*. New York: Oxford University Press, pp. 72–78.
Lewis, G., Pelosi, A., Araya, R., & Dunn, G. (1992). Measuring psychiatric disorders in the community: A standardised assessment for use by lay interviewers. *Psychological Medicine, 22*, 465–486.
Lewinsohn, P. M., Rohde, P., & Seeley, J. R. (1994). Psychosocial risk factors for future adolescent suicide attempts. *Journal of Consulting and Clinical Psychology, 62*, 297–305.
Liddle, J., & Joshi, R. (1986). *Daughters of independence*. London: Zed Books.
Lockhart, E. (1998). Audit cycle on young people presenting with self harm. *Psychiatric Bulletin, 22*, 100–101.
Lockhart, S. P., & Baron, J. H. (1987). Changing ethnic and social characteristics of patients admitted for self poisoning in west London during 1971–2 and 1983–4. *Journal of the Royal Society of Medicine, 90*, 145–148.
London, M. (1986). Mental illness among immigrant minorities in the UK. *British Journal of Psychiatry, 149*, 265–273.

Lopez, S., & Guarnaccia, P. (2000). Cultural psychopathology: Uncovering the social world of mental illness. *Annual Review of Psychology, 51*, 571–598.

Lukianowicz, N. (1972). Suicidal behaviour: an attempt to modify the environment. *British Journal of Psychiatry, 121*, 387–390.

Maccoby, E., & Jacklin, C. (1974). *The psychology of sex differences*. Stanford, CA: Stanford University Press.

Macdonald, C., & Parke, R. (1986). Parent child physical play: The effects of sex and age on children and parents. *Sex Roles, 15*, 367–378.

Maddox, J. C., Levi, M., & Thompson, C. V. (1994). The compliance with antidepressants in general practice. *Journal of Psychopharmacology, 8*, 48–53.

Madianos, M. G., & Economou, M. (1994). Schizophrenia and family rituals. *European Psychiatry, 9*, 45–51.

Madianos, M. G., Gefou-Madianou, D., & Stefanis, C. (1994). Adolescent drinking and alcohol related problems in a nationwide general pop. *International Journal of the Addictions, 29*, 1581–1599.

Madianos, M. G., & Stefanis, C. N. (1994). Symptoms of depression suicidal behaviour and use of substances in Greece. *Acta Psychiatrica Scandinavica, 89*, 159–166.

Madianos, M. G., Gefou-Madianou, D., & Stefanis, C. (1996). Symptons of depression, suicidal behaviour and use of substances in Greece. *Acta Psyciatrica Scandinavica, 89*, 159–166.

Maharajh, H. (1998). Transgenerational cultural conflicts and suicide among Hindu girls in Trinidad. *Caribbean Medical Journal, 60*, 16–18.

Mahgoub, O. M., Al-Freihi, H., Al-Myhaya, S. & Al-Nahdi, M. (1988). Deliberate self harm in the eastern region of Saudi Arabia: a hospital based study. *Annals of Saudi Medicine, 8*, 126–130.

Mahla, V., Bhargava, S., Dogra, R., & Shome, S. (1992). Psychology of self-immolation in India. *Indian Journal of Psychiatry, 34*, 108–113.

Mahy, G. (1993). Suicide behaviour in the Caribbean. *International Review of Psychiatry, 5*, 261–270.

Males, M. (1991). Teen suicide and changing cause of death certification. *Suicide and Life-Threatening Behaviour, 21*, 245–249.

Malik, G., Bilal, A., Mekki, T., & Kinani, H. (1996). Drug overdose in the Assir region of Saudi Arabia. *Annals of Saudi Medicine, 16*, 33–36.

Mani, L. (1989). Contentions traditions: The debate on sati in colonial India. In K. Sangari & S. Vaid (Eds.), *Recasting women*. New Delhi: Kali For Women.

Maniam, T. (1988). Suicide and parasuicide in a hill resort in Malaysia. *British Journal of Psychiatry, 153*, 222–225.

Marecek, J. (1998). Culture, gender and suicidal behaviour in Sri Lanka. *Suicide & Life-Threatening Behaviour, 28*, 69–81.

Maris, R. W., Silva, S. C., McIntosh, J. L., & Silverman, M. M. (2000a) *Review of suicidology*. New York: Guilford Press.

Maris, R. W., Berman, A., & Silverman, M. (2000b). Theoretical components in suicidiology. In R. W. Maris, A. Berman, & M. Silverman (Eds.), *Comprehensive text book of suicidology*. New York: Guilford Press, 26–61.

Marks, P. & Haller, D. (1977). Now I lay me down to sleep. A study of adolescent suicide attempts. *Journal of Clinical Psychology, 33*, 391–400.

Marmot, M., Adelstein, A., & Bulusu, L. (1984). *Immigrant mortality in England and Wales 1970–78*. Studies on Medical and Population Subjects. No. 47 OPCS. London: HMSO.

Marriott, M. K. (1976). Hindu transactions, diversity without dualism. In B. Kapferer (Ed.), *Transaction and meaning*. Philadelphia: Institute of Study of Human Issues.

Martin, G. (1996). The influence of television suicide in a normal adolescent population. *Archives of Suicide Research, 2*, 103–117.

Marttunen, M. J., Anott, M., & Henriksson, M. M. (1994a). Antisocial behaviour in adolescent suicide. *Acta Psychiatrica Scandinavica, 89*, 167–173.

Marttunen, M. J., Aro, H. M., Henriksson, M., & Lonnquist, J. (1991). Mental disorders in adolescent suicide: DSMIII R axes I&II diagnoses in suicide among 13–19 years in Finland. *Archives of General Psychiatry, 48*, 834–839.

Marttunen, M. J., Aro, H. M., & Lunquist, J. K. (1994b). Psychosocial stresses more common in adolescent suicide with alcohol abuse compared with depressive adolescent suicides. *Journal of the American Academy of Child Psychiatry, 33*, 490–497.

Mavreas, V., Bebbington, P., & Greely, S. (1988). Greeks, British Greek Cypriots and Londoners: A comparison. *Psychological Medicine, 18*, 433–442.

McCandless, F. (1968). Suicide and communication of rage. *American Journal of Psychiatry, 125*, 197–205.

McCulloch, J., & Phillip, A. (1972). *Suicidal behaviour*. Oxford: Pergamon Press.

McGibben, L., Ballard, C., Handy, S., Mohan, R., & Silveira, W. (1992). Deliberate self-poisoning in Asian and Caucasian 12–15 year olds. *British Journal of Psychiatry, 161*, 110–112.

McIntire, M. & Angle, C. (1970). The taxonomy of suicides as seen in poison control centres. *Pediatric Clinics of North America, 17*, 697–706.

McLure, G. (1984). Suicide in children and adolescents in England and Wales 1960–1990. *British Journal of Psychiatry, 65*, 510–514.

McMullen, C. O. (1989). *Religious beliefs and practices of Sikhs in Punjab*. Delhi: Manohar.

Meerloo, J. A. M. (1962). *Suicide and mass suicide*. New York: Grune and Stratton.

Meiselman, K. (1978). *Incest: a psychological study of causes and effects with treatment recommendations*. San Francisco, CA: Jossey-Bass.

Merrill, J. & Owens, J. (1986). Ethnic differences in self-poisoning: A comparison of Asian and white groups. *British Journal of Psychiatry, 148*, 708–712.

Merrill, J., & Owens, J. (1987). Ethnic differences in self poisoning: A comparison of West Indian and white groups. *British Journal of Psychiatry, 150*, 765–768.

Merrill, J. & Owens, J. (1988). Self poisoning in four immigrant groups. *Acta Psychiatrica Scandinavica, 77*, 77–80.

Milling, L., Campbell, N., Davenport, C. W., & Carpenter, G. (1991). Suicidal behaviour among psychiatric inpatients children: An estimate of prevalence. *Child Psychiatry and Human Development, 22*, 71–77.

Milling, L., Campbell, N., Laughlin, A., & Bush, E. (1994). The prevalence of suicidal behaviour among pre-adolescent children who are psychiatric inpatients. *Acta Psychiatrica Scandinavica, 89*, 225–229.

Monroe-Posey, R. (1985). The long term psychological effects of father–daughter incest in young adult women. *Smith College Studies in Social Work, 56*, 16–17.

Morris, B. (1994). *Anthropology of the self: The individual in cultural perspective*. London: Pluto Press.

Morrissey, R., Dickes, R., Abkoff, H., Alvir, J.-MJ., De Marco, A., & Kopelwicz, H. S. (1995). Hospitalising the suicidal adolescent: Investigation of decision-making criteria. *Journal of the American Academy of Child & Adolescent Psychiatry, 34*, 902–911.

Motto, J. A. (1965). Suicide attempts: A longitudinal view. *Archives of General Psychiatry, 13*, 516–520.

Mullen, P., Martin, J., Anderson, J., Romans, S., & Herbuson, G. (1993). Childhood sexual abuse and mental health in adult life. *British Journal of Psychiatry, 163*, 721–732.

Murphy, G. E. (1992). *Suicide in alcoholism*. New York: Oxford University Press.

Murugesan, G., & Hock, Y. O. (1978). Demographic and psychiatric aspects of attempted suicide – ninety six attempts. *Medical Journal of Malayasia, 33*, 102–112.

Myers, E. D. (1988). Predicting repetition of deliberate self-harm. *Acta Psychiatrica Scandinavica, 77*, 314–319.

Myers, K., McCauley, E., Caldron, R., & Tredes, R. (1991). The 3 year longitudinal course of suicidality and predictive factors for subsequent suicidality in youths with major depressive disorder. *Journal of the American Academy of Child & Adolescent Psychiatry, 30*, 804–810.

Naidu, V. (1980). The violence of indenture in Fiji. *Fiji Monograph Series, 3*. Sava, Fiji: University of South Pacific.

Nandy, A. (1980). *At the edge of psychology: Essays in politics and culture*. New Delhi: Oxford University Press.

Nandy, A. (1994). Sati as profit versus sati as a spectacle. In J. S. Hawley (Ed.), *Sati: The blessing and the curse*. New York: Oxford University Press, pp. 131–148.

Narang, R. L., Mishra, B. P., & Mohan, N. (2000). Attempted suicide in Ludhiana. *Indian Journal of Psychiatry, 42*, 83–87.

Narasimhan, S. (1998). *Sati: A study of widow burning in India*. New Delhi: HarperCollins.

Nasr, A., Vostanis, P., & Winkley, L. (1997). Child and adolescent self poisoning: Service related characteristics, *Psychiatric Bulletin 21*, 267–269.

National Centre for Health Statistics (1992). Advance report of final mortality statistics. *NCHS Monthly Vital Statistics Report, 40*, (8 Suppl.2).

Neeleman, J., Jones, P., Van, O. S. J., & Murray, R. M. (1996). Parasuicide in Camberwell: Ethnic differences. *Social Psychiatry & Psychiatric Epidemiology, 31*, 284–287.

Neeleman, J., Mak, V., & Wessely, S. (1997). Suicide by age, ethnic group, coroners' verdicts and country of birth: A three-year survey in inner London. *British Journal of Psychiatry, 171*, 463–467.

Neuringer, C., & Lethieu, D. (1982). *Suicidal women*. New York: Gardner Press.

Nissen, T., & Haggag, A. (1988). Parasuicidal snow wandering in the Arctic. *Acta Psychiatrica Scandinavica, 77*, 309–313.

Okasha, A., Lataif, F., & Sadek, A. (1981). Prevalence of suicidal feelings in a sample of non-consulting medical students. *Acta Psychiatrica Scandinavica, 63*, 409–415.

Oldenburg, V. T. (1994). Comment: The continuing inventions of the sati tradition. In J. S. Hawley (Ed.), *Sati: The blessing and the curse*. New York: Oxford University Press, pp. 159–174.

OPCS. (1992). *County monitors: Inner London and Greater London*. London: HMSO.

Ostamo, A., & Lonnequist, J. (2001). Attempted suicide rates and trends during a period of severe economic recession in Helsinki *1989–1997. Social Psychiatry and Psychatric Epidemiology*, *36*, 354–360.

Parasram, R. (1992). *Suicide and ethnic disadvantage. Academic and Research Committee Report*. Port of Spain, Trinidad: St Ann's Hospital.

Paykel, E. S., Prusoff, B. A., & Myers, J. K. (1975). Suicide attempts and recent life events. *Archives of General Psychiatry, 32*, 327–333.

Peterson, A., Awad, G., & Kendler, A. (1973). Epidemiological differences between white and non-white suicide attempts. *American Journal of Psychiatry, 130*, 1071–1076.

Petrie, W. M. F (1962). Religious life in Ancient Greece. In U. Thakur (Ed.), *History of suicide in India*. Delhi: Munshi Ram Manohar Lal.

Pfeffer, C., Hurt, S., Kakuma, T., Peskin, J., Sielker, C., & Hagabhairava, S. (1994). Suicidal children grow up: Suicidal episodes and effects of treatment during follow up. *Journal of American Academy of Child and Adolescent Psychiatry, 33*, 225–230.

Pfeffer, C., Kleinman, G., Hurt, S., Lesser, M., Peskin, J. R., & Siefker, C. A. (1991). Suicidal children grow up: Demographic and clinical risk factors for adolescent suicide attempts. *Journal of American Academy of Child and Adolescent Psychiatry, 30*, 609–616.

Plunmer, K. (1989). Lesbian and Gay youth in England. In G. Herdt (Ed.), *Gay and lesbian youth*. New York: Harrington Park Press, pp. 193–223.

Ponnudurai, R., Jeyakar, J., & Saraswathy, M. (1986). Attempted suicide in Madras. *Indian Journal of Psychiatry, 28*, 59–62.

Ponnudurai, R., Vivekananthan, V. R., Raju, B., & Shivakumar, T. S. U. (1991). Attempted suicide – a two year follow up study. *Indian Journal of Psychiatry, 33*, 291–292.

Price, J., & Karim, I. (1975). Suicide in Fiji: A two year survey. *Acta Psychiatrica Scandinavica, 52*, 153–159.

Priest, R., Vize, C., Roberts, M., & Tylee, A. (1996) Lay people's attitudes to treatment of depression: Results of an opinion poll for defeat depression campaign just before its launch. *British Medical Journal, 313*, 858–859.

Pritchard, C. (1995). *Suicide – the ultimate rejection? A psychosocial study*. Buckingham: Open University Press.

Rack, P. (1982). *Race, culture and mental disorder*. London: Tavistock.

Radhakrishnan, S. (1948). *Hinduism: A way of life*. London: HarperCollins.

Ramdin, R. (1994) *The other middle passage*. London: Hansib.

Recklitis, C. J., Noam, G. G., & Borst, S. R. (1992). Adolescent suicide and defensive style. *Suicide and Life Threatening Behaviour, 22*, 374–387.

Redfield, R., Linton, R., & Herskovits, M. (1936). Memorandum on the study of acculturation. *American Anthropologist, 38*, 149–152.

Ree, G. H. (1971). Suicide in Macuata province, Fiji: A review of 73 cases. *The Practitioner, 207*, 669–671.

Reed, J., Camus, J., & Last, J. (1985). Suicide in Canada: A birth cohort analysis. *Canadian Journal of Public Health, 6*, 43–47.

Reinherz, H. Z., Giacinia, R. M., Silverman, A. B., Friedman, A., Pakiz, B., Frost, A. K., & Cohen, E. (1995). Early psychosocial risks for adolescent suicidal ideation and attempts. *Journal of the American Academy of Child and Adolescent Psychiatry, 34*, 599–611.

Rey, J. M., & Bird, K. D. (1991). Sex differences in suicidal behaviour of referred adolescents. *British Journal of Psychiatry, 158*, 776–781.

Rich, C., Sherman, N., & Fowler, R. (1990). San Diego suicide study. *Adolescence, 25*, 855–855.

Roberts, R. E., Chen, Y. W., & Solovitz, B. L. (1995). Symptoms of DSM-III-R major depression among Anglo, African and Mexican American adolescents. *Journal of Affective Disorders, 24*, 36, 1–9.

Rodger, C. R., & Scott, A. (1995). Frequent deliberate self-harm repetition, suicide, and cost after three or more years. *Scottish Medical Journal, 40*, 010–013.

Roland, A. (1997). How universal is psychoanalysis? In D. Allen (Ed.), *Culture and self*. Boulder, CO: Westview, pp. 27–39.

Rosenthal, M. J. (1981). Sexual differences in the suicidal behaviour of young people. *Adolescent Psychiatry, 27*, 257–262.

Rossow, I. (1995). Regional analysis of alcohol and suicide in Norway: Some empirical considerations. *Suicide & Life Threatening Behaviour, 25*, 401–409.

Rossow, I., & Wichstrom, L. (1994). Parasuicide and use of intoxicants among Norwegian adolescents. *Suicide & Life Threatening Behaviour, 24*, 174–183.

Sainsbury, P. (1983). Validity and reliability of trends in suicide statistics. *World Health Statistical Quarterly, 36*, 339–348.

Salmons, P., & Harrington, R. (1984). Suicidal ideation in university students and other groups. *International Journal of Social, Psychiatry, 30*, 201–205.

Sahfi, M., Carrigan, S., & Derrick, A. (1985). Psychological autopsy of completed suicide in children and adolescents. *American Journal of Psychiatry*, *142*, 1061–1064.

Sangari, K., & Vaid, S. (1989). Recasting women. An introduction. In K. Sangari & S. Vaid (Eds.), *Recasting women*. New Delhi: Kali for Women, pp. 1–26.

Sato, T., Takeichi, M., & Hara, T. (1993). Suicide attempts by agricultural chemical. *Indian Journal of Psychiatry, 35*, 209–210.

Schneider, P. B. (1954). *La tentative de suicide, Etude statisque, clinique psychologique et catamenstique Neuchatel*. Paris: Delachauz et Niestle SA.

Schwartz, A. J., & Reifler, C. B. (1988). College student suicide in the United States: Incidence data and prospects for demonstrating the efficacy of preventative programmes. *Journal of American College of Health, 37*, 53–59.
Sedney, M., & Brooks, B. (1984). Factors associated with a history of childhood sexual experience in a non clinical female population. *Journal of the American Academy of Child & Adolescent Psychiatry, 23*, 215–218.
Seshadri, S., Srinath, S., & Girimaji, S. (1989). Deliberate self-harm in children. *Indian Journal of Psychological Medicine, 12*, 13–15.
Shaffer, D., & Fisher, P. (1981). The epidemiology of suicide in children and young adolescents. *Journal of the American Academy of Child & Adolescent Psychiatry, 20*, 543–565.
Shakin, M., Shakin, D., & Sternglanz, S. H. (1985). Infant clothing sex labelling for strangers. *Sex Roles, 12*, 955–964.
Shapiro, B. (1990). Guns and dolls. *Newsweek, 115*, 22, 56–65, 28 May.
Sharma, R. C. (1998). Attempted suicide in Hinarachal Pradesh. *Indian Journal of Psychiatry, 40*, 50–54.
Sibthorpe, B., Drinkwater, J., Gardner, K., Bammer, G. (1995). Drug use, binge drinking and attempted suicide among homeless and potentially homeless youth. *Australian and New Zealand Journal of Psychiatry, 29*, 248–256.
Simon, R., & Murphy, P. (1985). Sex differences in the course of suicidal ideation. *Journal of Youth and Adolescence, 14*, 423–433.
Singh, P. (1999). *The Sikhs*. London: John Murray.
Slap, G. B., Corters, D. F., Khadid, N., Marguiles, S. R., & Forke, C. M. (1992). Adolescent suicide attempters. Do physicians recognise them? *Journal of Adolescent Health, 13*, 286–292.
Smart, N. (1989). *The World's religions*. Cambridge: Cambridge University Press.
Soni-Raleigh, V., & Balarajan, R. (1992). Suicide and self-burning among Indians and West Indians in England and Wales. *British Journal of Psychiatry, 161*, 365–368.
Soni-Raleigh, V. S., Bulusu, L., & Balarajan, R. (1990). Suicides among immigrants from the Indian subcontinent. *British Journal of Psychiatry, 156*, 46–50.
Speechley, M., & Stavarky, K. (1991). The adequacy of suicide statistics for use in epidemiology and public health. *Canadian Journal of Public Health, 82*, 38–42.
Spirito, A., Brown, L., Overholsen, J., & Fritz, G. (1989). Attempted suicide in adolescence: A review and critique of literature. *Clinical Psychology Review, 9*, 335–363.
Spratt, P. (1966). Hindu culture and personality: A psychoanalytic study. Bombay: Manaktalas.
SSRC (1954). Acculturation: An exploratory framework. *American Anthropologist, 56*, 973.
Stack, S. (2000). Suicide: A 15 year review of the sociological literature. *I and II. Suicide and Life-Threatening Behaviour, 30*, 145–176.
Steele, R. (1977). Clinical comparison of black and white suicide attempters. *Journal of Consulting and Clinical Psychology, 45*, 350–363.
Stephens, B. (1985). Suicidal women and their relationships with their husbands, boyfriends and lovers. *Suicide & Life-Threatening Behaviour, 15*, 77–89.
Stiver, P. (1990a). *Dysfunctional families and wounded relationships Part I, Work in Progress 41*. Wellesley, MA: Stone Centre.
Stiver, P. (1990b). *Dysfunctional families and wounded relationships Part II, Work in Progress 41*. Wellesley, MA: Stone Centre.
Stiver, R. (1994). The role of gender in dependency. *American Journal of Orthopsychiatry, 64*, 636–639.
Stopes-Roe, M., & Cochrane, R. (1987). The process of assimilation in Asians in Britain. *International Journal of Comparative Sociology, 28*, 43–55.
Sudak, H. S., Ford, A. B., & Rushforth, N. (1984). Adolescent suicide: An overview. *American Journal of Psychotherapy, 38*, 350–363.

Straus, M. (1988). Abused adolescents. In M. Straus (Ed.). *Abuse and victimization across the lifespan*. Baltimore, MD: Johns Hopkins University Press, pp. 107–123.

Strauss, A. & Corbin, J. (1990). *Basics of qualative research*. Newbury Park, CA, Sage.

Suokas, J., & Loennqvist, J. (1995). Suicide attempts in which alcohol is involved. *Acta Psychiatrica Scandinavica, 91*, 36–40.

Surrey, J. L. (1991). The 'self' in relation: A theory of women's development. In J. V. Jordan, A. G. Kaplan, J. B. Miller, I. P. Stiver, & J. L. Surrey (Eds.), *Women's growth in connection. Writing from the Stone Centre*. New York: Guilford Press, pp. 51–66.

Swinton, J. (1859). *Journal of a voyage*. London: Bennett.

Taiminen, T. J., Kallio-Soukhaimen, K., Nokso-Koivisto, H., Kaljonen, A., & Helenius, H. (1998). Contagion of deliberate self harm among adolescent inpatients. *Journal of American Academy of Child and Adolescent Psychiatry, 37*, 211–217.

Taiminen, J. J., Saarijarvi, S., Helenius, H., Keskinen, A., & Korpilahti, T. (1996). Alexithymia in suicide attempters. *Acta Psychiatrica Scandinavica, 93*, 195–198.

Taiminen, T. J., Strandberg, J., & Kujari, H. (1996). Inpatient suicide on a general hospital psychiatric ward. Does experience with high-risk patients help to prevent suicides? *Archives of Suicide Research, 2*, 119–124.

Tatai, K. (1983). Japan. In L. A. Headley (Ed.), *Suicide in Asia and the Near East*. Berkeley, CA: University of California Press, pp. 12–58.

Taylor, E., & Stansfeld, S. (1984). Children who poison themselves. *British Journal of Psychiatry, 145*, 127–135.

Teoh, J. (1974). An analysis of completed suicide. *Annals of the Academy of Medicine, Singapore, 3*, 117–124.

Thakur, U. (1962). *History of suicide in India*. Delhi: Munshi Ram Manohar Lal.

Tinker, H. (1974). *A new system of slavery: The export of Indian labour overseas*. Oxford: Oxford University Press.

Topol, P. & Reznikoff, M. (1982). Perceived poor and family relationships, hopelessness and locus of control as factors in adolescent suicide attempters. *Suicide & Life Threatening Behaviour, 12*, 141–150.

Triandis, H. C., Leung, K., Villareal, M. J., & Black, F. L. (1985). Allocentric versus Idiocentric tendencies: Convergent and discriminant validation. *Journal of Research in Personality, 19*, 395–415.

Trivedi, J. K. (1997). Punishing attempted suicide – anachronism of twentieth century. *Indian Journal of Psychiatry, 39*, 87–89.

Tsoi, W. F. (1974). Suicides and attempted suicides with special reference to Singapore. *Annals of the Academy of Medicine, Singapore, 3*, 125–130.

Turner, B. (1997). The body in western society: Social theory and its perspectives. In S. Oakley (Ed.), *Religion and body*. Cambridge: Cambridge University Press, pp. 15–41.

Van Egmond, M. (1997). Sexual and physical abuse: Suicide risk factors. In C. Bagley & R. Ramsey (Eds.), *Suicidal behaviour in adolescents and adults*. Aldershot: Ashgate.

Van Egmond, M., Garnefiski, N., Jonken, D., & Kenkhof, A. (1993). The relationship between sexual abuse and female suicidal behaviour. *Crisis, 14*, 129–139.

Vandivort, D., & Locke, B. (1979). Suicide ideation: Its relation to depression, suicide and suicide attempt. *Suicide & Life-Threatening Behaviour, 9*, 205–218.

Venkoba Rao, A. V. (1983). India. In L. A. Headley (Ed.), *Suicide in Asia and the Far East*. Berkeley, CA: University of California Press.

Venkoba Rao, A. V. (1992). Parrsuicide and suicide: Some psychological considerations. *Indian Journal of Social Psychology, 8*, 3–7.

Venkoba Rao, A., & Chennian, R. R. (1972). Attempted suicide and suicide in 'students' in Madurai. *Indian Journal of Psychiatry, 14*, 389–393.

Venkoba Rao, A., Mahendran, N., Gopalakrishnan, C., Kota Reddy, T., Prabhakar, E.,

Swaminathan, R., Belinda, C., Andal, G., Baskaran, S., Prahee, R., Kumar, N., Luthra, U. K., Aynkaran J. R., & Catherine, I. (1989). One hundred female burns cases: A study in suicidology. *Indian Journal of Psychiatry, 31*, 43–50.

Wagner, B. M. (1997). Family risk factors for child and adolescent suicidal behaviour. *Psychological Bulletin, 121*, 246–298.

Wasserman, D., Varnik, A., & Eklund, G. (1998a). Female suicides and alcohol consumption during perestroika in the former USSR. *Acta Psychiatrica Scandinavica, 98*, 34–41.

Wasserman, D., Varnik, A., & Eklund, G. (1998b). Male suicides and alcohol consumption during perestroika in the former USSR. *Acta Psychiatrica Scandinavica, 86*, 76–78.

Weinberger-Thomas, C. (2000). *Ashes of immortality: Widow burning in India*. New Delhi: Oxford University Press.

Weitzman, N., Birns, B., & Friend, R. (1985). Traditional and non-traditional mothers' communication with their daughters and sons. *Child Development, 56*, 894–896.

Weitzman, L., Eifler, D., Hokada, E., & Ross, C. (1972). Sex-role socialisation in picture books for pre school children. *American Journal of Sociology, 77*, 1125–1150.

Westermarck, E. (1906/1962). Origin and development of moral ideas. In U. Thakur, (Ed.) *History of suicide in India*. Delhi: Munshi Ram Manohar Lal. (Original work published 1906).

Wetzler, S., Sanderson, W. C., Kelting, D., & Beck, A. (1997). Comorbidity and suicidality. In S. Wetzler & W. C. Sanderson (Eds.), *Treatment strategies for patients with psychiatric comorbididty.* NY: John Wiley, 295–306.

Wilkins, N. J. (1882). *Hindu mythology*. Calcutta: Rupa (reprinted 1989).

Williams, C. L., Davidson, J. A., & Montgomery, I. (1980). Impulsive suicidal behaviour. *Journal of Clinical Psychology, 36*, 90–94.

Wilmotte, J., Charles, G., & Depauw, Y. (1983). Detection des suicidants susceptibles de recedive dans l'année. *Acta Psychiatrica Belgica, 83*, 558–568.

Wilson, D., & Wormald, P. (1995). Battery acid – an agent of attempted suicide in black South Africans. *South African Medical Journal, 85*, 529–531.

Windle, R. C., & Windle, M. (1997). An investigation of adolescence substance misuse behaviors, depressed affect and suicidal behaviors. *Journal of Child Psychology and Psychiatry and Allied Disciplines, 38*, 921–929.

Wold, C. (1971). Sub groupings of suicidal people. *Omega, 2*, 19–29.

Wright, N., Trethowan, W., & Owens, J. (1981). Ethnic differences in self poisoning. *Postgraduate Medical Journal, 57*, 792–793.

Yamamoto, J. (1968). Japanese American identity crisis. In E. B. Brody (Ed.), *Minority group adolescents in the United States*. Baltimore: Wilkins & Wilkins.

Yasemi, M. & Sanei, N. (1994). Epidemiological study on suicide cases in the province of Kashan. Proceedings of Tehran University convention of Research in Psychiatry and Psychology in Iran. Cited in Mehrabi, F., Bayanzadeh, S. A., Atef-Vahid, M.,Bolhari, J., Shahmohammadi, D., Vaezi, S-A. Mental health in Iran. In I. El-Issa (Ed.), *Al-Junun-mental illness in the Muslim world.* Madison, CT: International University Press, 139–161.

Young, S. E., Mikulich, S. K., Goodwin, M. B., & Hardy, J. (1995). Treated delinquent boys substance use: Onset, pattern, relationship to conduct and mood disorders. *Drug and Alcohol Dependence, 17*, 149–162.

Zenner, W. (1996). Ethnicity. In D. Levins & M. Ember (Eds.), *Encyclopaedia of cultural anthropology*. New York: Holt, pp. 393–395.

Zimmerman, J., & Zayas, L. (1995). Suicidal adolescent latinas. In S. Caretto & D. Lester (Eds.), *Suicidal behaviour and women*. New York: Springer, pp. 120–132.

Zuckerman, D. (1989). Stress, self-esteem and mental health: How does gender make a difference. *Sex Roles, 20*, 429–444.

# Author index

# Subject index

For Product Safety Concerns and Information please contact our EU representative GPSR@taylorandfrancis.com
Taylor & Francis Verlag GmbH, Kaufingerstraße 24, 80331 München, Germany

www.ingramcontent.com/pod-product-compliance
Ingram Content Group UK Ltd.
Pitfield, Milton Keynes, MK11 3LW, UK
UKHW020017200926
475702UK00014B/1930

*9781138881501*